Practical Musicology

21st Century Music Practices

Series Editor: Simon Zagorski-Thomas

Contemporary Music Practice looks at the processes, techniques and technologies of making contemporary music. From performance and composition for the concert hall to music for theatre, screen and games and from the latest ideas about historically informed performance to electronic music and record production, this series uses innovative, collaborative formats to reflect the communal nature of the subject matter and the broad range of creative practices involved.

Practical Musicology

Simon Zagorski-Thomas

BLOOMSBURY ACADEMIC
NEW YORK • LONDON • OXFORD • NEW DELHI • SYDNEY

BLOOMSBURY ACADEMIC
Bloomsbury Publishing Inc
1385 Broadway, New York, NY 10018, USA
50 Bedford Square, London, WC1B 3DP, UK
29 Earlsfort Terrace, Dublin 2, Ireland

BLOOMSBURY, BLOOMSBURY ACADEMIC and the Diana logo
are trademarks of Bloomsbury Publishing Plc

First published in the United States of America 2022
This paperback edition published 2024

Copyright © Simon Zagorski-Thomas, 2022

For legal purposes the Acknowledgments on pp. vi–vii constitute an
extension of this copyright page.

Cover design: Louise Dugdale
Cover image © thegoodphoto/iStock.

All rights reserved. No part of this publication may be reproduced or transmitted in any form or by any means, electronic or mechanical, including photocopying, recording, or any information storage or retrieval system, without prior permission in writing from the publishers.

Bloomsbury Publishing Inc does not have any control over, or responsibility for, any third-party websites referred to or in this book. All internet addresses given in this book were correct at the time of going to press. The author and publisher regret any inconvenience caused if addresses have changed or sites have ceased to exist, but can accept no responsibility for any such changes.

Library of Congress Cataloging-in-Publication Data
Names: Zagorski-Thomas, Simon, author.
Title: Practical musicology/Simon Zagorski-Thomas.
Description: [1st.] | New York: Bloomsbury Academic, 2022. | Series: 21st century music practices | Includes bibliographical references and index.
| Summary: "A theoretical framework for studying how music is made as opposed to what is produced"– Provided by publisher.
Identifiers: LCCN 2021056293 (print) | LCCN 2021056294 (ebook) |
ISBN 9781501357794 (hardback) | ISBN 9781501392870 (paperback) |
ISBN 9781501357800 (epub) | ISBN 9781501357817 (pdf) | ISBN 9781501357824
Subjects: LCSH: Musicology. | Music–Performance–Research.
Classification: LCC ML3797.Z35 2022 (print) | LCC ML3797 (ebook) |
DDC 780.72/1–dc23
LC record available at https://lccn.loc.gov/2021056293
LC ebook record available at https://lccn.loc.gov/2021056294

ISBN:	HB:	978-1-5013-5779-4
	PB:	978-1-5013-9287-0
	ePDF:	978-1-5013-5781-7
	eBook:	978-1-5013-5780-0

Series: 21st Century Music Practices

Typeset by Integra Software Services Pvt. Ltd.

To find out more about our authors and books visit www.bloomsbury.com
and sign up for our newsletters.

Contents

Acknowledgments		vi
1	What is Practical Musicology?	1
	Theoretical interlude 1: *'As if'*	14
2	Methodology and methods	17
	Theoretical interlude 2: *Restriction, affordance and influence*	41
3	Context: Styles, tradition and identity	43
4	Context: Technology, uses and value	63
	Theoretical interlude 3: *The feeling of being*	78
5	Musicking	81
	Theoretical interlude 4: *Three modes of perception*	112
6	Learning and knowing	117
	Theoretical interlude 5: *The mechanisms of influence*	133
7	Communication and influence	137
	Theoretical interlude 6: *Belonging and not belonging*	158
8	Interaction and influence	161
	Theoretical interlude 7: *Authority*	178
9	Systems and networks	181
10	Some conclusions	199
Bibliography		217
Index		234

Acknowledgments

This book is the first in the new Bloomsbury 21st Century Music Practice series of which I am editor and it coincided with that explosion of workload for the majority of academics around the world that occurred when the Covid-19 pandemic meant that we had to transfer our teaching online. As series editor I tried to be forgiving and supportive to myself as author and I was, in turn, generously supported by Leah Babb-Rosenfeld, Bloomsbury's Music and Sound editor, and subsequently, when Leah went on maternity leave, by her colleagues Rachel Moore and Amy Martin. I would also like to thank Bloomsbury's anonymous peer reviewers as well as Stan Hawkins, Linda Kaastra, Eve Klein and Nyssim Lefford who looked at an early draft and were very effective and useful 'critical friends'.

The idea for the book grew out of the 21st Century Music Practice research network and I would like to thank Leah Kardos, Gonnie Rietveld and Chris Wiley for hosting our early events and the wider group of academics who participated in those events and the online activities that we subsequently undertook under lockdown. In particular, a group of colleagues at the University of West London – Andrew Bourbon (now at Huddersfield University), Emily Capulet, Mike Exarchos (now Creative Director at RT60), Sara McGuinness, Liz Pipe, Francis Pott and Dan Pratt – have encouraged the growth of these ideas through conversation and by collaborating in various practice and research projects. In addition, Amy Blier-Carruthers from the Royal Academy of Music was equally important in that regard. There is also quite a long list of research degree students – my own and others, past and present – who have challenged me to think about these issues in greater depth and breadth: James Bell, Isabel Campelo, Louise Cournarie, Jose Manuel Cubides, Agata Kubiak-Kenworthy, Yong Ju Lee, Jo Lord, Anthony Meynell, Christos Moralis, Gittit Pearlmutter, Tyrian Purple, Hammad Rashid, Caroline Russell, Gemma Storr and Susan Thomason.

I am grateful to my employers at the University of West London for providing a six week sabbatical which gave me the mental space to get around the last bend and reach the finish line. Further than that, my ideas have been continually stimulated by the wealth of discussion, presentations and reading that has come from the wider research community – the 21st Century Music Practice network, PRAG-UK, the Orpheus Institute, the Society for Artistic Research, the RMA Study Group on Music and/as Process, the Practice Research Assembly, IASPM and, of course, the Art of Record Production conference and association.

Lastly, and most importantly, I want to acknowledge the huge influence that my wife and daughter, Natalia and Alex, have had on my thinking. Although I am sure they would rather die than read this book, they have, nonetheless, had a massive impact on my thinking on these topics.

Simon Zagorski-Thomas. (February 2022)

1

What is Practical Musicology?

I am proposing that Practical Musicology is the study of how to 'do music better' and that, for the most part, this will involve researching by 'doing' and by studying how we make decisions about what 'better' is.

Why is it, just at the moment when everyone is getting fed up with arguments about the nature of practice research and wanting to get on with it, am I weighing in with another ontological argument that appears to be going over old ground? My point is that practice research and artistic research in music, while they have carved out quite a coherent identity, they have done so in a relatively homogenous set of musical practices. Much like artistic research in general, it has flourished in institutions which specialize in conceptually driven forms of creative practice and, as such, focus on particular types of knowledge.

In a recent presentation to the Scottish Graduate School for Arts and Humanities' Practice Research Assembly, I asserted that a key difference between autoethnography and practice research was that ethnography (of any type) is concerned with 'what happened' whereas practice research is concerned with 'how can I do it better?'. That principle was underlined in the recent reports on Practice Research by Bulley and Sahin (2021) for the Practice Research Advisory Group UK (PRAG-UK) which quotes David Cotterrel as saying it requires 'a self-reflexive approach to method, which is continuously subject to review' (Bulley and Sahin, 2021, p. 1.1.1.6). This is then expanded upon in point 1.1.2.4:

> This is what Pickering refers to as a 'dialectic of resistance and accommodation:' the practitioner chooses between multiple approaches to find what Schön has called their 'own way of combining them'.

For me, these skirt around a fundamental point: that practice research in particular and Practical Musicology in general involve the process of establishing their own quality criteria as part of the research process. They explore what 'better' is at the same time as establishing a methodology for achieving it. This is often implied rather than explicitly stated and is, I think, particularly made less 'visible' in creative practice that is conceptually driven. In the Orpheus Institute online video course on 'Artistic Research in Music – An Introduction', Paulo de Assis states, 'It is not research "of" something lost, but research "for" something to be invented' (Impett, 2019, p. 1.4 de Assis video (3' 18")). The Orpheus Institute course is very much focused on Western art music – from historically informed practice to contemporary art music with a conceptual basis. Thus, while artistic research, as it is emerging from its Northern European foundations, makes no ideological stipulations about the types of art practice that it is concerned with, the work of the European Artistic Research Network (EARN), PRAG-UK and the Society for Artistic Research (SAR) has, perhaps unsurprisingly, a strong leaning towards conceptual art. I say 'perhaps unsurprisingly' because these networks are based in university systems which have an obvious tendency towards intellectualizing artistic practice and there is a tendency towards art practice that has pre-existing ties to intellectual thought. Indeed, a lot of artistic research seems to be about exploring complex theoretical ideas through practice. The result – which is, of course, valid, useful and praiseworthy – is often to shine more light onto the theoretical idea rather than on the practice. That, however, provides me with more of a reason to propose a Practical Musicology.

I should point out that not only do I have no problem with conceptually driven art practice but I also 'do it' quite often. Some of my best friends are conceptual artists. I also do not think that this is a zero-sum game – that if some of us choose to theorize other forms of musical practice, that our aim is to belittle or reduce the influence of conceptually driven music. Nor am I trying to 'dumb down' music research by making everyone study popular music. I am trying to 'clever up' forms that are currently under-researched. If this seems like a defensive start to the book, I am only saying it because I have been accused of these things in the past.

Other 'types' of musical study that we need to be able to include:

- Developing an aesthetic approach to intertextuality
- Techniques for the control, development and aesthetics of micro-timing or expressive gesture
- Techniques for the control, development and aesthetics of instrument and production technology
- Creative strategies and aesthetics of tonal improvisation

- The aesthetics and politics of expectation and predictability in different contexts
- Distributed creativity and power/influence
- Strategies for performing identity
- The pleasures and benefits of different types of musical activity
- The ways in which musical activity can be used to change the world

The reason that I distinguish between practice research and Practical Musicology is that I think there are other 'ways in' to understanding how to do artistic practice better – e.g. research into music pedagogy might also involve a third person, non-participant researcher in an exploration of improving technique where the consideration of what constitutes 'better technique' is made an explicit part of the research process.

In January 2021 EARN held a conference and subsequently produced a book on The Postresearch Condition (Slager, 2021). It seems to me this reflects a dilemma in the Artistic Research community (and for quite a few members of the music research community) about the types of transferrable new knowledge. In many instances they seem to be about the presentation of artistic activity with an explanation of how the conceptual process worked – this is 'what happened'. Peter Osborne's keynote contribution to the book (Slager, 2021, pp. 5–13) provides an extensive argument about how art produced through the methods of institutional academic research is doomed to be bad art – or even not art at all. Hito Steyerl's response (Slager, 2021, pp. 13–15) argues that artists in academia are simply getting on with it and producing art – with or without funding and institutional support. In a mixed (online and offline) discussion at the 2021 Royal Musical Association Conference in Newcastle[1] about the Bulley and Sahin Report during a similar argument about the misery of creative practice in an institutional university context, I suggested that since virtually no money accrues to universities for practice as research but that their quality ratings are seen as important institutional markers, perhaps we could add a parallel stream of artistic ratings that simply peer reviewed the quality of the art. I agree with Osborne. Institutionalized art is unlikely to be cutting edge. Artistic research is unlikely to create great art because it involves doing two things at once. I would argue that the aim of artistic research is not to create great art, it is to create new knowledge about how great art can be made.

---

[1] Chaired by Scott McLaughlin on 16 September 2021.

Of course, these practice research activities provide data – case studies – that can be used to support or contradict ideas about how artwork suggests meaning. However, I would suggest that it only provides data about process if it includes evidence about why that path was taken rather than another: about how quality judgements led to a particular aesthetic. The Orpheus Institute's *Experience Music Experiment* (Brooks, 2021) provides evidence in this regard (i.e. case studies) and looks to frame this experience through Dewey's (1934) pragmatist approach. Huang, for example, discusses her aims as a researcher working through musical-gestural practice as 'providing insights for future creators, artists and academics in this field' (Huang, 2021, p. 35).

1.1 Background

Music making and the privately and publicly funded school, college, university and conservatory departments in which it is being taught are changing dramatically in the twenty-first century. This increased focus on the practices of music, famously termed *Musicking* by Christopher Small (1998), has seen a growth in popular music performance, ethnomusicology, electroacoustic/electronic composition, musical theatre and creative recording/production courses. There has been a similar growth in courses which combine managerial and entrepreneurial with musical skills to reflect the structural changes in the music industry. This has created a shift in balance in the sector away from the more 'traditional' courses in the analysis of the musical text in relation to classical music and the socio-economic contexts of audience engagement in relation to popular music. The focus of student attention – and in the contemporary demand-led education system, student attention is a, or even the, major driving force – has shifted from 'knowing what' to 'knowing how'. With the increased level of employment of practitioner academics that flowed from this change there has been a rise in demand for literature, networking opportunities and publication platforms centred on research in these areas. For me, the difference between training and education is in the way that you teach that 'how'. Training is pragmatic and teaches the equivalent of a flow diagram: if *a* happens then do *x*. If *b* happens, then do *y*. Education is theoretical and is about learning principles and mechanisms: why should you do *x* when *a* happens? Research is about providing the explanations and knowledge about principles and mechanisms and is therefore a necessary component of education. Indeed, the essence of education is to learn how to conduct research and, to me, it is also the essence of being a creative practitioner.

This volume is, therefore, an exploration of ways to conduct research into twenty-first-century music practice and, as such, is a venture into the psychology and sociology of music making. As I mentioned at the start of this chapter, Practical Musicology is the study of how to 'do music better'. And this is different to and distinct from the study of what is done. It is a first and second person approach rather than a third person approach. How can you and I do this rather than how did he or she do it? (Although, of course, third person knowledge is also useful in this first person context.) Ethnomusicology and performance studies are overwhelmingly concerned with what is done. What then is the difference between studying what is done and studying how to do it? After all, many ethnomusicologists study what is done by learning how to do it and many researchers in performance studies are performers who know how to do it and then write about what is done. So, while there is considerable overlap between this Practical Musicology and areas of ethnomusicology and performance studies, one key point of difference is the notion of individual aesthetics. Very often the goal of Practical Musicology will be to do something that is atypical or even unique whereas the goal of ethnomusicology and performance studies is to understand the typical. As we shall see throughout the book, an understanding of the typical is essential if you want to achieve the atypical but, more than that, we also need to understand why things are typical in order to be able to be atypical in successful ways. And 'successful ways' require the identification and application of quality judgements as part of the research process.

The term *musicking* that Christopher Small (1998) invoked in relation to participating in the activities of music has been a rallying flag for those concerned with these alternative branches of musicology but there is also the further divide between theoretical and applied research. I would distinguish Practical Musicology from applied musicology for two reasons. Firstly, this is a theoretical book – it mostly comprises theoretical research about how to 'do' music – and secondly, applied research is necessarily about specificity rather than generality. There can be both theoretical and applied research under the umbrella of Practical Musicology.

And while we're talking about what might fit under this umbrella – the pedagogies of practice are obviously included, as is a good deal of practice-research and autoethnography. It also raises the question of whether we can talk about twenty-first-century music practice as if it were a single 'thing'. Cook

(2018, p. 8) talks about bringing 'the distinct creativities of performance and composition together within a single overarching framework' mainly because of the perceived difference between an activity that has to happen in the moment (performance) and one that affords reflection and revision (composition), or what Burnard (2012) refers to as temporal mediations. Of course, outside of Western art music, these distinctions of immediacy and contemplation remain but do not fall into the same categories: recorded performances and sequencing allow for reflection and revision in the world of performance, and improvisation blurs the distinction between working in the moment and composition.

These types of disciplinary distinctions are also important for another reason. Several strands of important work are developing in parallel to each other with relatively little communication between them. A good deal of the theory in different subject 'silos' has areas of overlap and sometimes different language for the same or similar concepts. For example, ideas about performers and composers communicating with different 'voices' can be found in Judith Butler's (1988) extensions of Goffman's (1956) sociological theory of *dramaturgy*, Tricia Rose's (1994) and Ingrid Monson's (1997) use of Bakhtin's (1982) *heteroglossia* and Simon Frith's (1998), Philip Auslander's (1999) and Allan Moore's (2012) development of forms of *persona* in performance. And the notion of musical sound as the aural 'footprint' of energy expenditure can be found in Denis Smalley's *spectromorphology* (1997), Marie Thompson's (2013) use of *affect* theory and from cognitive musicology in the work of Eric Clarke (2005), Nicola Dibben (2013), Linda Kaastra (2008) and my own work (Zagorski-Thomas, 2018b). Of course, these are only some of the parallel developments that I do know about. These dramatic variations in terminology are often the most important barriers when we seek some cross-disciplinary connectivity. We cannot search for parallel threads without knowing what to search for. Hopefully though, conversations under this umbrella make it easier to find these points of connectivity and the additional insights we can absorb from other people's approaches.

Another feature of this cross-disciplinary approach is that it is also often concerned with different traditions, genres and styles. Indeed, these differences of musical culture were often the basis of the disciplinary distinction in the first place and were a driving force in the development of different concepts and theoretical tools within those disciplines. Why then, would I be so stupid as to propose drawing them together under this single umbrella when that is the basis of so much contemporary criticism of musicology? Surely, this is the polar opposite of what Philip Ewell was talking about when criticizing music theory's 'white frame' (2019). However, he was not proposing that music theory needed to widen the range of the repertoire it engaged with. He was suggesting that the theory was designed for white European art music and that therefore we need a wider theoretical frame; one that can accommodate a broader range of repertoire. The discussion that I saw about his talk focused mostly on the fact that he framed the anti-semitic Schenker as having produced a racist theoretical frame as well as being a racist person. It felt as though the larger point was drowned out by the furore surrounding that defensive backlash. Georgina Born (2010) has discussed the problems and the desirability of a relational musicology; of the difficulties of reducing or removing the hegemony of Western art music while at the same time retaining notions of value and aesthetics. Born's view is 'that the conceptual gains of the "impossible totality" project outweigh the risks of hegemonic intellection; unless we cast our nets wide and speak our analytical minds, as it were, there is no chance for others (and Others) to answer back' (Born, 2010, p. 224). Her approach, however, is that of the anthropologist/sociologist rather than the practitioner – the commentator rather than the participant. One of the key aims of this book is to seek to understand how the knowledge and understanding that have been generated and disseminated by researchers in this 'how is it done' world can be re-purposed into a 'how do you do it' world – and vice versa. Indeed, it could be seen as a way of reducing or removing the hegemony of reception-based or esthesic approaches in music studies in favour of a more equal balance with production-based or poeisic approaches.

This book sits within a discipline that has been transformed in recent years by notions of social constructionism, LGBTQ+ politics, intertextuality, audiovisuality and many others and it seeks to be part of that transformation. But it also needs to establish an identity before it can engage in a meaningful discussion of how it fits into the complementary and competing strands of thought in which it is enmeshed. So whilst, as will become evident, it draws upon these ideas to establish an identity, the focus is on using them in a practical sense and exploring how they relate to this theoretical model rather than explaining how this theoretical model fits into the history of music studies and musicology. Of course, a relatively slim volume of ninety thousand words is not going to be able to do justice to all that scholarship. What I hope to do, starting in Chapters 3 and 4 on Context, is to explore the ways in which some of these theoretical ideas can be used to 'do' music. The quote 'do what you can, with what you've got, where you are' is often attributed to Theodore Roosevelt but is in fact him quoting 'Squire Bill Widener' (Roosevelt, 1913, p. 336) in his autobiography. That piece of rather obvious homespun philosophy of course relies on you knowing what you can do, what you have got and where you are. That is where these theoretical models of knowledge, capacity, power, identity and technology can be harnessed into a Practical Musicology.

In each of the chapters, including this one, I will use an example from my own research practice to introduce some of the themes and draw further on these and the work of others to illustrate points as they are made. In 2015 I led the UK Arts and Humanities Research Council-funded Classical Music Hyper-Production and Practice-As-Research project in collaboration with Amy Blier-Carruthers, Andrew Bourbon and Emilie Capulet. The project consisted of a range of practical experiments that applied the record production techniques of popular music to classical music performance and recording. Although the project did involve some completed recordings and live performances at Birmingham University, the University of West London and King's Place in London, the main thrust of the research was concerned with the practice and the process of a much wider range of recording and live staging experiments. The production of finished artefacts and performances was a positive 'side-effect' in a few instances and the main research activity was through the process of 'doing'. We made singers and string players grub around in the filthy cellars and outhouses of the Bishop of Wrocław's seventeenth-century hunting lodge to record multiple types of reverberation, we recorded Shostakovich's 8th String Quartet using electric instruments and guitar effects pedals, we broke solo piano pieces down into multiple component parts that could be recorded and processed separately and we recorded a new piece for solo cello with eighteen channels of audio. Importantly though, it was also based on discussions with the performers and through score analysis to find musical reasons rather than technical ones. Although, of course, some of the experiments were more experimental than others … and that notion of experiments drew us into the question of whether we were using an inductive or deductive process and whether we were doing this to discover how we might use these techniques (and classify what they were) or we were trying to discover something more theoretical about how they worked on our interpretations. And, it seemed to me, we were doing all of those things at various times and to various extents, and sometimes we were doing them as insiders and sometimes we were looking for some kind of external perspective. These three dichotomies – inductive/deductive, practical/theoretical and emic/etic (insider/outsider) – were quite a crucial factor in setting me on the road to writing this book and I will return to them in more detail at the end of this chapter.

The Hyper-Production project and the responses to it also made me think about the impact of ideologies and value systems on research activity and the deeply subjective and political nature of even the most scientific forms of research. In this instance the notion of some music being more important or valuable than others came up in various forms along with a great many questions about whether there was a 'right' way to perform and record some of these pieces. That 'rightness' was sometimes framed in terms of the composer's intentions or the performer's agency and sometimes in terms of historical authenticity. In relation to Allan Moore's (2002) writing on authenticity, sometimes they were first person, individual creative, authenticity and sometimes third person, tradition-based or externally validated, authenticity. And those judgements were often framed as a question of why would you bother to do something like that?

1.2 Why bother?

The point of this book, as the first in this new series, is to stir things up a bit; to be a little provocative. The book is primarily about encouraging debate and discussion about the nature of music education and research. The world of research is being enjoined to ensure that it has impact in the wider world and to explain just what that impact might be. At the same time, with the increasing commercialization of the education system, music courses in contemporary practice – popular music, music technology, recording arts, musical theatre, film music, sound design, etc. – have grown in demand: a logical extension of the contemporary notion that if you are going to have to 'buy a degree' and be a consumer of education then it ought to have a direct bearing on your prospective career. While I disagree profoundly with this philosophy of education, it does force us to face the question of what music education and music research are *for*. Education and research systems have always struggled to find a place that lies in between the preservation of the existing power structures and the radical world of new knowledge that threatens them. This type of metaphor, however, tends to foster the idea that there is a single monolithic power structure. Obviously, this is not true. Just to draw on Adorno as an example: while as a Marxist he had very radical ideas about the upending of the capitalist economic structure, he can be seen to have very conservative views about the value of different forms of music. And while he may have written some intriguing fragments about gender, the male dominance in the power structure of the Frankfurt School tells a more one-sided story.

And it is the same in the hierarchies of power within both the academic and the cultural worlds of music. It may be messy and constantly changing but there are several well-established currents. Around the world, Western classical (or art) music has a higher cultural status than other forms of music. In addition, other forms of art music have a higher cultural status than folkloric or popular music forms. However, popular music is widely recognized as having all the economic muscle. Despite the fact that most 'popular' music does not make much money, the minority that does, produces the vast majority of revenue in the whole sector. And folkloric music is often given cultural status by governments wanting to use it for some kind of political or nationalist agenda. As far as the people who make music are concerned there are similarly complex hierarchies of power. Culturally, those who create 'newness' of some kind are usually valorized over those who produce highly skilled versions of what already exists and yet the economics works in reverse. It is much easier to sell somebody something that they already know that they like, and that counts for Jukebox Musicals re-selling familiar songs in a new context, music that falls within clearly well-established and popular styles, or the programming of classical music festivals with the same litany of history's greatest hits.

But what of the academic world? The university system has, for the most part, been built on the value of theoretical rather than practical knowledge. While the education of doctors and lawyers might provide exceptions to this rule, theoretical mathematics and physics trump computing and engineering in the hierarchy of the academic world, and musicology departments have been seen as more high-brow than conservatoires. And when popular music entered the university system in the 1980s it was the theoretical study of fandom, gender, race, sexuality, sub-culture and semiotics that was adopted rather than how to 'do it' or even to study the sound of it. The 'know how' subjects of popular music performance, record production, musical theatre, music management and other derisively termed 'cash cow' courses sit at the bottom of the hierarchy. That, in turn, means that staff in these areas tend to be afforded less research time in their contracts and this is compounded by the fact that staff tend to be professional musicians who have turned to teaching – the aforementioned practitioner academics or academic practitioners – rather than career academics. All of this means that there is both a less developed theoretical basis to poeisis than to esthesis and that those who are teaching it are less steeped in that theoretical knowledge. In addition, the theoretical basis that does exist tends to be focused on technique rather than expression – how to move your fingers, breath, operate the machinery, etc. rather than how to influence an audience's interpretation through particular gestures, metaphors or formal structures.

Practical Musicology obviously needs to be built on a firm theoretical basis. My view is that multiple methodologies provide a richer understanding than competing interpretations, but the book also seeks to ensure that these varied ways of documenting and analysing musical practice are nonetheless compatible with our scientific knowledge about how the brain, body and environment work. The difference between observing a phenomenon in laboratory conditions where certain variables are removed or fixed and observing it in the 'real world' is extremely apparent. If you want to observe the phenomenon of rhythmic entrainment you will get very different results if you study how accurately a group of subjects can tap their finger to recorded music (or a click) than if you study how they dance in a club on Saturday night. And, of course, they are likely to behave very differently if they know you have come to observe them dancing.

This section comes under the heading of 'why bother?' and the notions of subjectivity and pragmatism are at the heart of the question of motivation. Why we bother to study one phenomenon rather than another – or use one type of approach rather than another – is intimately tied up in our individual and cultural identity: who we are, where we are, where we want to get to and why? A subjective and ideological aspect of all research is the choice of the research question: what is it that we would find useful to know? The Bloomsbury 21st Century Music Practice series and the research network it grew out of reflect two different ideological slants in this regard.

On the one hand there are practitioner-researchers who are driven by the desire to understand their practice so that they can do it 'better' and of course, each of them has their own agenda about what constitutes 'better'. This may relate to questions of aesthetics or technical quality but it may also relate to communication or representation. I may be concerned with the elegance and coherence of the musical metaphors I'm creating. I may be concerned with the skill and virtuosity I am using in regard to some performance technology. Or I may be concerned with creating the 'right' type of experience for the audience or participants, or with accurately representing a set of views and getting them across effectively. This tripartite differentiation between different types of practice research can be broadly categorized as artistic, pragmatic and activist. In short, this approach to research is primarily concerned with a set of subjective criteria that define a positive outcome for the researcher. They are the criteria for deciding how effective the research activity has been. There needs to be a justification: the criteria which inform the decision that will be made need to be laid out so that others can establish whether they accept and/or agree with the subjective decision. And those criteria should be laid out in terms of the potential ramifications of deciding one way or another. It is different to be an 'anti-vaxer' (although I am not) based on the science of personal risk probability versus public good than it is on the basis of a rejection of that science. And it is different to want classical music to be taught in schools because of evidence that performing notation-based music increases learning capacity in other subjects than it is to believe that it is an inherently superior form of music.

The subjective value system of Western art music is deeply embedded in musical education. We cannot easily remove that subjectivity and ideology but we can explore it as an explicit part of music theory. Ethnomusicology has mostly sought to deal with this issue by being descriptive about judgement, value and quality – by trying to describe the participants' value system. In a Practical Musicology we need to be able to use it and not just describe it. Within popular music studies we have yet to address a fundamental problem. Classical music performance and composition pedagogy has a relatively homogenous value system – a widely accepted set of criteria by which we can judge performance and, perhaps to a lesser degree, composition. Popular music doesn't have that kind of homogeneity – you can't judge a punk rock performance or composition using the same criteria as you would for reggaeton, K-Pop or grime. And this is why practical popular music courses suffer either from students feeling (and being) judged by the wrong criteria or from the perception that they are being judged with lower standards. So my quest for a Practical Musicology is about creating a theoretical framework that brings the subjectivity of judgement, quality and value into the frame and allows music theory to move beyond what Ewell calls the white racial frame (Ewell, 2019) – and other frames based on hegemony and power such as gender, sexuality, class or other constructions of socio-economic and cultural difference.

This brings us to the second of the ideological slants mentioned above which is that there are researchers into practice who are driven by a similarly broad agenda about which features of practice are important enough to warrant being studied. This slant is to do with the subjective choice of a research question rather than the subjective estimation of what constitutes quality in relation to a research question. Rather than wanting to be better at what they do, they choose to study and/or do a particular thing because they perceive it to be a better thing than another thing or things. In some instances, as I've mentioned, this is because a general principle such as novelty is considered more important than virtuosity, and in others it may be something like 'certain general features of classical music are more important than those of popular music' – that harmonic complexity is more important than rhythmic energy, for example. And these subjective choices are complex – they can be about the complexities of status and power as well as the perhaps more mundane issues of taste.

And so, circling back to the 'why bother?' question, the aim of this book is to lay out a theoretical framework with a clear pragmatic purpose. It seeks to provide a series of mechanisms by which music practitioners of all stripes can use both existing and new theoretical work to inform their activity and make it more effectively reflect their intentions. I shall be bringing together a range of existing ideas, I shall be synthesizing some new theory from existing work, and I also hope I shall provide a model for how future new ideas from esthesic research can be incorporated into poeisic/practice research. Thus, for example, new developments in queer theory, such as opacity or temporality, are a way of looking at a problem from a different perspective – one that highlights some of the assumptions that have underpinned previous ways of thinking. Existing theory such as opacity and temporality can be explored as potential tools for creative expression as well as being more abstract socio-cultural forces or phenomena. But before we move on to that section, I want to explore an important epistemological detail of my thinking – and to introduce the idea of these theoretical interludes which will discuss some of the ideas in more technical detail.

Theoretical interlude 1: '*As if*'

Research, and the various forms of knowledge that result from it, is about simplifying the messy reality of life into useful chunks that can be easily communicated to others. Whether that involves agreeing on categories or establishing generalized rules or axioms, it is about the process of reduction. The pragmatic approach that I take is that working 'as if' this knowledge is true should be undertaken as long as it produces useful results. Rather usefully, that approach is also the living embodiment of the theories I use – that human thought and theories are not descriptions of reality. We do not 'know' what reality is and it is too complex for a complete or accurate description. Any description is necessarily a schematic representation, a simplification that attempts to remove the background noise so that we can understand general principles. General principles are necessarily incomplete descriptions and they are subjective (as in, they only exist in the 'mind' of the subject not the 'reality' of the object). As such, they are metaphors for reality that are always created with an ideological goal in mind – e.g. we want a theory of matter that allows us to do certain things – build bridges, predict gravitational forces, calculate the length of time since the big bang. Engineers and architects can build bridges based on the assumption (simplification) that matter behaves 'as if' Newtonian theories are true. Cosmologists use quantum theories even though they know that there are inconsistencies in the results produced by existing theories. It is enough to know that if we work 'as if' some theory is true that we will achieve useful results. More than that though, theories do not represent the way the world <u>is</u>.

If we wanted to build a theoretical model that described the universe completely and accurately, it would actually <u>be</u> another universe. On a more prosaic level, a musicology that explained twenty-first-century music practice on a sub-atomic level wouldn't be very useful even if it was more accurate in some empirical sense. Most cultures have some equivalent of the metaphor 'you can't see the wood for the trees' and our choice of theoretical approach in any given instance should be governed by whether it would be more useful to think in terms of 'the wood' or 'the tree' (or even the molecules or sub-atomic particles that are gathered together in the entity we call a tree). We choose our level or form of categorization based on what would be useful for the task in hand. By allowing for theories that work 'as if' a certain schematic representation or metaphor is true – we decide what is and is not important in a given situation and for a given purpose and judge the theory on whether it provides useful results. That does not mean that we cannot apply rules of logical rigor and tests as to whether the evidence or predictions produced are in accordance with our observations. But we might find, especially in relation to doing something musically 'better', that several very different metaphorical 'as ifs' tell us several very different useful things. Within the world of science, these levels and forms of categorization are seen as part of a unified and consistent whole. I may, working at the level of the wood for example, have discovered a statistical correlation between de-forestation and insect populations and it is unlikely that anyone is going to be interested in the relationship between the behaviour of sub-atomic particles and this phenomenon. They are, however, likely to be concerned that my theoretical explanation is consistent with established scientific knowledge even if no-one explicitly tests that consistency. One of the primary mechanisms through which knowledge progresses is this notion of consistency with existing knowledge. And, of course, when that existing knowledge is flawed (and it always is) the way that it creates inconsistency provides important evidence about the nature of the flaws. If the theoretical 'as if' that I propose as the relationship between de-forestation and insect populations – perhaps a general assertion that de-forestation reduces food supplies and insect habitats – is not consistent with other evidence then it may be necessary to explore some further complexities – perhaps what the forest is replaced with, the specific species of tree and insect, etc.

The same is true of theories about music practice. They may sit outside current theories by examining new forms of practice or new forms of audience engagement, for example, but they can still be examined against the evidence of existing knowledge and that allows us to critique both the new theories and the existing ones in terms of their consistency.

2

Methodology and methods

2.1 Some important themes

There are four main concepts or themes which have emerged out of my research and my writing about it. I have found that they weave in and out of the narrative and crop up in a variety of different ways but that they also reflect some fundamental features of the way I think about music – and, indeed, about the way I think about thought. The detail and nuance of these themes will emerge as they are explored through the book, but in essence they are:

1. The importance of **convergence** and **divergence** as a basic structuring concept in human thought and culture – from the basics in embodied cognition of 'me' and 'not-me' to the complex cultural (and musical) concepts of 'similar' and 'different' or 'insider' and 'outsider'.
2. The way that our perception and interpretation of **restriction** and **affordance** shape our activity in, and understanding of, the world. This is predicated on the idea that the basis of thought is embodied (i.e. action) and that this emerges from our understanding of the possibilities for action – the affordances – and, conversely, of the restrictions that prevent or hinder action.
3. A categorical distinction between three types of thought: **automatic** activity like empathy, learned **subconscious** activity and calculated **conscious** activity. This may be better understood as a field of continuity or a three-way interactive intersection.
4. Our capacity for the **schematic representation** of phenomena by re-casting something complex in a simplified or distilled form based on a limited set of categories, features or activities. An important feature of this is that we also apprehend and appreciate the form of the representational system as well as the phenomenon that is being represented.

These four themes have emerged out of the theoretical basis of my ideas about how we 'do' music and they will continuously crop up in various ways throughout the book as the details of this theoretical basis emerge. As I have said, these themes will provide the mechanisms by which various aspects of theory can become creative tools for practitioners.

2.2 Three dichotomies

But before we start on that, I want to discuss the three dichotomies, mentioned earlier, that are important in practice research where they have a somewhat different flavour than they do in 'traditional' research. It is important to bear in mind the 'as if' aspect of theory as each of these dichotomies is useful in some ways and misleading in others. It is also important to remember that this book is not solely about practice research (or artistic research or practice-as-research) despite the fact that these next three sections focus on that. As we shall see, it is also very much about drawing on research from other 'traditional' areas, but these sections are concerned with methods and the definitions and methods in those 'traditional' areas of research are already firmly established. I do, however, feel I have something to say about methodology in practice research – and in particular about these three dichotomies or continua: inductive/deductive; practical/theoretical; emic/etic.

2.2.1 Inductive and deductive

The difference between inductive and deductive research methods is often characterized as bottom-up and top-down and, to some extent, reflects a similar dichotomy in cognition and problem-solving. There are two mechanisms at work in the brain. The first is induction where we learn from experience. As patterns of behaviour, perception and existence emerge in our lives, they become the 'well-trodden pathways' of the brain; they get marked as more or less probable in certain situations and more or less likely to produce successful outcomes. They form our habits, our expectations and our expertise. They become the learned **subconscious** activity mentioned in Section 2.1; responses and patterns of behaviour that we do not need to think about because they have become wired into our brains through repetition and positive or negative reinforcement (Bear, Connors and Paradiso, 2007, pp. 23–54). The most basic version of this process is the model for induction: if you gather enough data in a randomized fashion then patterns will emerge from that data which reflect aspects of the phenomena in question. These can be to do with categories or causality – phenomena that have features in common and phenomena that have chronological structures in common. This process of bottom-up learning has been mapped onto studies such as computer-based AI neural networks which 'learn' through this number crunching process (Schmidhuber, 2015) and through 'big data' studies (Kitchin and McArdle, 2016) which operate in a similar fashion.

This inductive approach to research also underpins grounded theory. However, the 'purity' of the inductive process in the brain is compromised as soon as patterns start to emerge. Once certain knowledge about the world becomes embodied in these pathways – or schema to give them a technical term – the existing patterns influence how new patterns are formed. This is because the existing patterns are not just to do with what we perceive, but are also enmeshed with what we do as well. Our behaviour becomes conditioned by what we know – and that influences the types of new experiences that we have (and therefore learn from). And in the theoretical models of grounded theory, personified strikingly by the split between Straussian and Glaserian paradigms (Strauss, 1987; Glaser, 1992), the ways in which pre-existing knowledge can be incorporated into the data coding process are recognized as being crucial to its effective operation.

The second mechanism, deduction, is also characterized as top-down. In the 'traditional' scientific method this could be characterized as forming a hypothesis and then designing experiments that might prove that hypothesis to be wrong. Experimental evidence cannot prove something to be right but the lack of 'disproof' can be taken as evidence of the hypothesis' reliability, i.e. that we can proceed for the time being 'as if' it were true. The cognitive mechanisms of top-down processing in the brain are less firmly established than the bottom-up. However, my theoretical framework is partially built upon the neural theory of metaphor (Lakoff and Johnson, 2003; Feldman, 2008) and the idea that there is a process by which schema which have features in common can be identified and mapped onto one another. And embedded in this process is the ability to construct hypothetical schema based on these overlaps (Lakoff, 1990; Fauconnier and Turner, 2003) which can, in turn, suggest blended interpretations or possible courses of action. In short, the process of **conscious** problem-solving – and more contentiously, intuition – involves the construction of hypothetical knowledge from previous experience which can then be tested either through its compatibility with other aspects of remembered experience or through new experimental activity.

Turning, then, to how this has an impact on practice research, I am going to use the example of my 2012 research networking project, Performance in the Studio (PitS), which was funded by the UK Arts and Humanities Research Council (AHRC). During the PitS research network, eight researchers observed the same 'staged' recording project which was also extensively documented. Each of the researchers brought their own theoretical and interpretational agenda to the project but the basic approach was to observe and use the documentation in an inductive process. Of course, strictly speaking, this project lies more in the realm of Stévance and Lacasse's *research creation* (2018) than practice research or auto/ethnography. Unlike *research creation* the creative activity was commissioned and fully financed by the research project rather than being a semi-autonomous project that the artist was working on regardless. This is important because it was envisioned and designed as a data-gathering project – hence the notion of it being inductive, despite the aforementioned 'theoretical and interpretational agenda'. The researchers, Amanda Bailey, Amy Blier-Carruthers, Anne Danielsen, Mine Dogantan-Dack, Morten Michelsen, Thomas Porcello, Alan Williams and myself, were augmented by the fact that two of the participants, Andrew Bourbon and Mike Howlett, were also researcher practitioners. In addition, the fees paid to musicians involved both performance and their inclusion in the research process through interviews and discussion. Indeed, partly because the project was a research network concerned with knowledge exchange rather than being focused on knowledge creation, the amount of data produced by the project was greater than the formal outputs – although the repository of the audio-visual documentation of the weekend session in the four-room studio complex plus the pre- and post-production interviews itself constituted a major output. And the notion of the project as an inductive process was mostly embodied in the networking aspect: the range of interests and approaches that this interdisciplinary band of researchers brought to the table meant that there was quite a broad range of pre-existing knowledge that had an impact on the (informal and communal) data coding process. This collaborative approach therefore diffused the distortions that researchers' pre-conceptions can bring to an inductive methodology.

On the other hand, the Classical Music Hyper-Production project, also funded by the UK AHRC and also involving Amy Blier-Carruthers and Andrew Bourbon as co-investigators (along with Emilie Capulet), provides an example of a more deductive approach. Although it was a practice-driven research process, the 'hypothetical' involved in the planning and execution of these experiments was the notion that techniques drawn from popular music record production could be used to stimulate new interpretations of pieces from the classical repertoire. This hypothesis drove the development of a series of ideas for practice-led recording research. Indeed, further than that, this deductive approach also extended to a more micro-level as well. For each of the recordings, the various participants discussed the potential metaphors and musical imagery that could be employed in the production process. Thus, for the Debussy piano recordings and performances, Emilie Capulet (who performed them) and the team discussed a range of metaphors that were appropriate to the musical materials and the ways in which they could be implemented (Bourbon and Zagorski-Thomas, 2017; Capulet and Zagorski-Thomas, 2017).

It is hard to imagine what 'pure' versions of either of these approaches would be. An idealized inductive process would have to sample all data randomly without any selective process and, even if that were possible, the process of pattern matching still needs to be based on some hypothesis of what constitutes a 'pattern'. The patterns that we, as humans, identify are based on the hypothetical 'conclusions' that evolution has embodied into our physiology based on its history of 'experiments' – i.e. life. An idealized deductive process would start from a hypothesis that has emerged from pure logical principles but, of course, all of our hypotheses emerge from the 'dirt' of our experience. Neither of these approaches can exist in these idealized forms but there is definitely a continuum of some kind between the more inductive process of 'unguided' experiential learning where patterns emerge out of experience and the more deductive hypothesis- or research question-driven process. Of course, when it comes to inductive research (rather than inductive thought processes) there still needs to be a research question: we may not know the specifics of a hypothesis but we will have a ball park area in terms of the problem we are trying to solve or the subject area in which we are seeking new knowledge. An inductive research question will outline a problem area to be explored and a data set in which to look for patterns. In terms of practice research, this might involve engaging in practice 'instinctively' (i.e. using an existing habitus of **subconscious** learned behaviour) and learning from experimentation, versus a deductive process of hypothetical **conscious** experimentation – choosing some metaphor or technique as a guiding principle for exploration and testing the validity or usefulness of the approach.

2.2.2 Practical and theoretical

Positioning practical and theoretical as opposites is frequently done but is also problematic. You might equally say that the opposite of practical is impractical and the opposite of theoretical is un-thought-out. However, practical and theoretical are often opposed through terminology such as 'applied' and 'blue sky' research. The distinction being between research that has a clear and specific practical goal and research that is 'merely' about extending our knowledge and for which a 'use' may or may not be found. Once again, although the two extremes are more likely than the extremes of the induction/deduction dichotomy, the more widely populated territory is along the continuum rather than at either end. If we think of the continuum as progressing from the goal of solving a single problem to the goal of providing more generalized knowledge, the middle ground progresses through the territory of a solution that can be applied in a small variety of similar contexts into knowledge about principles and techniques that can be applied in a wider range of contexts. It is hard, but not theoretically impossible, to imagine a solution to a specific, one-off problem that is so esoteric that it cannot help in any other context and it is equally hard to imagine a principle, rule or 'law' which has no practical applications.

Historically, in universities, the theoretical is seen as a more 'pure' form of research because abstract and generalizing knowledge purports not to be driven by the ideological imperative of a selected problem. Of course, the purity or otherwise of knowledge that can be applied in a wider set of contexts and the intellectual superiority of this type of knowledge over that which solves a specific problem are both ideological judgements. And the choice of what one seeks to understand in this 'pure' way is also an ideological decision but the notion of 'practical' research involves decisions about 'good' and 'bad' or 'right' and 'wrong' ways of doing something and that involves a further journey down the ideological road. However, that additional journey, making value judgements about potential outcomes, seems more useful than the seemingly arbitrary one about which form of knowledge is 'better'. An example such as historically informed performance illustrates a research agenda that is driven by an ideological stimulus such as historical authenticity over the more established stimulus of individual creative expression. Very often in the world of research these ideological positions are portrayed as truths self-evident because they are well-established historical and cultural conventions such as 'art should be valued more than folklore' or 'capitalism and democracy are inextricably linked'. And, of course, the choice of what to study next is always ideologically informed by what was studied before and what kinds of knowledge emerged. The research agenda is just as driven by Vygotsky's *zone of proximal development* (Vygotsky, 1980) as the teaching agenda is. Indeed, the subtitle of this book – with its reference to 21st Century Music Practice – is dogged by a lot of ideological baggage but the aim is to be as simple and literal as possible; to explore the similarities and differences between any forms of musical practice in the twenty-first century. This might range from Japanese Dubstep or Australian musical theatre and from Irish traditional music played by French musicians from Toulouse to Brazilian thrash metal or K-Pop.

How do these distinctions between the practical and theoretical play out in a Practical Musicology? I have already pointed out that both the applied and the theoretical have a place in a musicology concerned with practice – researching how you or I can 'do' music. It might be tempting to be drawn into comparing them with the distinction between the technical and conceptual in music. However, technique can become quite generalized and concerned with broad principles of ergonomics or physiological control and the conceptual can be very specific – considering the most effective metaphor to be applied in a very specific or singular context. In a similar manner, activity that focuses on the realism of what is being represented versus work that focuses on the elegance or virtuosity of the **representation** can equally exist in either of these forms. We might consider that realism equates to specificity but the hypothetical can be realist as well as the 'real'. Hypothetical realism is based on general principles being used to create a hypothetical instance. And the elegance or virtuosity of a representation can rely on the specifics of an instance as much as on the generalities. On the other hand, the distinction between mental processes such as empathy and learned **subconscious** responses versus **consciously** calculated metaphors provides a better fit. The raw guttural ('method') response can be seen as relating to the specific circumstances that triggered or suggested it while a crafted and stylized approach is based on the consideration of whether this is the appropriate context: a process that requires us to make some generalizations about the context we are in.

Returning to the Classical Music Hyper-Production example, we can also see how there is a connection between the induction/deduction dichotomy and this practical/theoretical one. A data-driven, bottom-up process seems, at first sight, connected to a specific application while the hypothetical, top-down process of deduction relates to a generalized, theoretical approach. However, of course, induction is driving towards a theoretical outcome and deduction involves testing theory in specific situations. One of our experiments during the trip to Poland was to record Mozart's string quartet number 19 (KV465) performed by Małgorzata Filipowicz (vln 1), Anna Olszewska (vln 2), Kamila Barteczko (vla) and Anna Kulak (vcl) and arranged by myself. It was recorded to a click track in a series of different spaces in a sixteenth-century palace at Piotrowice Nyskie in southern Poland in June 2015. The current owners of the palace keep poultry in the grounds and we knew in advance that the constant noise floor of geese, chickens and turkeys meant that the recordings would not produce a usable final recording. This was practice research in a starker sense than usual: the process of experimentation was the only 'output' as such. The arrangement involved changing very little musically but fragmented the parts so that they could be recorded in different spaces. The inspiration for this was an analysis of the Kings of Leon's 'Sex on Fire' (Zagorski-Thomas, 2014a) and, in particular, the use of different spatial acoustics in various sections of that production that roughly corresponded to the notion that louder passages were staged in larger spaces. The seven spaces that were used were:

1. The master bedroom with a domed ceiling. This provided a small chamber reverb and the majority of the recording was done one instrument at a time.
2. A medium-sized barn space where the recording was done one instrument at a time with a close microphone and another about four meters above the player in the roof.
3. A corner of a small living room with each player recorded individually with a close microphone and heavy curtains and blankets to deaden the acoustic.
4. A small basement with a low ceiling and stone and brick walls and floor. The quartet played together because the dampness in the basement made it difficult to work there for long periods of time.
5. A cow shed where the ceiling consisted of a series of parabolic domes which created very intense comb filtering and resonant reverberation. Each player was recorded separately.
6. A large barn where the recording was done one instrument at a time with a close microphone and another about thirty meters away.
7. The ballroom where a short segment was recorded with the quartet playing together.

We were therefore making very site-specific decisions about which features of the ambience we wanted to capture and how the microphone placement was going to help with that. Indeed, the resonant, comb filtering of the cow shed produced by the parabolic domes of the very distinctive ceiling was the result of two days of experiments before the string players arrived where myself, Andrew Bourbon and eight of our masters students recorded a range of sounds using different microphone arrays to explore the acoustic potential of this unique space. Thus, on the one hand, the research process involved highly site-specific experiments and decisions and yet, given that we knew that it would not result in any usable recordings, the results were general and theoretical. The process allowed us to think about the practical and musical implications of transferring these techniques from popular music to the classical string quartet without the pressure of having to produce pristine and potentially commercial results. Interestingly, many of the results told us very specific things about the practicalities of how to make general principles work in specific contexts. For example, within popular music practice, it is common to use different forms of ambience on different instruments in an ensemble – perhaps a shorter reverberation time on rhythmic instruments and a longer one on melodic instruments. The general principle is to match reverb times to instrument note lengths and to maintain clarity by preventing a build-up of reverberation tails that mask the onsets of new rhythmic notes. Our experiments suggested a good deal of additional detail and nuance to this general principle – in some instances allowing us to think explicitly about tacit knowledge that we had already been using and in other instances providing new insights. The point I am making in relation to this practical/theoretical dichotomy, though, is that there is a continual interaction between these two forms of knowledge. Any specific application of general theoretical knowledge not only produces specific knowledge about this particular context but also enriches the theoretical knowledge itself. It is a single circular progression. The mechanism will be explored throughout the book but is particularly related to the discussion of schema in Chapter 5.

2.2.3 Emic and etic

The third of these dichotomies relates to the nature of the researcher as either an insider or outsider. Whereas in ethnography these terms are used to distinguish between a participant researcher and an external observer, in practice research, where to be a researcher is to be a participant by definition, the distinction relates to how initiated one is into the participant role – to be an insider is to know what you are doing and to be an outsider is to be an ingenue. Or it can also relate to how your role fits into the social structure of the participant community. These are, of course, two of the ways in which the theme of **convergence** and **divergence** manifests itself in practice research. Do you share the habitus, language, knowledge and values of other participants? My musical experience was more as a song writer and performer in my early career and I gradually crept into the world of recording and record production. On a more nuanced level, my performance skills as both a vocalist and a guitarist combine elements of both the insider and the outsider. My taste was quite eclectic but also changed quite dramatically over the years so I did not become steeped in a particular musical scene which also meant that I was more of a 'jack of all trades' than a master of one. With the onset of MIDI I was also drawn into drum, keyboard and sample-loop programming which further exacerbated the broad but shallow nature of my performance skills. In many ways this broad set of skills was very useful for arranging and communicating musical ideas to those who were more expert performers than I was. It also, however, fostered an element of imposter syndrome: the feeling that I was not a 'proper' musician. On the other hand, my experience as a sound engineer and producer fostered an entirely different set of emic/etic reactions. As I mentioned, I gained entry mostly as a self-taught engineer. The apprentice-style experience and knowledge that I gained was through freelance work and because I had the kind of mind that could read through technical manuals and understand and learn from them. This gave me quite a strong knowledge base – one that I worked at quite extensively – but without the social capital that working and learning through an established studio complex in the conventional studio apprenticeship model provided. I became an insider through knowledge and an outsider through socialization in a community that I thought I was a member of. In the Polish Piotrowice Nyskie recordings for the Classical Music Hyper-Production project, after a few years as a full-time researcher and lecturer, I was surprised at how much of that insider/outsider self-image returned. I realized that on the recording side, all of those insecurities about being an outsider in the recording community had virtually disappeared. On the other hand, even working with comparatively young and inexperienced musicians (they were mostly recent graduates of the Wrocław conservatory), I was much more nervous about directing the performances of both the string quartet and the SATB vocal quartet than I needed to be.

The emic notion of having confidence in your abilities as a participant is one feature of this idea. It can take several forms relating to feeling you have the correct detailed technical skills to be a competent member of the team, a sufficient 'big picture' overview to delegate to a team with specific skills and the social aspect that grows out of a knowledge of the ways of being, thinking and talking that are common in this community. At the same time, the etic notion of being an outsider is similarly affected by your sense of the 'rightness' of your role. In many ways, the roles of leadership and delegation establish aspects of an etic persona as much as an emic one. The 'big picture' is, almost by definition, an outsider perspective and yet, if we return to our 'can't see the wood for the trees' metaphor, you have to have some insider knowledge about what trees are in order to know what a wood is, but you also have to be outside of the wood in order to see it properly.

The emic/etic question also brings us back to the notion of subjectivity. Does your immersion in the activities that are under investigation make you more or less likely to understand them? There is a long history of discussion in anthropology and ethnomusicology about, on the one hand, the benefits of an external perspective and, on the other, the problems of looking at one culture from the perspective of another. The idea that there is a neutral or normative perspective that flows from the objectivity of the scientific method is useful in some ways and problematic in others. Of course, this is also a vital issue in practice research, and the question takes us back to the roots of the tensions inherent in both deductive and inductive reasoning: what kinds of understanding do we bring to the conceptualization of the problems we face? What difference does it make to our research if we share the same *habitus* (Bourdieu, 1993) and categorical distinctions in relation to the processes we are studying as the participants in those processes? While there is no absolute right and wrong in regard to this, we do need to be aware of the types of distortion and potential 'blindness' to certain features that both emic and etic approaches can bring.

2.3 Types of knowledge

In the first chapter, I talked about the way that practice research is, almost by definition, based on case studies – on specific examples of practice. If part of our definition of research is that it must be transferrable knowledge as well as being new, then it should produce general principles that can be applied in different contexts. And by general principles, I certainly do not mean general aesthetics. I mean the types of mechanism through which we can workshop our own aesthetics – whether those are forms of socially **convergent** aesthetics that appeal across a broad range of demographics or more specialist and niche **divergent** aesthetics. I have identified four types of new knowledge based around the theoretical model that will be elaborated upon throughout the book and which also relate to the four types of aesthetic appreciation that I will outline in Chapters 5 and 6. These categories have been designed to provide scope for including a broad range of musical styles and traditions as well as a wide variety of roles and activities, while maintaining the potential for representing transferrable knowledge through general principles.

2.3.1 The relationship between problem-solving and technical skill

As I will elaborate in the rest of the book, the **inductive** and **deductive** distinction involves two different types of knowledge. The inductive process involves learning by experience and repetition. The notion of technical skill involves creating a kind of script or flow diagram where particular patterns of perception and action are reinforced by the achievement of goals: when particular patterns of perceptual stimulus are present, we learn that certain actions will move us towards a goal or sub-goal. Many of these forms of skill exist in the **subconscious** mode of thought – although it is important to maintain a distinction between subconscious and non-verbal. Tacit knowledge – things that we know how to do but cannot explain – can be **conscious** or **subconscious**. One of the features of inductive learning is that, as the patterns become more and more reinforced in our brains, the detail becomes **subconscious**. Infants work hard consciously at learning how to walk but it eventually becomes a subconscious process for most of us, most of the time. The deductive process, on the other hand, is about creating a hypothetical: patterns of perception and action that have not been experienced but which seem possible based on previous experience and which would move us towards a goal or sub-goal. It involves making connections between existing patterns by finding aspects of commonality to suggest a possibility or affordance. I might learn from observing my family and copying them that black currants taste good (inductive) and see various other forms of berry in the hedgerows and use the deductive process to test whether they also taste good. This might produce positive results in the case of blackberries or sloes and rather different results in the case of deadly nightshade.

There are many ways in which these two types of knowledge can manifest themselves and be combined to achieve some musical goals. In Anthony Meynell's

PhD (2017) he explored various recording and processing techniques from the 1960s that were associated with psychedelia. One set of experiments explored the process of tape phasing compared to later electronic phasing techniques. The performative possibilities of 'playing' the gestural shape of the phasing sound by using the tape vari-speed knob became obvious through the inductive experience of doing it. This and other examples of changes in technology produced several specific historical case studies which might suggest possibilities to other recordists for using them in contemporary contexts. However, it also suggests a broader principle of looking at electronic interfaces from the perspective of identifying parameters that could be controlled differently and, in particular, of allowing gestural control of parameters that have been automated in some way.

2.3.2 The relationship between the development and emergence of quality judgements and methods

The subject of quality judgements as a key part of the research process is going to come up repeatedly in the book. As I will discuss in more detail in the methods section below, Practical Musicology and various forms of practice and artistic research differ from other forms of research in that the quality criteria for judging the success or otherwise of the research process are negotiated as part of the methodology and not set 'externally' as part of the definition of the paradigm or as the unstated ideology that underpins and predicates the research question. While it is possible for a Practical Musicology study to be conducted outside of practice research, I am not aware of any that have explicitly included the development and emergence of quality judgements in the research process. I can think of several studies in the fields of record production and performance pedagogy that have an implicit aesthetic aim underpinning a study of practice but not studies that embed aesthetics in the research. Of course, describing an aesthetic and the way in which it was negotiated and emerged from the process does not constitute sharable knowledge about how aesthetics emerge.

Charulatha Mani's (2021) performance experiments for her PhD and subsequent research have involved exploring the creative possibilities of singing repertoire from early European opera using ornamentation techniques drawn from Indian Karnatic music. Although Mani does not frame the aesthetic decisions extensively through the lens of first person expression, the notion of historically informed 'aptness' and a gender theory inflected re-evaluation of what constitute appropriate forms of expression for a female Karnatic vocalist are central to the development of the technique. The danger with a study like this is that it could easily become a process split in two: between a comparative historical study into the similarities and differences between ornamentation in the two traditions and a highly creative application of those ideas in performance. Mani's work not only uses the sonic and haptic outputs of performance experiments to conduct the comparative study. She also uses both those experiments and the historical research to develop an aesthetic approach that relates vocal ornamentation to both the sound and sensation of doing it and is also founded on an explicitly stated ideological motivation: de-colonizing Western music practice. By comparing what she does to the 1960s and 1970s historically informed performance movement in the UK (and the fact that it was not 'historically informed' but 'came out of nowhere' (Mani, 2021, p. 74)), she points to the importance of who you are when you reinterpret early music.

2.3.3 The complex aesthetic relationship between the expected and the unexpected

There is no reason that Practical Musicology needs to be based on the strongly psychology-inflected theory that I am outlining in this book but that is my choice as outlined above. That is why these four types of new knowledge are not framed in terms of the theory I outline. But in the past half-century, theories about the psychology of expectation (e.g. Lerdahl and Jackendoff, 1996; Huron, 2008) have become important within mainstream musicology and, of course, in any musical tradition the process of pedagogy is based on what is expected practice. And in many traditions, mature exponents are expected to produce some form of unexpectedness. However, music psychology has focused on the practices of Western art music for the most part and, generally, with its avoidance of explicit questions about quality – about what might be 'good' or 'bad' ways of fulfilling or not fulfilling expectations about harmonic progression – has focused on how it is done. In line with Ewell's (2019) exultation to widen the net of music theory, Practical Musicology can contribute towards a broader pattern of research into expectation that ranges from the macro-level of which styles or traditions should exist in which contexts (c.f. the discussion of Charulatha Mani in the previous section) to the micro-level of expectations about timing in groove.

I am currently working on an audio-visual album of songs called *Failing Upwards* which, all being well, should appear at roughly the same time as this book. While the album is unashamedly intertextual – drawing on rock, hip hop, jazz, soul, Congolese rumba and electronic dance music – I am also continually working on little details that reference other styles, songs and historical periods. The aim is to create something that is relatively familiar and expected in terms of what popular music is, while at the same time providing a multitude of small-scale references, clues and hints that afford and encourage multiple listenings. As such, the project is an exercise in how I think the expected and the unexpected can work together.

2.3.4 The mechanisms for creating metaphors relating theory to artistic, pragmatic or activist practice

In Chapter 1 I drew the distinction between artistic, pragmatic and activist forms of practice research and I will revisit that idea in the section on methods below and later in the book. With or without that distinction, musical practice is always informed by some kind of theory – whether through the expectational rules of tension and release in Western harmony, something more poetic such as the association of Indian *raga* with times of the day, or the association of popular music with particular types of lifestyle or identity. Using the term 'metaphor' in the cognitive sense of Lakoff and Johnson (2003) rather than as a purely linguistic device, some aspect of the musical sound or the activity which produces it is mapped onto some aspect of meaning: particular 'dissonant' intervals mapped to psychological tension, scalar patterns with atmospheric conditions or particular timbres with tropes like rebellion or sophistication. However, analogies like these do not get to the heart of the matter. The metaphors are more complex and nuanced than this because they are based on extended narratives and the contexts in which they occur. And, as I mentioned in relation to expectations, these can work on the micro and the macro level – as can the kinds of general principles that emerge from the research.

In one of the Orpheus Institute's online videos Tom Beghin discusses an example of his work on the pedalling in the middle movement of Beethoven's fourth piano concerto (Impett, 2019, p. 2.2 Tom Beghin's videos) where his experiments with a recreation of Beethoven's 1803 French Erard piano are combined with a musicological analysis of the piece to suggest performance strategies. The experience of the precise and specific mechanism that Beethoven was playing with has inspired a musical metaphor through which pianists can explore his work on modern instruments.

2.4 Methods

The identification of these types of new knowledge provides a framework for identifying goals and outlining specific research questions or problems. This, then, forms a basis for the methodology of Practical Musicology but we also need to identify some specific methods. The methodological impetus for identifying these methods is two-fold and goes to the heart of the identity of this approach. Firstly, as I have mentioned several times, the identification and/or development of quality judgements has to be documented and analysed in some way. Secondly, the types of new knowledge that are being sought will inform and define the way they should be represented. Some forms of tacit knowledge may be best represented through audio-visual media, and other knowledge may be best represented through language. That, however, is not sufficient as a distinction. The features that we need to show, the perspective that we need to take, the type of narrative structure that we need to represent: these will all help to determine the form of documentation and the subsequent analysis and representation of that analysis.

There are three types of output that musical creativity produces. The first two – an artefact or a performance or event – provide a common basis for distinction, but the third – a set of instructions to others about how to produce the musical output – are usually lumped into the category of artefact. Goodman (1968) introduced the distinction between autographic and allographic works of art and writers such as Gracyk (1996) have talked about it more specifically in music. Autographic work relates to the creation of a unique output such as a painting and allographic relates to something reproducible like a book where the uniqueness of the object or activity is not important. This, of course, also relates to Benjamin's (1969) writing about the aura of a unique artwork and mechanical reproduction. Table 1 maps these two axes onto some descriptions and examples.

Table 1 Types of musical output

	Artefact	Performance/Event	Instructions
Autographic	Unique artefact e.g. audio installation	One-off performance or event	One-off instructions e.g. a theme for improvisation
Allographic	Reproducible artefact e.g. recording	Repeatable performance or event	Transferrable instructions e.g. score

In the presentation I gave for the Practice Research Assembly of the UK Arts and Humanities Research Council's Scottish Graduate School for Arts and Humanities in 2021, I was asked to outline some principles for publishing practice research across a range of arts disciplines. I distinguished between three forms of practice research: artistic, pragmatic and activist. I also used Table 2 as a way of distinguishing them from each other and from autoethnography, action research and applied research. It should hopefully be clear that, given that Practical Musicology is partially defined in terms of including quality judgements in the research goals, the artistic and pragmatic forms of musical practice research fall into that definition. The fundamental difference between

Table 2 Defining characteristics of various forms of research that can involve artistic practice

	Quality Judgement Type	Research Goals	Methods	Reasoning
Autoethnography	Accuracy of interpretation (communal)	To understand	Qualitative	Inductive
Practice Research (artistic)	Aesthetic (individual)	To understand and improve (improvement criteria part of the research problem)	Qualitative	Inductive and deductive
Practice Research (pragmatic)	Aesthetic (communal)	To understand and improve (improvement criteria part of the research problem)	Qualitative	Inductive and deductive
Practice Research (activist)	Ideological	To understand and improve (improvement criteria set in the research question)	Qualitative	Inductive and deductive
Action Research	Measurable/ ideological	To understand and improve (improvement criteria set in the research question)	Quantitative or qualitative	Inductive
Applied Research	Measurable/ ideological	To improve (improvement criteria set in the research question)	Quantitative	Deductive

autoethnographic and practice research is that autoethnography aims to find out how something is done and practice research is about how to 'do it better' or more effectively. This relates to the idea that the establishment of the criteria for improvement is part of the research process. When and how those criteria for judging quality, benefit and improvement are set is what distinguishes action research and applied research from practice research. Research in those areas mostly establishes measurable quantitative criteria in advance. However, I would also add the caveat that there are blurred boundaries between most, if not all, of these paradigms.

If we think about the research process through the metaphor of a journey, we can ask three questions. Where am I going? How do I get there? And how will I know when I'm there if no-one has been there before? This last question may seem an odd aspect of the metaphor in this modern world but we should remember that when explorers like Columbus travelled west to try to circumnavigate the globe they assumed they had arrived in some part of India when they arrived in the Americas. They didn't know how to identify their destination. The question of 'where do I want to be?' is usually quite clear in terms of the type of artefact being produced. Although, perhaps unusually, I thought I was making an audio album when I started the *Failing Upwards* project and the way that the video element became embedded into the music production ideas emerged later and took me by surprise. However, what is often less clear is the number of songs; the way they have merged into a more singular conceptual entity; the musicians who are involved; the arrangements, the lyrics, the music and the intertextual ideas; and the issues about temporality and opacity. All these things have been developing and are continuing to develop through the process of creation. The negotiation and development of the criteria for quality judgement are part of the practice research process and this journey metaphor reflects the fact that, even more than in standard qualitative research, the research question is constantly being clarified and revised during the research process. To labour the journey metaphor, even when I know where I am going there will be detours for toilets, petrol and food and I may decide to use the Park & Ride instead of the city centre car parks. When I don't know exactly where I am going and what it looks like, I am also changing my ideas about what my destination is. The research question and the methodology have to embody a recursive process. I reflect and revise my judgement of what constitutes a good outcome and how that can be achieved. Thus aesthetics (quality judgements) and the appropriate methods for documentation and analysis are part of this ongoing iterative and recursive journey.

Everything that we want to document and analyse in Practical Musicology is a subjective phenomenon, a phenomenon of the mind. Even when we are looking at people, objects and actions we are looking at what they are doing to suggest meaning for other people. In that sense, all of the 'documentation' is 'representation'. There is not a finite set of data to be 'captured'. As I mentioned earlier there are features that we need to show, perspectives that we need to take and types of narrative structure that we need to represent. We can represent this information with a temporal focus or a spatial focus. We can deconstruct it in various ways and we can represent it through various processes of internal narrative.

2.4.1 Temporal focus

By using the term 'temporal focus', I mean documentation and representation methods that use time as a structuring principle and/or manipulate temporal relationships to bring out ideas and relationships. Perhaps the most obvious of these methods is the idea of a timeline as a structuring principle: representing your practice based on the order in which it happened. This might be a literal timeline where time is represented on an axis and activities, phases or events are placed in chronological relation to that axis. Or it might be a series of snapshots – e.g. various versions of files from my album, *Failing Upwards*. During the development and production I saved versions with new date stamps when something that felt significant changed. A second type of media-based documentation involves telescoping or otherwise altering the temporal structure of the original activities. Thus varying the speed of a video playback with either time-lapse (which increases the speed) or slow motion provides another temporal perspective that can encourage different forms of interpretation. And thirdly there is the idea of a structural analysis – a schematic representation of time, of phases of activity that are a basic form of interpretation – as well as documentation of what happened – a practice akin to thematic coding of interviews in the social sciences.

2.4.2 Spatial focus

Spatial focus refers to not just observing something over time but observing the same phenomenon from a variety of perspectives. Just as we can playback media at different speeds, we can zoom in and out to view more detail or the bigger picture. During one of the first recording sessions on *Failing Upwards* with the Congolese guitarist Kiamfu Kasongo I made a video where you can see me directing him but if you zoom in you can see what his hands are doing in detail. And, of course, in order to represent aspects of practice in ways that explicate tacit knowledge about a particular feature, we might combine the spatial and temporal: zooming in and slowing down, for example. Just as I talked about the schematic representation of the temporal aspects of the activity, we can also use visual representations of spatial relationships. This can be relatively literal, as in a diagram to demonstrate lines of sight or physical groupings or it can relate to spatial representations that are part of the process. It might be used to demonstrate how editing software translates temporal and aural information into the spatial realm on the computer screen and how that can be used to suggest new musical relationships or different ways of conceptualizing structure. A third form of spatial focus is the possibility of presenting multiple perspective of the same phenomenon simultaneously. An obvious example of multi-perspective data capture would be having several camera angles filming the same moment. In the recording world we also do the same by capturing the same performance with multiple microphones. On the *Failing Upwards* recordings there are two drummers, Winston Clifford and Jasmine Kayser, who were playing together in the room and were recorded with sixteen separate microphones. Each with a different spatial relationship to a different part of the drum kit and allowing for multiple configurations that could be used to highlight different features of the performance and their interaction.

2.4.3 Deconstruction

The notion of deconstruction is something that crosses over with the various schematic and structural representations we've talked about already. It is about re-representing information in a different way that brings out or allows us to find relationships or features that weren't visible in the raw data. So, for example, I might simplify a complex set of interactions into categories of influence – of when it happened and who it was. We can also create multi-modal representations that combine complex information from different types of sensory experience. We could, for example, show the sixteen channels of audio mentioned above with some split screen footage of the two drummers. Thus, the deconstruction process creates something that is simplified but it can combine multiple simplified perspectives into a complex representation. By presenting multiple dimensions simultaneously in a form that can be explored slowly over time, creative visualizations[1] provide opportunities for understanding relationships and connections between different aspects of data (e.g. McCandless, 2012; Krum, 2013). Another technique that popular music scholar Phil Tagg uses is the notion of substitution or commutation (Tagg, 2000). This can be either a hypothetical or real substitution to see what the effect is – imagining or trying out the same melody on a trumpet and a saxophone and also imagining or hearing how it affects our interpretation. Obviously this is something we do all the time in practice when making decisions between alternative strategies but it also needs to be formalized into the documentation process.

2.4.4 Internal narrative

The fourth of these methods is the creation or documentation of an internal narrative. Well-established techniques such as reflective journaling and stimulated recall are found in ethnography and autoethnography. In keeping with my repeated assertions about Practical Musicology, a third important factor here is concerned with identifying goals as the outcome of quality judgements. Indeed, once goals are identified they should form an integral part of any reflective journaling, interpretational phenomenological analysis and stimulated recall. And, of course, we may choose to represent our internal narrative and the journey towards crystalizing our criteria for quality judgements and aesthetics through a range of non-verbal representational systems: sequential examples of how our practice, or the outputs, got 'better'. That way, we can reflect on which features are changing and how and get to a more explicit definition of 'better' and thence to some general principles about 'betterness' and how it emerges. This question of quality judgements should be formalized in the methodology and should be regularly assessed and documented. Given that much of what we might be seeking to uncover and analyse is likely to be tacit knowledge, it makes sense that techniques to explicate motivations, patterns of behaviour and habits might be useful. There are techniques such as mind maps, Rogerian therapy (Rogers, 2003) and Kelly repertory grids (Fransella, Bell and Bannister, 2004) which can provide insights and lateral thinking about these internalized narratives. And, of course, discussing your research and your findings with

---

[1] Or auralizations or potentially other modes of perception like haptics which might afford new forms of representation.

other practitioners and practice researchers provides a hybrid form of member checking or participant validation (Birt *et al.*, 2016; Candela, 2019).

2.5 Forms of analysis

As can be seen from the description of these categories of methods mentioned above, there is no distinct boundary between these methods of representation and the forms of analysis required to produce the new knowledge. This is true in all forms of research – that any form of data capture or representation is based on preconceptions about what is being analysed or represented. Where we point the camera or the microphone, when we start and stop recording, which questions we ask: these are all predicated on assumptions about what is important and what is unimportant. That is also why pilot studies and test runs are so important. They provide valuable information and clues about what you might be missing or how you might be wasting resources on documenting some aspect that is unimportant.

It will become clear throughout the book that I consider a key part of analysis to be based on the twin process of categorization and feature recognition. All of the forms of documentation mentioned above relate to the identification of features through which we can categorize and the identification of relationships through which we can also categorize. There are a broad range of techniques for analysis in other disciplines which provide techniques and tools for conducting these types of feature extraction. Textual analysis of the musical outputs we produce provides features that can be used to explore the development of aesthetics. The narrative techniques of autoethnography and interpretative phenomenological analysis can both work in a similar manner. Indeed, we can draw from anywhere if it appears relevant. The important points are to identify the research goal, bear in mind the principles of identifying quality judgements and the appropriate form for the 'data', think about the characteristics of your research journey's end (and how you will recognize them) and then choose the appropriate methods.

2.5.1 Roles

One final feature of analysis in Practical Musicology is something that will emerge later in the book – the types of agency that practitioners can adopt. The trouble with categories or typologies – despite them being part of the very stuff of research – is that they are 'as if' phenomena. There are never cut-and-dried definitions, so we must always allow for blurring of borders between them. It is also important to remember that in any given project one person can perform several different roles simultaneously (or sequentially) and several people might perform the same role.

I would start by identifying enablers – those who create the pre-conditions or the context in which music making can take place. These include indirect agents such as instrument makers, technology designers and manufacturers, promoters, managers, patrons. There is definitely a blurring of the boundary between enablers and instigators. Instigators can be direct creatives like composers who write a set of instructions or producers who give instructions about what to play. However, they can also be people who commission works which means that they may well also fall into the category of managers. However, before we discuss managing the process, let us mention the creators. These are the people who actually make or manipulate sounds in some 'real-time' process: musicians, performers, etc. Coming back to managers, I mean this in the general sense of the term rather than the word's industry-specific usage. These are people who manage and enable the process of making sounds. Finally, there are the editors: people who engage in some post-hoc manipulation of the sounds that were made – they may edit instructions/scores or they may edit recordings. Some jobs often span several of these roles – sound engineers often engage in creative manipulation of sound during the recording process, manage the recording and edit it afterwards. Many musicians combine instigator and creator and often it includes some element of managing the process.

USEFUL QUESTIONS

These boxes will come into their own in later chapters when we get to the pragmatic details of the theory. However, in this chapter, I would like to preview some of the ideas that will relate to the four themes mentioned earlier:

Convergence and divergence:
In what respects do you consider yourself an insider or an outsider?
> How do you categorize what you do in terms of the roles mentioned above?
> In what circumstances have you learned/acquired your skills inductively through repetition?
> In what circumstances have you used or extended your skills deductively?

Restriction and affordance:

How would you define your practice in terms of the things you do not or cannot do?

How and when do you think about 'what comes next?' during the flow of your musical practice?

Where are the borders between the possible and the impossible in your practice?

What are the things you can do now that you could not do a year ago and why?

Three types of thought – automatic, subconscious and conscious:

Which aspects of your practice are so engrained that you no longer think about them?

What happens when you think about them and try to alter them in some way?

Think of an image or metaphor used in a piece of visual art and apply it to your practice

Schematic representation:
In what ways is your practice based on the ideas it expresses?
In what ways is it based on the ways it expresses them?
How are those two things related?

Theoretical interlude 2:
Restriction, affordance and influence

These three mechanisms – affordance, restriction (or inhibition) and influence – are the three pillars of this theoretical framework. Affordance and restriction are really flip sides of the same coin – the possibility or impossibility of doing something and my approach to them goes beyond Gibson's (1979) original formulation of the ecological approach to perception in which he considered affordances as the empirical possibilities for action and interpretation that were inherent in the environment. My approach is based on the subjective comprehension of affordances which involves a broader interpretation of 'ecology' to include our understanding of the socially and psychologically constructed affordances and restrictions that surround us in the world. Influence is the process by which desires and the opposite (phobias? Dislikes?) become programmed into our cognitive system. At base, they are chemical rewards/discouragements that establish the mechanisms of pleasure and pain or dislike. In particular they relate to the cognitive rewards of problem-solving (Bar, 2009; Canestrari *et al.*, 2018) and the relief of the stress that is caused by unresolved interpretations. Put bluntly, making sense of the world around us has become a driving force in our biological make-up.

When some form of interpretation or course of action is recognized as having the potential to solve some cognitive or practical problem that we are facing then we adopt it as a strategy. This doesn't have to be based on reason or logic. Emotions and feelings (longer-term mental states which can make emotional triggers more likely) are mechanisms for by-passing slower processes of reason (Sloman, 1990; Damasio, 2000, 2011). So influence is the process by which a desire for a positive reward or fear of a negative result is translated into goals – and hence the propensity to act in a particular way. When I say 'these three mechanisms' it relates back to the notion of 'as if' mentioned in the introduction. They are categories of activity that exist in our minds rather than physical things, forces or mechanisms in themselves. They are one of the important tools of thought and are constructed through the establishment of well-worn neural pathways, the result of experience, that allow us to perceive and construct notions of similarity and difference between experiential phenomena. These are phenomena that involve both action and perception – indeed they also include the perception of one's own action, the feeling of doing something. Therefore restriction, affordance and influence become built into the way we react in given contexts. They become part of our musical practice and are constantly being shaped by new actions and experiences. Some may become 'baked in' and difficult to change but others are constantly shifting in response to our actions and experience (of action).

Part of what the next chapter seeks to do is to explore intersectionality by looking at the commonalities of influence, restriction and affordance that a whole range of contextual factors have on music making. Although I argue that these three mechanisms work as metaphors on a range of levels – from the individual, to the interpersonal, to the cultural – the idea is based on a theory of the mind involving thinking as a process rather than what might be called object-based approaches such as semiotics or knowledge-as-information metaphors. Under this process-focused approach, there is no such 'thing' as a message or knowledge or information to be communicated or acquired, there are only processes in which the likelihood of various forms of activity undertaken by any participants changes.

My activity may be restricted or inhibited, encouraged or afforded, or influenced – i.e. not actually causing an action to happen or not to happen, but indirectly, and either implicitly or explicitly, making an action or a type of action more or less likely. This happens through my perception of my surroundings in conjunction with my previous experience. On the individual level, from my experience as a trumpeter and my perception of the nature of a watering can, I might perceive the affordance of turning it into a musical instrument by blowing noisily into it. On the interpersonal level, I might be influenced by the increasing excitement exhibited by my fellow musicians and my audience to 'push' the tempo of my performance (and thus influence my co-performers to do the same – or to try to 'pull me back'). On a cultural level, as a woman, I might feel that certain tropes about 'appropriate' feminine identity in relation to technology inhibit my desire to become a live-sound engineer for rock groups – or the inhibitions that I see implicitly manifested in others (through the absence of women for example) might influence me to go ahead and do it anyway.

3
Context: Styles, tradition and identity

In November 2017 I went with Sara McGuinness on an Erasmus+ funded exchange trip to Cuba where she had arranged, in conjunction with El Alamaçen collective, Yaniela Morales and Sonia Pérez Cassola, to record members of the *Muñequitos de Matanzas* – a Grammy-nominated Cuban Rumba group founded in 1952. The recording was one of the first steps in what has become known as the *Cuban Music Room*.[1] It is an immersive audio-visual format, devised by Sara, in which the final result is a 'room' created by four large screens arranged in a square. The musicians in an ensemble are back-projected onto each screen so that they surround the audience. Behind each screen are a pair of speakers which playback the audio of the particular musicians projected onto that 'wall'. We had eight musicians from the *Muñequitos* – lead vocals (and clave), three backing vocals (one of whom played hand percussion), three hand drum players (*quinto, tres dos, tumba* and *cajon*) and a wood block (*cata*) player – and two dancers. The experience in the *Cuban Music Room* is that the projections are almost life-size (each screen is 3 m × 2 m) and the audience can walk around inside the 'room', observing the musicians at close quarters and hearing the detail of their individual performance or move back and observe and hear the ways they interact with each other. Audiences at the Pitt Rivers Museum in Oxford and La Linea Latin Music Festival in London engaged with the installation in an entirely different manner than they would with a normal video or a live concert. They danced and they listened but they also walked around, pointed, had conversations and drew each other's attention to little events and details.

The audio-visual recording was made in the courtyard or *solar* in Matanzas, Cuba where the group started seventy years ago and many of the current players are the children or family members of the founders. The musicians played with

[1] http://www.c21mp.org/practice-research-publications/sara-mcguinness/

their backs against the four walls of the *solar* facing the four cameras in the centre. Each had a close microphone on their instrument to keep the sounds separate so that we could create the four separate stereo mixes – one for each screen – in post-production. Rumba is a musical form steeped in tradition that developed around the time that Cuba abolished slavery in the late nineteenth century and which is a syncretic music born out of various West and Central African musical forms combined with Spanish influenced choral music. While deeply traditional, it is also continuously evolving and the *Muñequitos* had a reputation for innovating – particularly in the interactions between the *tres dos* and *tumba* hand drums and later when they started to incorporate the kind of break-downs found in the timba popular music style in the 1980s by dropping out the low hand drums. These are musicians who are both following and breaking 'rules' and whose 'rules' have been set by years of tradition and yet are also constantly being changed. It is also a musical style that was forged by the politics and economics of race in Cuba and where musical gender roles are just beginning to break down. It is a highly traditional musical style that has very strict 'rules' about the types of instrument technology that should be used and yet the *Muñequitos* are also highly skilled and experienced recording artists – familiar with the latest recording technologies and techniques. Cuban rumba retains a strong social and community function while at the same time gaining a platform at international festivals where audiences politely listen rather than joining the communal singing and dancing. In addition, from being a low status musical form in the post-slavery, pre-revolutionary period, the Cuban government has elevated it into a national institution through formal structures such as the Ministry of Culture, Conjunto Folklórico Nacional de Cuba and Instituto Cubano de Antropología.

There are, therefore, two aspects of this project which we can focus on through the lens of Practical Musicology: the development of the technical process and the development of the aesthetic. Both of these aspects were thoroughly interrelated: we were working with what was possible and we were working with some 'big picture' goals and they were constantly interacting and influencing each other. This was further complicated by having different participants with different priorities: McGuinness is primarily an academic practitioner (musician) who also trained as an ethnomusicologist and a sound engineer. Morales is an anthropologist specializing in Cuban musical culture. Pérez Cassola works mostly in documenting and promoting Cuban musical culture and moves between the public and private sectors. El Alamacen collective are an arts co-operative based in Matanzas making films and recordings with local artists. My researcher hat was primarily to do with exploring how these various parts of the jigsaw could fit together and helping Sara and El Alamacen with the recording side. While we did that, Yaniela and Sonia documented the recording process and interviewed the participants. It is thus quite a multi-faceted research endeavour and only a relatively small component of it falls into the Practical Musicology category. In addition to adding to the already quite extensive documentation of Cuban Rumba and to the *Muñequitos* in particular, Sara and I have presented on the nature of the format as a form of ethnomusicological documentation and Sara and Sonia are currently discussing and writing about the format's potential as an educational tool in music. The link that can be found in the footnote is to Sara's initial practice research output and is interesting in that it encompasses elements from all three of the types outlined in the first chapter: artistic, pragmatic and activist.

One of the aims of this book is to deal in intersectionality – to explore what we have in common as well as what makes us different from each other. This kind of universal approach got off to a bad start as a reverence for Western art music and the tools that have been developed to analyse it, were used as the yardstick by which to measure and describe other musical forms and traditions. In the Introduction I mentioned Phillip Ewell's (2019) lecture on music theory's white frame as a warning about tradition-specific music theory. The re-invention of comparative musicology in recent years (Clayton, 2007; Born, 2010; Clayton, 2012; Savage and Brown, 2013), of course, happened in a world of increased contextual sensitivities – stemming from cultural theory, the 'new musicology' of the 1980s and 1990s, popular music studies and ethnomusicology. This comes in part from a sense that we were in danger of throwing the baby out with the bath water but also reflects a recognition that the study of the text/baby is impoverished without a study of the context/bath. The juxtaposition of text and context is not however a simple matter of etymology. One is not a corollary of the other. For example, while in a score-based approach to musicology, the music practices used to perform a particular score might be seen as part of the context in which a work exists, in a practice-based approach the texts of musical representation could be seen as part of the context in which music practices emerge. If we are to seek commonalities between examples of practice as disparate as Bach and Dubstep then we also need to understand the similarities and differences in their contexts. And in order to define their context we also need to delineate the nature of the phenomena being studied. There is, of course, no dividing line between music practices and the context in which they exist but it may be useful to progress 'as if' one exists. If we limit the definition of music practices to the physical and mental activities that directly produce musical sounds, transform them or interpret them, then we can start to think of context as the physical, social, cultural or economic factors that encourage, inhibit or influence the occurrence or the nature of those activities. As discussed above, the sound that the *Muñequitos de Matanzas* make – either in the *solar* itself or the sound that emanates from the speakers of the *Cuban Music Room* – is restricted, afforded and influenced by their traditions, their identity, the technologies involved, the function of the musical activity and the value that they and others place on it. Sara's practice research output is not about the *Muñequitos* per se, but about how the *Cuban Music Room* developed through the practice of creating it. Nonetheless, her sensitivity to the musicians' (and other participants') traditions and identity, the technological affordances available to us, the proposed usage of the project and its potential value shaped the emergence of the process and are evident in the videos she made. Before getting further into the nuts and bolts of Practical Musicology – the processes themselves – the rest of this chapter and the next look at ways of mapping theories about the wider contexts of music making onto those practices.

3.1 Musical styles and traditions

The musical culture into which we are born and by which we are influenced in our most formative years is a crucial factor in this definition of context. If we start with the basic level of affordances as described by Gibson (1979), our affordances for activity – including our interpretation of what is happening in and around us – are determined by what is physically possible given the body we inhabit and the environment in which we find ourselves. In terms of sound, the shape and size of our vocal cords, mouth, nasal and sinus cavities determine the types of vocal noises we can emit but what we hear of them is also determined by the acoustic properties of the enclosed and semi-enclosed spaces in our surroundings as well as by the physiology of our hearing system. These physical limitations both afford and restrict the types of sound we can make and, in turn, the types of sound that other humans can and will make and, therefore, what we expect to hear from them. The limits of pitch and dynamics might vary according to the size and strength of the person and certain types of timbral variations will not only be learned as possible but also be used for the recognition of individuals as well. Affordances and restrictions are not only about what is possible and impossible, they also reflect what is more or less likely in different situations based on previous experience. In this model, I go further than Gibson and, in addition to these physical affordances and restrictions, there are also psychologically, socially and culturally constructed ones as well. In these instances, what I believe is possible or likely affects my affordances for action and interpretation. Thus, if I grow up within a particular musical culture my expectations about musical activity – what is 'normal' or 'abnormal' to do or hear – are shaped by that experience. I have expectations about what kinds of noises a human voice can make that are, in some part determined by what is physically possible, but also by what is normal in my experience. It will include affordances for what constitutes music; what particular instruments sound like; where music is likely to be heard or made; what style a particular melody is; even whether a particular sound constitutes an 'appropriate' variation of a tune I am familiar with, i.e. that this is something that I already know rather than something new. So these affordances and restrictions delineate not just what is possible but what is more likely or appropriate in a particular context based on our prior experience.

Of course, even in the least cosmopolitan of worlds we will know others who like and make music that is different from our own. That the variety of our experience is an important influence is the basis of theories of *intertextuality* and Burns and Lacasse (2018) have edited a collection based on how these can be applied to popular music, including my own contribution on how *intertextuality* relates to this theoretical model and vice versa. There has been much discussion about the definition and categorization of styles, genres and traditions and, of course, they are labels that demarcate and identify commonalities of practice (and the sounds that they produce). Unfortunately, that is not a particularly useful definition for the complexities of the naming conventions that have developed in response to distinctions of chronology, geography, identity, economics and culture and the various levels of scale and detail at which they are applied. However, it is useful for considering how these conventions work. There are two main ways in which we acquire our musical (making and listening) habits and aesthetics and they relate to the distinctions we made between **induction** and **deduction** in Chapter 2 – and which will further emerge throughout the book as a primary structuring principle in the brain. On the one hand, there is what we have described so far – the mostly automatic, bottom-up or inductive processes of acclimatization and familiarization that happen as we stew in the juice of our lives – and then there is the top-down or deductive process of seeking out the less-common, unfamiliar and the 'difficult' forms of music that are foreign to our everyday experience. Our aesthetics are constructed through the extent to which the chemistry of our brains 'enjoys' or is 'stressed' by unresolved interpretations and to which we have developed successful strategies for their resolution. These strategies may be more established in certain areas than others – aural skills, language acquisition, visual skills, manual dexterity, abstract mathematical skills, personal relationships – and, whether by nurture or nature, some individuals seem to be better at developing them than others. However, while aesthetics and these various forms of intelligence are intimately connected, that is not to say that the aesthetics of problem-solving or resolving interpretations is in any way more important or 'better' than the aesthetics of allowing unresolved interpretations. It is easy to imagine that both have their own evolutionary advantages and disadvantages.

The musical styles and traditions that we enjoy, understand and can participate in are, then, determined by and continually altering through these two mental processes. There is a good deal of **subconscious** tacit knowledge that simply flows from the expectations generated by our experience and there is also **conscious** engagement that flows from trying to understand unfamiliar, new or difficult experience. And there are countless examples of musicians who have moved between styles and traditions or collaborated with musicians from other backgrounds. Once they engage through a **conscious** deductive process of making sense of these new styles or traditions, they then begin the **subconscious** inductive process of learning through their everyday experience in these new contexts. Even within the experience of a single musician we can see very different forms of influence. Claude Debussy's response to jazz and ragtime was relatively crude and simplistic compared to his nuanced and sophisticated response to Javanese gamelan. In both instances, his responses were individual and separate from the musical cultures rather than participatory. His response remained deductive, based on listening to records and in concert, rather than inductive, immersing himself in the experience of a musical culture. This doesn't necessarily mean that he understood gamelan better than he understood jazz, just that, looking back, the deductive resonances that he drew upon appear to have stimulated his compositional practice in a richer manner. White British blues musicians like Eric Clapton and Keith Richards, on the other hand, may have started in this purely deductive manner of observing, listening and copying, but, later, they also played with many of their heroes and participated in a broader inductive community that, while it maintained a white British slant on an African-American culture, developed a more nuanced and immersive understanding.

These musical styles and traditions exist within the broader context of society and, depending on the culture, our exposure to these practices is likely to be affected by economics. Whether it is payment for the commodification of the music practices of others (concerts, recordings, etc.) or for the opportunity to acquire skills in those practices ourselves (e.g. music lessons), different cultures will have different mechanisms by which this happens. Toulouse-based band Doolin' play Irish traditional music despite being French. Members of the band come from a range of musical backgrounds – rock, jazz, classical, French and Italian folk styles – and they made their way into Irish traditional music through a variety of routes. The Irish traditional music scene has quite a firmly established infrastructure and hierarchy based on apprentice-style relationships and formal competitions but there is also the informal participatory activity of the pub session. The reliance on a traditional canon of repertoire and arrangements makes entry into the immersive, informal sessions relatively easy and convivial for newcomers. Four of the members of Doolin', Wilfried Besse (vocals and accordian), Guilhem Cavaillé (fiddle), Jacob Fournel (tin whistles) and Josselin Fournel (bodhrán) – those who play 'traditional' instruments rather than electric bass or guitar – have all studied with musicians in Ireland and engaged with the formal competition system. Their success requires them to walk a line between these types of markers of authenticity, the traditions of the form and the various innovations and variations that they bring from their other musical experience:

> 'French in origin – though easily mistaken for Irish musicians – this sextet … brings a fresh approach to Irish music. Inspired by the purest tradition, Doolin' combines instrumentals, vocals and original compositions in a resolutely modern style. The arrangements, at times taking their inspiration from pop-rock, folk, jazz, funk or even rap (and always in the best taste), emit great energy. That's Doolin' – Irish music with a French touch!' (Doolin official website: http://www.doolin.fr/english/biography)

Of course, various forms of Celtic rock and Celtic fusion are part of a much wider movement of cosmopolitan and eclectic fusions and evolutions in a range of 'traditional', folk and 'world' music forms that demonstrate the ways in which **divergence** and **convergence** are negotiated. On the one hand, Doolin' can exploit their status as 'outsiders' (i.e. not being Irish) by exploring their **divergence** from tradition – especially given their focus on touring in mainland Europe and North America – but a great deal of their musical identity is also bound up in being able to play inside a nationally defined tradition to which they don't belong.

In a 2020 presentation entitled 'Would You Award Björk or Jimi Hendrix A Practice-Led PhD? – what form does new knowledge take in popular music?' for the IASPM UK & Ireland branch online conference,[2] I employed the conceit of a 'Fantasy Supervision League' based on the Fantasy Football version in which I imagined I was supervising various musicians through practice-based PhDs in order to explore how they could contextualize their practice as research. I will be using this 'Fantasy Supervision League' idea at various points in this book and I am going to start with Josselin Fournel from Doolin'. Focusing on the single element of musical styles and traditions, I would suggest that Josselin could explore the line he walks between traditional bodhrán technique and the innovations that he has brought in from his popular music and jazz background. Using some of the temporal and spatial focus methods outlined in Chapter 1, he could undertake a thematic analysis which categorized phrases both in terms of the tradition or style (e.g. Irish traditional, jazz, rock) but also in terms of a developing aesthetic (what works well and what does not?).

However, this also brings up the question of who determines the parameters within which performers of a style should operate? Shah and Scheufele (2006) suggest that 'opinion leadership is a consequence rather than a cause of civic participation' and I would suggest that this is as true of the types of cultural leadership involved in style and tradition forming as it is for politics. Stakeholders in a community are more likely to be conservative in their tastes and, therefore, to have narrow ideas about what constitutes an authentic form of variation or creativity. Radicalism is, by definition, the territory of 'outsiders' but the causality is important to consider. This way of thinking suggests that you are more likely to be radical if you are an outsider rather than that radicalism will cause you to become an outsider. The earlier discussion of inductive and deductive approaches to the emergence of new styles also

---

[2] https://london-calling-iaspm2020.com/simon-zagorski-thomas-university-of-west-london-uk/

resonates with the notion of interpretive flexibility (Pinch and Bijker, 1987) from theories of the social construction of technology which can also relate to cultural phenomena like musical styles. Once the **conscious** deductive phase of exploring new ways of doing something is replaced by the **subconscious** inductive process of learning through experience, that experience is absorbed rather than questioned and our interpretation becomes inflexible unless we consciously return to a deductive process. Outsiders are more likely to engage in this deductive phase and therefore will still possess interpretive flexibility and a propensity to question the existing way of doing things. These deductive and inductive processes also relate to Moore's typology of three forms of authenticity (Moore, 2002): the first person 'I' of the performer/artist, the second person 'you' of the immediate audience, or the third person 'they' of some established authority. Whereas first person authenticity emerges from the interpretive flexibility of the deductive process, second and third person authenticity emerge from the inductive 'absorbtion' of an externally pre-established value system. In addition, as Moore points out that these are ascribed rather than inscribed qualities, the choice of which type of activity to engage in involves an inherent judgement of whose ascription is the most important. Sometimes this will be a **conscious** decision as part of the deductive process and sometimes it will be inherent in the tacit knowledge of the **subconscious** inductive process. Returning to Josselin's imaginary PhD, those questions about categorizing aspects of his performance in terms of a developing aesthetic could be given an added dimension of nuance by exploring these three modes of authenticity in parallel. If he also categorizes them according to his own individual expression (first person), 'crowd-pleasers' (second person) and authentically 'Irish' (third person), how do they map onto the stylistic and aesthetic categories? His association with five times All-Ireland bodhrán champion, Junior Davey, and Josselin himself being runner-up in the competition signify his convergence with tradition, but can he similarly identify elements from his (non-Doolin') prize-winning performance as more or less individually expressive and more or less expressive of 'traditional' excellence? To turn this into a more longitudinal PhD-style study, it would also make sense to document and compare examples performed in front of different audiences and in a more generic tour rehearsal context. In the heat of the moment, does he instinctively adjust his playing in different contexts and, by using methods such as schematic representation and hypothetical (or real) substitution, can he identify patterns or invariant properties?

USEFUL QUESTIONS

Understanding the nature of the tradition or genre and using an analysis of it to consider affordances, inhibitions and potential influences:

What are the core identifying features of the tradition or genre that you are working in?

Do you want to be mainstream or an outlier of some sort?

If you want to be an outlier, what are the features that you are abandoning, changing or subverting?

Why have you chosen those ones and what are you going to do to them?

How do these issues relate to your feelings of creativity and authenticity?

3.2 Identity

Gender, sexuality, disability, class and race are often bracketed together as a particular type of contextual phenomenon that needs to be taken account of within analysis. In recent years this has frequently come under the heading of identity politics. However, they are each complex mixes of more fundamental phenomena – embodied or physiological differences, psychological differences and socio-cultural differences – which are related to the individual, interpersonal and cultural levels mentioned above in relation to influence, restriction and affordance. Obviously, the extent to which, and the ways in which, these types of differences combine in these phenomena is the subject of a complex discursive process about the inscribed/ascribed, the personal/social and about the power relationships and ideologies of categorization. They all have a very powerful effect on whether, when, where and how we feel we are included in social situations (**convergence** and **divergence** again) or have any power and influence in them, and that in turn has implications for the types of musical practices we engage in and how we are likely to be affected and shaped by them. And the economics and ergonomics of access are also deeply intertwined with these factors as well. It is also important to remain vigilant about the evidence in relation to the inscribed and ascribed debates that are often framed as nature versus nurture. The science has sometimes been interpreted in ways that produce enlightenment and sometimes misinterpreted in ways that result in oppression, inequality and bigotry. These range from the complex history of genetics and eugenics (e.g. Galton, 1904; Allen, 2001; Haker and Beyleveld, 2018) to recent discoveries about the chromosomal ambiguities in sex and gender (Ainsworth, 2015).

What can I say that has not already been said by the many (much better qualified) theorists in these areas? The question returns to practicality. What are the mechanisms by which we can use complex ideas about power, culture, identity and interpretation in practice? My proposal is to break down these ideas into strategies for the identification, enactment and/or avoidance or transcendence of restrictions, affordances and influences. How can we create representations, distortions (such as parodies) or metaphors for the behaviour of particular agents which suggest, signpost or provoke interpretations based on these kinds of ideas?

What kinds of generalities can we draw out of, for example, studies about race and ethnicity in popular music? There are many ways in which race and ethnicity have been used to define nationhood and communal identity through music (Stokes, 1994) – e.g. in China (Stock, 1995; Jones, 2001), India, Pakistan and Afghanistan (Srivastava, 2004; Baily, 2015), South Asian music in the UK (Bakrania, 2013; Hyder, 2017), the United States (Rose, 1994; Stratton, 2015) and what has been called the Black Atlantic legacy of the slave trade (Gilroy, 1993). These relate to both the affirmation and the denial of identity on the basis of race and ethnicity and, as such, can be related to restriction, affordance and influence. For example, both Jones (2001) and Srivastava (2004) point to how, in China and India, respectively, notions of national identity were encouraged in the face of multiple regional languages and cultures through the use of popular music and film music. Additionally, both of these examples illustrate the ways in which gender roles were affected – allowing women professional roles in the music industry, albeit by using child-like voices as a way to sidestep prejudices associating women in music with sexual promiscuity and prostitution. By drawing audiences in through the seemingly non-political portal of music, inductive processes could be instigated which normalized a national language or which blurred regional differences by blending and juxtaposing different musical styles. However, we should not be too eager to claim victory (or even significant influence) for examples of activist art without evidence of change. The recent (2020) rediscovery of the film footage (released as Summer of Soul) from the 1969 Harlem music festival demonstrates how flashes of activity and optimism can be buried by the dominant narrative.

However, activist works obviously do have an effect but the extent to which they 'work' is less part of the pro-active Practical Musicology and more part of the retrospective gaze of history. Practical Musicology is more concerned with the music maker's intent – artistic, pragmatic or activist – than with the aftermath.

Using Jimi Hendrix as another 'Fantasy Supervision League' example, looking at his performance of *Star Spangled Banner* at the Woodstock Festival in 1969, I would get him to undertake a stimulated recall analysis exploring the ways in which he juxtaposes sounds that are mimetic of warfare (Clarke, 2005) into the musical narrative. Many aspects of the activist stance are best expressed through language and his internal narrative expressed through reflective journaling, stimulated recall and goal identification would be important in this research. Was the choice to parody and subvert this piece of music in this context, to do with its use on sporting occasions and some similarities with the festival? Were the drivers explicit (e.g. Vietnam or civil rights violence) or a more general metaphor about the disintegration of the United States?

The notions of deterritorialization and reterritorialization (Deleuze and Guattari, 2004) are broadly sociological and relate to any notion of identity through which one leaves or occupies some territory. So while this can relate to women 'reclaiming the streets', gay people 'coming out of the closet' or senior citizens taking temporary ownership of shopping precincts through 'mall walking', it also relates to indigenous (or existing) populations who have power over, or have lost power to, immigrant populations. Thinking of cultural territory like music in this way can be done both in terms of the physicality of venues, jobs and media presence – how access and control can pass from one group to another – and in terms of musical traditions – such as white British men claiming some ownership of African-American blues, Frenchmen doing the same with Irish traditional music or Koreans doing the same with hip hop and rap. This allows us to extend the notions of restriction and affordances into individual morality and social mores. When and where are the barriers set which prevent or allow us to cross into particular moral, social or cultural territories? Why were the personal and social circumstances right in 1929 for Li Minghui, an eighteen-year-old woman, to break existing taboos about women singing in public and record the song 'Mao Mao Yu'? (Jones, 2001). On a personal level there was the psychological barrier of it being, in her prior experience, something that women did not do and yet, at the same time, having worked in a touring children's singing troupe, she was habituated into the practice of singing – two inductive processes that started to clash as she became an adult. And on a wider note, her experience of it being something that women did not do was part of a social phenomenon in China that stretched back into its history. This song, by using Chinese nationalist language of mandarin instead of the widely used local languages, was a call to the modern twentieth century notion of the Chinese nation. In addition, there is the added dimension that the leader of the children's troupe of performers and the composer of this song, was her father, Li Jinhui. If she were wanting to document this practice and frame it as research through a deterritorialization and reterritorialization theoretical lens, the first step would be to identify some ideas of territory in her practice: perhaps looking for boundaries between being a singer as a girl and as a woman, between tradition and modernity, between the local and the national, between obedience and independence. The question of whether documentation of aspects of her practice which embody these territories and the boundaries between them are best created in their 'natural habitat' (her working life as a singer) or through re-enactment is one for the researcher to explore.

It is remarkable both how quickly history can be re-written and how long memories and traditions can last when displaced or reterritorialized. This works both in terms of normalizing authority – i.e. erasing the past when you have overthrown an existing system – and maintaining traditions and dignity when your system has been overthrown and replaced or you have been forcibly displaced into a new culture. It can also often be seen in the ways a diasporic immigrant community maintains the folklore of 'home' – the third person authenticity of induction and maintaining a tradition being valued above the first person authenticity of deduction and creative variation. This often results in diasporic communities being more 'traditional' than 'home'.

Inductive forms of activity can also be characterized as repetitive and notions of repetition have been theorized in a variety of ways in relation to race and ethnicity. Deleuze (2004) has theorized stereotyping as repetition rather than generalization; as based on a connectivity that is to some extent, arbitrary rather being based on principles or observed categories. This distinction mirrors the bottom-up induction versus top-down deduction model. Although the idea is often attributed to Josef Goebbels, Isa Blagden (1869) wrote 'If a lie is only printed often enough, it becomes a quasi-truth, and if such a truth is repeated often enough, it becomes an article of belief, a dogma, and men will die for it.' The process of familiarization and habituation that both Deleuze and Blagden refer to, reflects the fact that while repeated experience in the physical world is usually a marker of the reliability of the experience, in the world of **representational systems** like language and music, it can be used to reinforce something unreliable or even unpleasant. We have all had the experience of having a tune that we do not like stuck in our heads and this works via the same cognitive mechanism as propaganda, fake news and bigotry. The notion of the counterfactual – a real or hypothetical example that runs counter to some simplified, distorted or wrong idea that has become established through repetition (like the attribution of the idea to Goebbels) – has become an important tool in addressing the distortions inherent in the way the winners have written history. And, of course, it has a similar power in the way that it can inform practice research; artistic, pragmatic or activist. Li Minghui and Jimi Hendrix both embodied counterfactuals that undermined stereotypes simply by existing.

A further way that the notion of repetition has been used in theorizing race and nationality relates to the way it is embedded in a culture itself. On the practical side, Gates (1988) introduced the notion of repetition into the discussion of race through the term 'signifyin(g)'. This is based on his assertion that African-American culture is based on communal repetition as a form of reinforcement and that this is at odds with Western/European individualism. The notion of a cultural difference being that one culture is communal and the other individual is, of course, a gross simplification but the idea is based on the more nuanced idea of pragmatism in the world of post-slavery America – that having less power encourages a more communal approach to life – and on the twentieth century American ideology of individualist capitalism which largely excluded African Americans. Where the communal is based on conformity, it is based in the inductive – on learning through the **subconscious** process of repetition. This process of communal repetition as reinforcement relates to what Tang (2016) has discussed in the context of South and South-East Asian student stereotyping and their reactions to it being about trauma and parody as two forms of repetition. They appear to be at odds – the negative, victim-like repetition of trauma versus the subversive, ownership of parody (a deliberately distorting form of repetition) – and yet both of their uses in present narratives are about an idealized and unrealistic 'solution': making marginal alternative histories visible through the identification of trauma; and about belittling the dominant paradigm through parody. These result in the maintenance of a separate, parallel minoritarian culture that is not the aim of liberal multiculturalism but which fosters 'Model Minority' stereotypes – like hard working and studious South and South-East Asian student stereotypes (Tang, 2016, p. 5). Indeed, minoritarian cultures have frequently been built upon a stereotypical notion of inherent musicality – another form of 'model minority' – which is cultivated and exploited in ways that foster a self-fulfilling prophecy.

The notion of repetition is so deeply ingrained in studies of race and/in performance that Colbert, Jones and Vogel (2020) felt the need to draw together a range of racial and temporality theory other than repetition. While the performance studies work focused on repetition is mostly in theatre, installation / activist art and movement studies, it has a lot of useful things to say for Practical Musicology and so does this kind of work that looks at other forms of temporality theory. Colbert *et al.* (2020) and their contributing writers look at notions such as the after-life of activities, morphologies of gesture, the counter-factuals that can grow out of re-enactment, and dichotomies such as presence and absence. As we progress further into this book it should become clear how these ideas can also be considered and utilized through these mechanisms of affordance, inhibition and influence and the concomitant theories of cognition, communication, action and interaction. Briefly stated, though, these ideas relate to the structures that emerge in the mind through this process of inductive learning. The notion of after-life (Colbert, Jones and Vogel, 2020, pp. 15–17) relates to the way that a modular and bounded schema – the mental representation of an event or activity – is problematic: that there is always some further affordance that needs to be considered or accounted for. In Tina Post's chapter (Colbert, Jones and Vogel, 2020, pp. 123–6) looking at morphologies of gesture in boxing and dance, we can explore this further through the contextual understanding of gestural schema as animal or mechanical.

While these ideas are not as established within music performance studies, they are certainly being explored within popular music studies. Stan Hawkins (2016) is among many looking into queerness in popular music and drawing on notions of temporality (Taylor, 2010) and opacity (de Villiers, 2012, 2015) in other ways. Whereas the performative notion of temporality in theatre studies often focuses on the specifics of repetition and re-enactment, queer theory and race and gender studies (e.g. Butler, 1990, 2006) also address the general repetition of life and its structuring role in oppression, conditioning and the mechanics of power. Thus, queer time in terms of lifespan structures can be opposed to heteronormative reproductive time which is also part of the process of maintaining patriarchal dominance through the dissonance between normalized working-life temporality and reproductive temporality. Opacity – the notion of how visible or invisible particular features of one's identity are to others – takes us back to the distinction made at the beginning of this section between embodied or physiological differences, psychological differences and socio-cultural differences. Whereas race, gender and physical abilities have embodied characteristics which, while they can be more or less visible, make certain identities more transparent and, therefore, obvious and apparent, others, such as sexuality, nationality, neurodiversity and socio-economic distinctions, are more apparent through behaviour than appearance. The nuances of performativity that relate to these features of identity can be explored, as discussed above, through physical, psychological and culturally constructed restrictions, affordances and influences.

Going back to the Hendrix PhD example of *Star Spangled Banner*, I would steer him towards taking a couple of ideas from queer theory as a way of structuring his ideas. Firstly, temporality – looking at the ways in which he disrupts musical time in this performance. How does he decide upon and interpret these interruptions in the timeline of the tune? Is this process of temporal disruption intended to encourage an audience to make subconscious references into conscious ones by placing them into a new context? While the elements of Hendrix's PhD we discussed earlier were strongly language-based, this process is much better suited to modes of audio-visual documentation and representation. Most obviously, this could be explored through the process of substitution: creating multiple versions that alter the length or the type of the temporal disruptions in the timeline of the tune. Secondly, he could explore the idea of opacity – how he would discuss this performance in terms of the ways in which he subverts the sonic world of his virtuosity through the dilettante visuals – the way he goes beyond the presentation of effortlessness into a self-consciously throw-away delivery?

Pender (2016) describes the career of Australian actor and musical theatre star, Tony Sheldon, in terms of the various moments at which a 'brave' decision was made. We can think of this as decisions to refuse and subvert a particular categorization or to side with the subordinate participants in a social order – but also how that mostly involves assuming some new categorization or joining (or forming) some alternate social grouping. However, many of the traumatic aspects of his early career relate to the inductive process of being socialized or conditioned into harmful or self-destructive behaviour. Discussing the 1973 Ensemble Theatre production of *Goldilocks and the Three Bears R Certificate,* Pender says:

> Not knowing any better and determined to please the director, Sheldon explains that he 'tore himself apart' every night. But he would cry all the way home because he was raw with the effort of actually having become hysterical night after night, without knowing how to manage the shattering outbursts of anger in performance. Without techniques for performing the outburst, he could not detach, so it took a personal toll on him as the actor. (Pender, 2016, p. 4)

Identities are formed through behaviours which balance the individual with the communal and this balancing process can happen through the inductive triggering of **subconscious** learned behaviour or the deductive **conscious** process of problem-solving. Moore's (2002) first person authenticity versus second and third person forms can be aligned with Bakhtin (1982) and Monson's (1997) use of *heteroglossia* as ways of theorizing our ongoing process of balancing the value of fitting in and being different in various ways and at various times. All of these theoretical models owe a debt to Goffman's (1956) *dramaturgical* model of behaviour but an important element in all of the subsequent developments lies in the way that they relate to the notion of doing as thinking (e.g. Gibson, 1979; Lakoff and Johnson, 1999; Noë, 2004; Clarke, 2005; Ingold, 2011). It is the patterns of our behaviour, including our language use, as they emerge from the specificity of our bodies, that both form our identity as we experience it and which make it apparent to others. **Convergence** and **divergence** can emerge from both inductive and deductive behaviour. Of course, there is also the question of how much we <u>can</u> fit in or be different. Our perception of the value of these types of behaviour flows from the idea of influence. Our expectation of how useful, beneficial or pleasurable – or the opposite – a given activity and the resultant experience will be is a hypothetical prediction based on previous experience. Whether and how we act upon those influences are determined by our perception of the restrictions and affordances involved, i.e. can we do it? Sheldon's decisions about wanting to belong or be different in any given context can thus be explored in terms of restriction, affordance and influence but that the perception of these possibilities is predicated on the structure and balance of previous inductive and deductive experience and learning. I will explore the notion of influence more fully in Chapters 7 and 8 but, from the perspective of using the micro-sociological notions of *dramaturgy* and *heteroglossia* in a case such as Sheldon's, I would suggest that the documentation and representation of the process should aim to expose various categories of restriction, affordance and influence. These might include various types of aims and goals: financial, prestige, physical and mental health, social connections, ideology, morality/ethics, etc. Documenting and reflecting upon how various phases of activity and their concomitant decisions about action occurred, provides the potential for identifying various patterns and mapping them onto these theoretical concepts. This allows the research journey to include the development of personalized strategies for decision making – one of the many ways in which the pro-active identification and development of quality judgements can be incorporated into this Practical Musicology.

Sheldon's experience of directors in the Australian theatre and other mentors from the acting world who were either nurturing or bullying also highlights the importance of understanding power relationships. As we have seen in the earlier discussions of identity, power is more often institutionalized through repetition, conformity and routine than through enforcement. Rose (1994) examines hip hop through Bakhtin's (1982) dialogic approach, exploring the varied and sometimes contradictory voices of participants. She describes 'public' and 'hidden' social transcripts that document the narratives and interactions between the dominant and subordinate participants in the social order. In terms of restriction and affordance, there are embodied and physiological factors such as visibility (e.g. in the visible signs of race as opposed to nationality or class), socio-cultural factors such as the quality and nature of available education, economic factors, etc., and the psychological factors such as how an individual responds to these broader factors (e.g. acceptance or rebellion). Rose's study demonstrates how ideologies of categorization – perceiving oneself as someone who can and can't do various things, who is or is not a member of a particular category – are a crucial part of the mechanisms of power. How are we making the decisions by which the features which define categories are established? Once again this relates to the personal and the social – are we accepting a particular group's established categories and, if not, what are the criteria we are using for establishing our own individual and competing categories? I will be exploring categorization in more detail in Chapter 5 and power in Chapter 9.

USEFUL QUESTIONS

Embodied, physiological and physical/ecological differences:
How can you exploit or subvert your own physiological nature or the physical nature of your surroundings?

What are the restrictions you perceive as preventing you from achieving your goals?

What are the influences that are shaping your goals and how should you be questioning them?

What is the basis for the categorical definitions you use and how do they restrict and afford particular types of activity?

For example: Constructed androgyny – how has it been done so far and how could you do it differently?

Subverting an appearance or an environment by performing in a dissonant manner. What is influencing your interpretation and how could you be influencing others?

Psychological differences:
For example – choosing to control aspects of your opacity
Which aspects of your behaviour create transparency or opacity?
What kind of persona does this construct?
Are you a deliberately opaque/caricature-like persona or do you strive to present a transparent/authentic one?

Socio-cultural differences:
Playing with the social constructions of temporality and the ideologies of categorization

Remembering that temporality can work on multiple levels – micro to macro – what are the affordances available to you to manipulate them?

How can you influence an audience's (or other performers'/participants') perception or interpretation of them?

4

Context: Technology, uses and value

4.1 The technologies of music practice

Aside from singing and a few limited activities such as hand claps, music practices are highly reliant on technology. From the simplest bone flute to the latest digital audio workstation, the practices of music are hugely influenced by our access to and understanding of these technologies. Although organology is considered a relatively minor tributary in the waterways of musicology, ecological studies of musical traditions have explored the development of instrument types based on the available resources in a geographical area and the way that localized craft skills afforded improvements and adjustments. There is a direct line of connection between these ethnographic studies to work on the social construction of technology where, for example, Cecily Lock (2004) examines the influence of the Broadwood piano mechanism on Haydn's writing style, Mark Katz (2004) wrote about the influence of turntable technology on the development of hip hop or Paul Théberge (1997) discusses the effect that the commodification of upright pianos, synthesizers and recording technology had on the practices of popular music making in the twentieth century.

Returning to the example of Sara McGuinness' *Cuban Music Room*, I discussed the fact that the project involved technology from the twin perspectives of production and presentation or distribution. While I have just mentioned production or *poeisis* technologies ranging from a bone flute to a digital audio workstation, we also need to think about the technologies of distribution or *esthesis*. On the one hand, there are various technologies associated with the distribution of a physical product that allows an audience to hear music: recordings and their multifarious formats but also sheet music, music boxes, player pianos and other mechanical and electrical devices for playing music. On the other hand, there are technologies which afford audience engagement with live performance: mechanical and electrical amplification and venue design. In addition there are a few technologies that straddle both areas: various forms of audio and audiovisual broadcast and streaming media. The *Cuban Music Room* used existing technologies in new configurations rather than seeking to develop new forms. Rather than using newly emergent 360° video formats, virtual reality headsets and binaural recordings that were additionally processed based on directional information from head-tracking technology, Sara wanted to maintain the communal experience of musicking. Thus, while these virtual reality technologies reflect individual consumption as an ideological driver in the design and implementation of new consumer technology – an isolated and personalized immersive experience – the principle behind the *Cuban Music Room* was to create a form of immersive recording and playback media that could be experienced in the company of others. Instead of the 360° video format, Sara chose to record the musicians facing inwards, arranged in a square around four 'normal' cameras. This decision was based on the restrictions and affordances of these technologies. The 360° video playback is projected onto a circular or dome-shaped screen from the centre and if the audience approaches the screen they get in the way of the projection and cast shadows – even with contemporary short throw projectors. Having four large flat screens, inside which the audience walks around, allowed us to use back projection and avoid the shadow issue. In addition, we wanted the audio recordings to be directional – the sound of whoever was projected on a particular screen should come from the direction of that screen. We experimented with various ways of achieving this and settled upon recording with closely positioned microphones on each sound source to isolate each one as much as possible. We then created four stereo mixes – one for each screen – that represented what was happening on that screen. Thus, there was a stereo mix of all three of the hand drum players, another of the three *coro* singers along with their hand percussion, another of the lead vocalist and another of the *cata* player. However, Sara also wanted to reproduce the ambience of the open-air courtyard or *solar* in which the performance happened and so each stereo mix was replayed into the *solar* through speakers the following day and re-recorded to create four separate tracks of ambience. In the installation space, each screen has a pair of speakers behind it so that the mix of the audio changes as audience members move around the 'room' – the hand drums get louder when you walk towards them, etc. In the 'Research Narrative' video on the c21mp.org website[1] McGuinness presents the relatively crude 'proof of concept'

---

[1] http://www.c21mp.org/practice-research-publications/sara-mcguinness/

prototype that demonstrates the evolution of the technical set-up – an example of the documentation of 'versioning' through a temporal/timeline approach.

Decisions about which technology to use are often driven by novelty, fashion, availability and economics rather than the detailed and explicit discussion about ideology and aesthetics that was used in the *Cuban Music Room*. Having said that, availability and economics, especially during the site-specific recording phase in Cuba, had an influence on microphone and camera choices. Writers such as Théberge (1997) and Taylor (2001) have explored the increasing commodification and commercialization of production technology and others have discussed the mythologies that have grown up around instrument technologies such as electric guitars (Waksman, 2001) and violins (Barclay, 2011). Pinch and Trocco (2004) conducted a study of how the marketing and promotion of the Minimoog synthesizer transformed the fortunes of the instrument, Small (1998) discusses the many social, cultural and economic factors that influence concert hall architecture and I (Zagorski-Thomas, 2010a) have written about the complex interaction between the developing design and aesthetics of drum kit technology and the sound of recorded drums in popular music. All of this research, and a good deal more besides, demonstrate that choices of musical technology go far beyond musical aesthetics and technological possibility and that the social construction of music technology is a complex and nuanced process.

The theorization of the social construction of technology problematized the notion of technological determinism in the latter part of the twentieth century. The determinist approach was initially associated with the positivist and modernist idea of progress as an inevitable, pre-determined tide. In some ways, of course, the ecological approach is determinist. Some features of our environment produce physical affordances and restrictions which limit our choices – including the 'choice' of what technology it is possible to develop at any given time and place. However, there are two important caveats to this. One is that simply because a development is possible or impossible in a given context does not mean that we will inevitably recognize that. This leads to the second, which is that we may or may not develop what is possible and we may or may not continue to try to develop that which is impossible. And trying to achieve something that is currently impossible sometimes leads to a series of transitional developments which can subsequently make the impossible possible. On the grand scale, we can think of the story of human flight that has unfolded over several millennia but we can also think of technological problem-solving on the micro-scale. In educational psychology, Vygotsky (1980) developed the notion of the *zone of proximal development* – the limited set of affordances for learning that a given individual can perceive at any given moment. Harry Partch, the twentieth-century composer, developed an increasingly complex series of microtonal musical instruments (Gilmore and Johnston, 2002), starting by having a cello's neck fitted onto a viola in 1930 and, through an incremental process, to ensembles of custom-built string, reed organ and tuned percussion instruments with evocative titles such as Chromelodeons, Cloud Chamber Bowls and Harmonic Canons. Partch became fascinated by the just intonation approach to tuning in his twenties and developed a tuning system based on the harmonic series that divided the octave into forty-three unequal subdivisions. This then required the development of this series of new musical instruments that allowed his musical imagination to make these previously hypothetical sounds real. The process develops through the now-familiar pattern of interactions between deductive and inductive thought: the deductive process of imagining a hypothetical sound-world based on his tuning system followed by the inductive process of exploring the lived experience of playing each of these instruments. Of course, although Partch did much of the instrument design and construction himself, he also used other instrument makers and this kind of process is more usually highly communal or distributed – the development of human flight being a case in point. Partch as a practice researcher could obviously use all four forms of documentation (temporal focus, spatial focus, deconstruction and internal narrative) to demonstrate how various affordances, restrictions and influences were revealed by this process of *proximal development.*

One further important process in the development of musical technologies relates to ways in which it divides and distributes the activities of musical labour. In the early history of music, if I wanted a musical instrument I would have to make it. The division between musicians and instrument makers was established early in most musical traditions and Harry Partch's decision to bridge this divide seems eccentric. However, it should also be remembered that just as Caribbean musicians re-purposed oil cans to make steel drums, many electronic music composers have re-purposed computers to do the same. In 1977 John Chowning used the Stanford Artificial Intelligence Language (SAIL) to implement his Frequency Modulation sound synthesis technique and create a piece called *Stria* for the Paris Institut de Recherche et Coordination Acoustique/Musique's (IRCAM's) first major concert series (Clarke, Dufeu and Manning, 2015). And many electronic composers utilize commercial products such as Max/MSP, Raspberry Pi and Arduino which can be programmed in unique ways to create new pieces of music and new musical instruments. In addition, the various technologies of music notation from around the world and throughout history have also allowed for the division of labour between composers and performers – an example where interpretive flexibility has reduced so much that it seems like a 'natural' division. And the roles of various instruments in musical cultures are partly constructed by the physical affordances for musical patterning that they offer and partly by other non-musical factors such as portability, the ease with which they can be acquired and learned, the status of the social grouping from which they emerged or that some virtuoso or charismatic character popularized their use at a particular juncture. For example, there was a dramatic change in the fortunes of the guitar in American popular music after the 1940s – partly through the development of electrical technologies that opened up a new sound world and a new set of playing techniques – but also with the huge expansion of folk-derived singer-songwriter styles from Leadbelly and Woodie Guthrie to Bob Dylan and Joni Mitchell.

These narratives of social construction, it should be remembered, also undermine the modernist notion of innovation by reminding us that technologies have long lives (Edgerton, 2006). Musical instruments are remarkably persistent technologies in many ways and there is a constant tension between conservatism and innovation in organology: just as constant as the one I discussed in relation to musical traditions. Very few instruments emerge relatively fully formed from an inventor's mind like the saxophone or the theremin. Mostly, they are based on changes or improvements to existing instruments and often do not change their name: the trumpets, flutes, French horns and clarinets of Haydn's period were very different instruments than the ones we generally hear today. They are made of different materials and there have been many innovations in relation to mouth pieces, valves and key mechanisms. Despite this narrative of innovation, there is still a constant demand for antique and vintage instruments such as Stradivarius and Guarneri violins (Barclay, 2011) or 'classic' electric guitars (Rogers, 2005). This has also translated into the recording and electronic music worlds where some older analogue equipment not only is highly valued in its original form but also, importantly, is being carefully emulated and marketed in digital software form: a process that Taylor (2001) describes as *technostalgia*. This tension between conservatism and innovation is, therefore, similarly driven by the inductive processes of habit and tradition and the deductive processes of innovation and the hypothetical as a driver of change. One of the experiments we conducted for the AHRC Classical Music Hyper-Production project was a contemporary re-imagining of Haydn's Piano Sonata XIV:50 in C major. The inspiration for the experiment was in historical studies of his work in London in the last years of the eighteenth century and of this piece in particular (Harrison, 1997; Van Oort, 2000; Lock, 2004; Zagorski-Thomas, 2019b). The process, as can be seen from the presentation on the C21MP.org website,[2] drew heavily on metaphors relating to the ways that the innovative pedal and key-action technologies introduced by Broadwood & Sons inspired Haydn to write very differently to pieces he wrote for existing Viennese-style pianos. The metaphors in the Hyper Production example are not directly related to these types of sustain and note-sounding but relate to contemporary manipulations of spatial audio and timbre in a broader sense.

I have already mentioned the notion of interpretive flexibility (Pinch and Bijker, 1987) in relation to musical styles and traditions and how it relates to the mechanisms of affordance, restriction and influence. The history of musical instrument and recording technology is littered with examples of what Andy Keep has labelled *creative abuse* (Keep, 2005) where 'users' of the technology come up with new ways of utilizing a technology that go beyond those intended by the designers. Almost by definition, most of the early historical examples of instrumental performance innovation go undocumented until their impact feeds back into instrument design and manufacture or their uptake by composers through notation. Hampl's development of French horn hand-muting and hollow wooden mutes in the eighteenth century (Smith, 1980) is one of the few documented examples. Even in the twentieth century, with examples like electric guitar distortion and multi-track recording, there is seldom a single person or narrative and they are often contested by rival claims of being the 'original'. Oudshoorn and Pinch (2003) as well as Akrich and Latour (1992) have used terms such as program/antiprogram and subscription/de-inscription to theorize how technology users develop their own alternative, and sometimes even subversive, ways of utilizing devices which were designed with something different in mind. These antiprograms can be developed either through inductive processes in what we might call the ingenue approach – of developing a technique through 'doing' in a way that is experimental and uninformed by previous conventions or learned technique. Alternatively, they can be deductive, where a user deliberately thinks of ways or experiments with ways in which a particular problem can be solved or goal achieved by using the technology

[2] http://www.c21mp.org/practice-research-publications/simon-zagorski-thomas/

in a new way. Lying somewhere in between these two processes, the user may stumble on something by accident – through a faulty or clumsy, yet nevertheless inductive process of usage – which encourages or stimulates them to think (deductively) about the affordances of the technology in a new way.

If I were Joni Mitchell's practice-based PhD supervisor and we were looking at her album *Hejira* from 1976, I would suggest that she focus her research on her guitar technique and the ways in which her experiments with non-standard tuning and FX pedals have impacted on her song writing process. I would suggest she try to disentangle the causality between these two elements and their relationship to guitar technology. Looking at demo recordings or videos of key moments in which the ideas for these songs emerged, can she demonstrate how the specifics of the tuning system and the pedal technologies available to her encouraged the physicality of certain musical gestures above others? And what are the ways in which the timbral qualities of those gestures influenced her choice of a harmonic structure – that certain chord voicings maintain the timbral 'soundscape' while others disrupt it? Once again, the key to a successful presentation of this research is in finding ways to focus on the salient features – the invariant properties (as opposed to those which vary from instance to instance and can therefore be disregarded as non-salient) that produce the affordances, restrictions or influences that lead to new knowledge. These might also require re-enactments to produce temporal or spatial focus possibilities as well as contextualization through deconstruction and internal narrative techniques.

USEFUL QUESTIONS

Which technologies are you using and why?
Be as broadly inclusive as you can about this and consider everything – from your phone to your note book, from your chair to your nail clippers. Of course, you can discard most of them, but avoid as many preconceptions about what is important as you can.

Why was the technology developed and what was it designed to do?
American ordinance worker Vesta Stoudt had the idea for duct tape (to make a plasticized, waterproof cloth tape) to seal ammunition boxes in the Second World War. When her factory bosses turned down the idea she wrote directly to President Roosevelt in 1943, the idea was adopted and she received a government commendation and a Chicago Tribune War Worker Award (but no royalties).

What other things can it do?

One of the most interesting and thought provoking conference presentations I have seen was about the history of duct tape in crime at the 2012 Society for the History of Technology conference in Copenhagen by Tisha Hooks (see Hooks, 2015). Obviously, even the idea of sealing ducts was a later addition to its uses and seems to be a corruption of the earlier term 'duck tape' (invented around 1900 and made with non-waterproof cotton duck cloth). Although duct tape is not primarily a musical technology, it is used extensively in the music sector – from fixing down and hiding electrical cables in live and studio sound, to fixing broken or loose instrument or microphone stands, to dampening the resonance of drum skins.

Why are you using it? Are there reasons other than pure functionality that have influenced the choice?

4.2 The uses of music

Ethnomusicologists and musical archaeologists have, of course, conducted extensive studies across a huge range of traditions and cultures into the functions and uses of music. The majority of this work has concerned itself with the nature of the music, the nature of the social activity and the function that the music performs. Steven Pinker (1997) famously sparked long-lasting controversy by comparing the evolutionary development of the arts to cheesecake and pornography – as side effects of the real purpose of cognitive evolution (Carroll, 1998; Fodor, 2000, 2005; Pinker, 2005). At the same time, theories about the evolutionary advantages of music (Wallin, Merker and Brown, 2001) have pointed to parent-infant bonding, co-ordination of physical activity and nurturing social cohesion as potential candidates – and, of course, there is no reason why it could not be some combination of all of these rather than one. The reasons for the evolution of a trait – or more accurately, the physiology that affords such a trait – are not the same as the uses to which it is put once it has evolved. I am arguing that our musical activities have developed in parallel to other processes which have emerged through the development of the brain – the **induction/deduction** distinction being just one of many that I will be making – but that I do not recognize the same process of causality that Pinker identified. That is in part, though, because I think Pinker's identification of 'the arts' misses a great deal of the point. By associating the arts with cheesecake and pornography, it suggests that they are a development based on pleasure, entertainment and gratification. As mentioned in the second theoretical interlude above, problem-solving is associated with the chemical pleasure processes in the brain (Canestrari *et al.*, 2018) and, to that extent, the arts share that characteristic with cheesecake and pornography as much as they also share it with mathematics, science and engineering. The adaptive process is far less specific than the development of a capacity for literature or visual art or music and Carroll (1998) points to research about an ongoing and more general process of increased brain connectivity. In addition, music involves two other important features: entrainment and representation. The facility to engage in both of these are general, highly important adaptations (and either absent or less developed in other species) which afford a range of evolutionary advantages. I discuss the Pinker argument because while, as I said, the reasons for the evolution of a trait are not the same as the uses to which it is put once it has evolved, they are related. So, in the following, I am going to explore a few of the potential uses of music through the examples of video games *Final Fantasy IX* with music by Nobuo Uematsu (2000) and *Assassin's Creed Odyssey* with music by The Flight (Joe Henson and Alexis Smith 2018).

There are two aspects of this that relate to music and mood. On the one hand there is the idea of music helping in temporary mood synchronization – either with other individuals in a community or, as in the case of these computer games, as the way of setting the mood in a particular scene or phase of game play. In *Assassin's Creed Odyssey* we can look at this on two different levels. On a socio-cultural level, the use of harp and flute sounds and hand percussion provides a generally folk-inflected pseudo-genre that matches the Ancient Greek/Spartan theme of the game. On the more moment-to-moment level, the music also provides significant cues as to the current environment and potential impending action. Simple harp or lute tones provide a backdrop to functional conversations in the game, low drones demarcate some significant piece of information and faster more complex music accompanies travel and movement. Although there are 150 different tracks used in the game, it is necessary that the player can recognize changes – the safe places, when a quest has been completed, character themes and how themes are changed to help the narrative structure of this Role-Playing Game. On the other hand, given that this is a game, it also reflects the ways in which music can be part of the process of play-acting. There is no actual danger and yet the action of the game and the supporting role of the music create a sense of excitement (Collins, 2013;

Aska, 2017). It has been proposed (Juslin and Sloboda, 2001) that various forms of performance – music, theatre, games, etc. – allow us to work through and rehearse moods, emotions and formal scenarios without the stress of a real cause or implication.

The idea of using music to physically entrain your activity with others for a specific purpose (e.g. work songs) or for creating more general social cohesion through the ritualization of activity (e.g. dancing or communal singing) relies on synchronizing one mode of perception or activity with another. This seemingly simple activity appears to be an important indicator of the ways in which humans think differently to other species. There will be more on that later in the book but, given that computer games have only very recently started integrating interactivity between the user and the sound, how does this relate to this kind of sound to picture synchronization? *Final Fantasy IX* utilizes many 'set piece' scenes and interludes which are like short film or television, sound to picture segments. Our brains are designed to ascertain a general interpretation of what is happening in our world rather than separately calculating 'what can I see?', 'what can I hear?', 'what am I touching, tasting or smelling?' (see for example McGurk and MacDonald, 1976). This produces the Pinker-esque cheesecake add-on phenomenon that we perceptually fuse unrelated perceptions that are in some way synchronous or gesturally similar. However, we also (mostly) notice the incongruity of these types of synchronization and they can become interpreted as a special or significant version of the activity. In the finale to *Final Fantasy IX* which involves a set-piece segment built around a song by Nobuo Uematsu called *The Melodies of Life*, the final gesture is of the character Zidane turning his head to look wistfully off into the distance and the movement is synchronized with the penultimate arpeggiated chord – the last chord, of course, reserved for the title frame. While these forms of synchronization may be melodramatic clichés in one sense, they are also the basis for ritual in many cultures – for making something ordinary seem special through the addition of music. An extended version of this effect is to use the pulse of music to structure time – from the timing of an elegant procession down the aisle by playing a wedding march to the musical tension-building that accompanies a clock countdown in a television game show or the encroaching 'danger' as the Space Invaders in the eponymous computer game move further down the screen. Practical Musicology about these sorts of 'functional' music can use creative practice to explore these types of multi-modal synchronizations and the symbolic meaning that can arise from these types of everyday ritual.

Something that is perhaps less frequently studied is the way in which the music, and the practices that make it, is shaped and influenced by the use/function to which it is put. Obviously, the usage determines the budgets available in the commissioning and production process and the huge increase in video game usage between 2000 and 2018[3] has also resulted in music production budgets for large-scale games around the time of *Assassin's Creed Odyssey* being as high as $500,000.[4] That has dramatically changed the sound of computer games. But the function of both commercial and art music affects aesthetic decisions beyond the scope of budgets. Recorded orchestral performances are likely to be slower and quieter than live concerts (Blier-Caruthers, 2010, 2011) and record companies regularly produce different mixes of the same track for different formats and markets. When I visited Cuba I witnessed a broad range of more or less sanitized versions of *son* and *rumba* depending on whether the venue was aiming at tourists or locals. The role of competition in music is also a complicated phenomenon, with, for example, Eisenberg and Thompson (2011) noting that keyboard improvisations performed in competition were judged as more creative than those outside and Dudley (2003) investigated how colonialism and nationalism influenced performance aesthetics in steel band and other performances in Trinidad Carnival competitions. Once again we return to the ways in which the inductive processes of tradition (or colonial oppression) and the deductive processes of conscious variation work in complex ways together. Returning to the members of the *Muñequitos de Matanzas* who performed in the *Cuban Music Room* example, the use of this performance – recording it for the immersive audio-visual format – required them to configure the ensemble in an unfamiliar way but in the familiar environment of their home *solar* with a small audience of friends and people who live there. The balance of sound that each of musicians heard was unfamiliar because they were arranged in a square and the vocal amplification was configured differently and the volume was kept low because of the recording. On the other hand, the energy and the acoustics of the *solar* – a place where they had literally grown up learning and performing this music with their families during the seventy-year history of the ensemble – were more than just familiar.

---

[3] *Assassin's Creed Odyssey* sold a reported 10 million units in the two years between 2018 and 2020 (https://venturebeat.com/2020/05/14/ubisoft-says-11-games-sold-over-10-million-copies-each-in-ps4-xbox-one-era/) while Final Fantasy IX sold 5 million units between 2000 and 2018 (https://www.ign.com/articles/2016/02/09/final-fantasy-9-available-now-on-ios-and-android)

[4] https://www.quora.com/How-much-does-it-cost-to-develop-modern-PC-games-like-Assassin%E2%80%99s-Creed-CoD-or-NFS

Whether we are dealing with professionals in a highly commercialized environment or with community music making, the social function of the musical activity has a major impact on how that activity is conducted. Even when there is a normalized mode of 'art/entertainment' presentation, the details of the function that the musical activity is serving manifest themselves in the environment, the resources, the personnel, the additional participants and how they respond and in a broad range of other social and cultural factors that influence how the participants think about the process. If I were Courtney Cox's practice-based PhD supervisor (the guitarist with Iron Maiden tribute band, Iron Maidens) and we were looking at the 2012 YouTube video of their cover version of *Genghis Khan*, I would suggest that the uses of this performance, i.e. as a tribute band performance, suggest the use of the notion of authenticity as a structuring feature in her PhD. If we use Allan Moore's three-person approach to authenticity, how much of the performance does she consider to be first person authenticity? And from a representational system – form and content – approach, are there voicing and fingering innovations that she has bought to this performance? Are there musical touches that she is introducing? Licks, or links or flourishes? And how do these relate to the third person authenticity of being true to the Iron Maiden original or what she considers to be the appropriate musical language of heavy metal? Finally, her character shines through in both her facial expressions and her body language: how does this work as a performance of her own identity and as a cipher for Iron Maiden's Adrian Smith in terms of second person authenticity? If the research question involves establishing what sort of criteria help to make a 'better' tribute band, it would make sense that there are many practice-based studies in the classical music world that can help.

USEFUL QUESTIONS

What are the social functions that your musical activity is performing?
How does it relate to the various proposed evolutionary values of musical activity?
Synchronizing emotions
Synchronizing activity
Social cohesion
What can you do to make it perform those functions better?
What purpose might it serve to undermine those functions in some way(s)?

4.3 The value of music

Also inherent in the development and structure of musicology are implicit judgements about the cultural value of different musical traditions. The very notion of musicology emerged at a time when the system of patronage and sponsorship for classical music was shifting from the private model of the aristocracy to the public model of government and when popular or vernacular forms of music were demonstrating a financial value through various forms of commodification. And while we may all have individual taste, not all aesthetic decisions carry the same weight. For a whole range of reasons, certain people's opinions matter more than others on both the supply side and the demand side. Whether in terms of private or public patronage and sponsorship or in terms of the commercial 'gambles' that promoters, venue owners, publishers, record companies and broadcasters may choose to take, those on the supply side have to make decisions about supporting styles of music, artists and individual projects. The decisions about what to fund are the result of a complex negotiation between what they think there is demand for (or will be after the lead-in time of the project) and what they think is good. And of course, the supply-side is also strongly invested in influencing demand through advertising and through demand-side gatekeepers such as journalists, critics and other forms of influencer. As such, we can see that determinations of value and quality are strongly influenced by power: not just the enabling power of money but also the influential power of who you know, what you know and who is prepared to listen to you. However, value and quality are not the same thing. In an ideal world, perhaps, value would be a social representation of quality. If the notion of quality is ascribed rather than inscribed – if beauty is in the eye of the beholder rather than inherent in that which is beheld – then the value of a piece of music (or any artwork) should be the result of the number of people who appreciate it: much like consumer demand determines price. However, as discussed, the social construction of value is not an egalitarian process and some consumers' demand is more equal than others.

If, therefore, value is a manifestation of power, Bourdieu's model of the various forms of capital provides a useful way of engaging with the notion of musical hierarchies. However, while Bourdieu's notion of capital has usually been thought of in relation to a 'zero-sum' game, a competition in which some gain dominance and power over others, it can also be thought of as a collaborative tool for producing an increase in the overall good. Thinking of music in terms of cultural capital, it seems by no means a given that an improvement in the status of one form of music has to lead to a reduction in the status of another. To use an example to explore the nuances of Bourdieu's theory of capital as mechanisms for restriction, affordance and influence, the English National Opera's 2019 staging of Philip Glass' *Orphée* directed by Netia Jones is based on Jean Cocteau's 1950 film of the same name. Financial capital is clearly evident in terms of a project funded in subsidized theatre and through the obvious expense of the staging. By drawing on Cocteau's film it demonstrates cultural capital on several layers – as Netia Jones describes it in the ENO promotional materials 'Orphée is a mirror of a mirror, or a "mise-en-abîme" – an opera of a film of a play of a poem of an opera, in which everything reflects on something else'. You literally need to know a lot about culture in order to get to the bottom of this staging. It also demonstrates quite an unusual version of social capital. Instead of the usual 'who you know' benefits that the term intimates, this relates to a form of benefit from association – that Philip Glass might be seen to benefit from associating himself with Cocteau. For example, the *Guardian*'s 17 November 2019 review by Tim Ashley says: 'the score, with its throbbing rhythms, looping figurations and elegant vocal writing doesn't, however, have the impact and drive of his earlier operas, and the tension occasionally dips in the second act' and yet 'it all adds up to stylish, at times disquieting entertainment, beautifully done'. In short, the subject matter, narrative, staging, direction, performances and conducting make up for the short-comings of the opera. And for those of us who are not sufficiently informed to benefit from understanding and engaging with all the nuances of this wealth of cultural capital, we can instead absorb the symbolic capital: the simple act of being present at the event makes us 'cool' by association. On a very basic level, these various types of capital either afford or restrict our willingness to listen to and value a particular voice: one of the definitive forms of influence.

How do notions of the value of music fit into Practical Musicology? If I were Shoukichi Kina's practice-based PhD supervisor and we were looking at the track *Haisai Ojisan* from 1972, I would suggest that he could explore the notion of value in relation to intertextuality, focusing on songwriting and ideologies of musical style. There's a clear tension here between the Okinawan folk style and the American rock influence and yet they are also complementary in terms of their sonic content, tonality and the gestural shapes employed. How does this song work in terms of performing his identity? The traditional form and the use of the sanshin (Okinawan lute-style instrument) perform a national

Okinawan identity that marks him out as simultaneously belonging to that tradition and as resistant to both Japanese and American occupation of the island. At the same time, the rock arrangement and the slightly rebellious and yobbish lyrical content perform a counter-cultural identity that is deliberately provocative towards that traditional Okinawan identity. How do the various identifying features of these styles work together and could he use the idea of convergence and divergence to these styles and traditions as a way of describing his own idiolect? The more established forms of practice/artistic research that I discussed in the first chapter would connect these ideas through an internal narrative – normally a text-based thesis – that writes about these contextual ideas and aspects of his songwriting and performance. As I will argue in the following chapters, a Practical Musicology should embrace both this conceptual perspective that takes ideas from micro-sociology and cultural theory as well as perspectives that seek an inductive understanding of instinct, tacit knowledge and the development of aesthetics in a practical context. I would encourage Shoukichi Kina into a process of deconstruction and re-representation of the minutiae of his practice so that he can infer some more general features and principles about what he considers appropriate or inappropriate, 'better' or 'worse', or more or less meaningful and in which ways.

USEFUL QUESTIONS

What are the various forms of financial, cultural, social and symbolic capital that are in play in your work? How can you deconstruct or re-represent your practice in ways that explore how the tacit, implicit and subconscious elements of your musical activity are related to these notions of value?

Either in terms of the power that accrues to you? Do some forms of activity make you feel more powerful than others?

Or in terms of the power that accrues to other participants or to your audience/ consumers?

How might these things be having an impact on the perceived value of what you are doing?

Is everything pulling in the same direction?

Do you want it to?

Theoretical interlude 3: *The feeling of being*

The theoretical heart of this framework centres on practice, process and 'being', not only because this is a *Practical Musicology*, but also because the embodied cognition model that underpins it operates on the basis that all knowledge is fundamentally a knowledge of how to do something or how it happens. Knowledge of facts and 'things' is a higher-level abstraction predicated on action. As we will further explore in Section 5.2, the primary way in which neurons work is to create commonly activated pathways based on both perception and action. When we perceive a sequence of events X, activity Y has in the past resulted in sequence of events Z. Going back to those themes of restriction and affordance, the way that we construe 'things' is in terms of their behaviour – both in terms of the way that they act and in the ways in which our perception of them changes when we act. In terms of my dog, for example, there are sights, sounds and smells that he stimulates in my perceptual system through his own activity but my perception of his shape is also based on the way that the image of him on my retina changes as I move and as the light changes, and on the sensations of touch I receive as I pet him. In short, my conception of my dog as a 'thing' is made up of pathways of neural behaviour – patterns that result from both his and my own doing. And these behaviours are multi-modal – the aural patterns of how he sounds are connected with visual patterns of how his mouth moves, for example.

Research such as O'Regan and Noë (2001) also leads to the notion of humans in general, and, for our purposes, musicians in particular, being active participants in a multi-modal world where there is no qualia-like difference between the sensation of different neurons firing. It does not feel different when a neuron fires that is sensing sound than when one fires that is sensing light. It does not even feel different when a neuron fires that is controlling a muscle movement than when one is sensing a muscle movement. Noë (2004) proposes that the difference between sight and sound is not in the qualia of the sensations but in the types of patterns and morphologies that these input stimuli produce in the brain. Visual data is different in structure to aural data and other types of sensory data and that is what makes them feel different. We learn what sight feels like and we learn what hearing feels like and they feel different because of the patterns and the shapes they trigger in our neurons rather than because the triggering of a sight neuron feels different to the triggering of a hearing neuron. And the same is true of all our perceptions, both those that relate to the outside world, such as sight, sound, taste, smell and touch, and those that relate to our internal world, such as hunger, thirst and the many forms of proprioception (e.g. joint position, movement, muscle effort, balance). Further to that, I am suggesting that the difference between sensations of agency and internal/external stimulus is to do with learned parallels between different modes of perception. As an infant I learn which brain activity is 'me' (e.g. the sensation – including the sight, muscle control and proprioception – of me moving my arm) and that which is 'not-me' (e.g. something passing across my visual field that is not caused by me) because of the ways in which these multiple modes of brain activity are related to each other. The following chapter delves deeper into the notion of affordance and how the representational systems our minds use in the processes of *musicking* can be modelled and used to explain and analyse examples of practice.

These three conditions – that the differences between 'types' of sensation are shape-based rather than qualia-based, that the multi-modal nature of cognition is inherent at the most basic level, and that there is also no qualitative difference between the sensation of doing something and the sensations of perception – provide the neural substrate for ideas about expression and interpretation that have manifested themselves in spectromorphology (Smalley, 1986, 1997, 2007; Zagorski-Thomas, 2018b), affect theory (Thompson and Biddle, 2013) and in grounded/embodied cognition (Lakoff and Johnson, 1999, 2003; Feldman, 2008). This, of course, destabilizes the notion of agency and subjectivity but the idea that there is no qualitative difference between the sensation of doing something and the sensations of perception is born out by the phenomena of mirror neurons and mirror systems (which we will look at further in the Chapter 6) and by the ability to 'hear' imagined sound or to 'see' imagined visualizations. It should not be seen as a way of denying agency or free will but it does require us to think about them differently.

I should also point out that the identification of organized large-scale networks in the brain is a recent development in neuroscience (Deco, Jirsa and McIntosh, 2011; Power *et al.*, 2011; Chen *et al.*, 2013; Chand *et al.*, 2017). These have been characterized as the Salience Network (SN), the Default-Mode Network (DMN) and the Central-Executive Network (CEN). Although there is some research on the brain structures involved in each of these networks, it is not important for our argument and it also seems that they rely on communication and interaction between different areas of the brain. It is tempting to consider the DMN and the CEN as **inductive** and **deductive** respectively and perhaps even the SN as the mechanism for deciding between them. Whether that turns out to be a fruitful avenue or not, the DMN emerged from research about what constituted a 'resting state' in brain activity when conducting brain imaging. The SN monitors and responds to the homeostatic demands of the body (Seeley, 2019) – the mechanisms that aim to maintain a healthy system but which also responds to pleasure and pain. The CEN deals with decision-making and problem-solving in the pursuit of goal-directed behaviour (Menon, 2011).

5

Musicking

During the 2020 Covid lockdown, I created some collaborative pieces with Congolese guitarist, Kiamfu Kasongo a.k.a. Burkina Faso (see Video 5.1 on the website[1]). I sent him some basic rhythm tracks in various related keys, time signatures and tempos and asked him to record me some rhythm and lead parts. He is a well-known guitarist in the Democratic Republic of Congo but he's now a resident of the UK and I know his amazing playing through Sara McGuinness' Cuban / Congolese fusion band, Grupo Lokito. I wanted to create some pieces that edited his performances into tonalities and cross rhythms that were uncharacteristic of Congolese music but that retained the fluidity and momentum of his normal playing style. He recorded around thirty tracks of guitar in these different keys, times and tempos and I edited them into five pieces (see Video 5.2 on the website for a short video about the making of these pieces). There are two things in particular about this project that relate to this chapter: the first relates to the theme, mentioned in Chapter 2, of three types of thought and the second is about the notion of categories that I discuss in Section 5.3.

I will explore how this theme of **three types of thought** can be applied to music at the end of this chapter and throughout the rest of the book. The way that it relates to the pieces I created with Kiamfu concerns the combination of **automatic** entrainment to a pulse in groove-based music; the use of **subconscious**, pre-learned shapes and gestures that many of us will hear as the Congolese or, less specifically, African-ness in his playing; and finally the manipulation and subversion of these tropes that require a more **conscious**, problem-solving approach to listening. Given that I am proposing that these three types of thought are therefore also the three mechanisms through which we can interpret music, it should be clear that these mechanisms provide the

---

[1] http://www.c21mp.org/practical-musicology/

basis for a theory about tension and release or confirming and confounding expectations. These mechanisms, along with the notion of representational systems that makes up the fourth theme from Chapter 2, also suggest a model for four types of aesthetic appreciation of music that I will tease out in this and the next chapter.

Bringing to mind or subverting categories is another feature of these Kiamfu pieces. One of the first things that jump out of the piece is that it falls into the category of guitar music – something that is not just defined by the way that guitar strings resonate but also by an implicit knowledge that we have of the type of movements that are possible with the hand. The fact that it sounds Congolese or African to many listeners is also related to the types of hand movement (albeit embodied as sound) that we have come to associate with those types of style or artist. Yet while the gestures fit into those categories, the way they fit together to produce larger phrases and tonal structures does not. The way that it subverts certain categorical conventions can be a source of interest or annoyance. Kiamfu himself, referred to them as 'crazy pieces'. One of my interests as a composer and producer is to find elements from popular music – particularly groove-based music – that can be used to provide new conscious, problem-solving, conceptual mechanisms for structuring my music. Western art music focused on tonality for a long time, exploring structures based on variations in harmony and melodic shape. In the twentieth century, in parallel to the development of conceptual visual art, this aesthetic shifted towards the sonic representation of complex ideas: serialism, minimalism, spectral music, *musique concrète* and a range of composers like Messiaen, Ives or Ligeti who developed their own individual conceptual frameworks. In the work that grew out of my PhD (see Chapter 7 for some examples), these Kiamfu pieces and even in some of my Classical Music Hyper-Production work (see Chapter 8), I am seeking an aesthetic that balances and values all **three types of thought** and uses intertextuality to subvert and examine aspects of value and authorship in both the roles of the participants and the features of the musical output.

Christopher Small's term *musicking* (1998), which gives this chapter its title, provides two important contributions in this area: the focus on music as a process rather than a 'thing' and the notion that there are many and varied ways of contributing to this process. The idea that my contribution to this piece was to commission Kiamfu to perform and subsequently to edit those performances together does not place me in the traditional role of a composer – although in the world of popular music it is not uncommon for a producer who works in this way to be considered the 'author' of the piece, much like a director in the world of film. So the role of this chapter is to bring together some theoretical approaches to the study of practice, process and 'being' under this heading of *musicking* and ideas from anthropology such as Tim Ingold's (2013) and work from psychology and cognitive science such as that by James Gibson (1979) and Alva Noë (2004). For me, these have all been an important part of bridging the gap between a musicology which examines the practice of music making and one which examines whatever kind of 'text' might be produced and how it can be interpreted.

5.1 Perception as action

Gibson (1979) and Noë (2004) in particular have contributed to the idea of perception as an active embodied process rather than as passively processing incoming 'data'. In addition, Ingold's writing on 'dwelling' or 'wayfaring' (2011) provides an anthropological slant on this understanding of living as an embodied activity in which our physical interaction with the world provides the core of our understanding. The theory which underpins this book is founded on the notion that the sensations of moving one's body are the same as, and intertwined with, the sensations of sensory 'input'. The pathways of behaviour in the brain are reinforced by repetition. We can describe this using the metaphor that when humans or animals repeatedly follow the same route in a terrain they create a path which through ease of use and habit becomes their default pathway. When we are first establishing the pathway it has to be done consciously but this process of habituation means it can eventually become subconscious: in the absence of any reason not to, it is what we always do in this context. These neural pathways are also either reinforced by pleasure or suppressed by pain or stress. The neurons which receive information from, for example, my eyes via the optic nerve, are learning successful responsive and reactive behaviour by organizing that information in successful ways: as pathways in the brain. These pathways reflect patterns of experience and patterns of my own movement that have produced desirable results in the past. These types of patterns on my retina along with these patterns in my ear have, when I have moved these muscles in the past, resulted in me getting fed. Eventually, I accrue enough of these patterns to identify them, as a whole, as 'mother' or 'father' – types of visual image and the results they produce. I learned to see, in the sense that my brain learned to simplify the complicated, chaotic and constantly moving stimuli from my retina, in the same way that I learned to walk.

Through Gibson's ecological approach to perception we have the idea that the brain's 'understanding' of the world is built up through this repetitive process of certain repeatedly-encountered phenomena producing particular affordances for action. More than that, though, perception is an active, exploratory and experimental process and that, as mentioned earlier, our understanding of the nature of phenomena is built on our experience of how they behave: either through their own agency or through the way our perception of them changes as we move around. Similarly, for Ingold, life as 'wayfaring' is participation in the emergence and continuation of the world. Living is a process of habituation in which the individual and the world they inhabit interweave and respond to each other in a continuous process.

In the pre-production session of my UK Arts and Humanities Research Council-funded project on Performance in the Studio, we put Jo Beth Young, a singer song-writer, in the studio with drummer Chris Taylor, bass player Jonny Bridgwood and producer Mike Howlett to work on one of her songs. Jo had produced a demo recording that she and Mike agreed had the wrong rhythmic feel and that was one of the first issues that they addressed in the pre-production / rehearsal session. She had played the guitar on the demo with a triplet-style 12/8 feel and they agreed it should be a 16th note feel instead (see Video 5.3 on the website[2] for a video of the session). With very little discussion the three musicians launch into a 16th note rhythm and play it for a little while until Mike stops them and expresses approval for the 'lovely feel'. They all agree that it sounds much better. Over the next two hours they work on the arrangement, discussing the chord changes, the structure, the length of the transitions between sections and the need to adjust the dynamics for the string parts that are yet to be written. Nobody mentions groove or feel again and yet there is a constant adjustment whenever they play (see Video 5.4 on the website for a representation of this process). There is a tacit and seemingly partially subconscious process of slowly adjusting their interlocking rhythmic patterns on drums, bass, guitar and voice through a process of responsive and reactive behaviour. Initially Chris moves some of the accents in his bass drum pattern and Jonny sometimes adjusts his part in response and sometimes stays the same. At one point Jo changes the accent of her guitar strumming from entraining to the kick drum to the snare drum and that seems to encourage an increase in tempo – although the tempo

---

[2] http://www.c21mp.org/practical-musicology/

had been creeping up in any case. There is a definite sense of everyone moving from a more tentative and edgy performance to a more relaxed and confident one and, apart from the fact that they are all becoming more familiar with the material, it also seems as if the shifts in all of their parts have been about finding the 'right' groove for the song.

There are two aspects of this that are pertinent to this chapter. Firstly there is the fact that both consciously and unconsciously, these musicians have been adjusting their activity based on their perceptions of what was happening. This perception is multi-modal and influenced by what is seen as well as what is heard. McGurk (1976) has long-since provided evidence that vision has an influence on hearing and equally there is evidence (e.g. Colley *et al.*, 2020) that performance and timing are similarly affected. Secondly, in addition to this constant process of adjusting performance to accommodate perception, this provides an example of the first type of aesthetic appreciation that I will be outlining over the next two chapters: the appreciation of 'correct' or 'expert' action. I mentioned the notion of finding the 'right' groove for the song and this relates back to what we were discussing earlier – the fulfilment of expectation.

USEFUL QUESTIONS

How can you make the acquisition of tacit knowledge into an explicit process and why is that not a contradiction in terms? Why is it useful to explore and document the ways in which these subconscious pathways have emerged through process and to question whether they are, indeed, 'right' or optimal?

> Using the process of stimulated recall to focus attention on the relevant details:
> Video an instance of your practice and watch it back
> Can you identify instances of subconscious, tacit knowledge?
> Are there aspects of it that you could improve or expand upon?

Use this type of critical reflection on audiovisual recordings of subconscious, tacit knowledge to guide a program of conscious practice which will deal with the issues that have been identified:

> Decide upon the criteria for 'improvement' and consciously practice that activity
> Develop a process of repetitive activity that will result in particular perception/response patterns becoming automatic.

5.2 Pathways and schema

Within neuroscience, the maxim that 'neurons that fire together, wire together' is a basic building block of our understanding about how the brain works. That is the basis of this organizational process by which our brain structures itself to respond flexibly in different situations. We may think first of the wiring together of simultaneous phenomena such as Pavlov's bell and his salivating dogs but it is not only simultaneous experiences that 'wire' together to create expectations, and therefore knowledge, about the world. Sequential experiences also become the well-worn pathways or schema that determine our expectations and aesthetics. The reason that Jo Beth and the others could find the 'right' groove was that their ideas of 'rightness' had developed over the years into a complex set of schema about normality, musical expertise and expectation – those neural pathways that emerged out of their musical 'wayfaring'. This process is the same for music and for all other types of activity that make up our human lives. These are in some part established by the common or universal experience of inhabiting the human form in the world and in others by the multifarious unique and individual experiences of our lived lives. We are all the same in many ways and we are all different in many ways and those 'ways' are the neural pathways that create schema, the cognitive structures of knowledge and expectation. Thus, if we rewind a little earlier in that pre-production session to the time when these musicians met for the first time, all three of them and Mike, the producer, are experienced session musicians and have a well-established schema relating to how professional greetings and introductions at the start of a session work. There is a formulaic process involving enquiries about recent work, anecdotes about extraordinary working experiences (both good and bad) and, often, music or musician-related jokes. It is a schema like the 'what do you do?' ritual at parties that not only serves to break the ice and start conversations but also establish hierarchies of expertise and experience. A schema like this is similar in some ways to a script but is more flexible and will contain conditional branches – if they say A, I should respond with B, but if they say C then … - and ultimately is designed to lead towards the possibility of the much less rigidly structured schema of normal conversation. A musical schema might be relatively rigid – as in the process of reading sheet music – or, as in this example, might involve a set of strategies for steering a piece towards a sonic structure that we perceive to be competent, fluid and to complement the melodic line that it accompanies. In many ways it is about habituation but it is also built on the notion of goals: on the idea that there is one or more desirable results. Indeed, one of the key reasons that schema become reinforced is that they lead to positive results or, if they lead to negative results, to suggest strategies for avoiding them. In this instance I would suggest that there are a range of desirable characteristics for each of the player's parts that can co-exist in complex ways.

There is a trope in the world of psychology to talk about different 'types' of knowledge but I would suggest, that much as Noë used the notion of all neurons being 'the same' to propose a solution to the problem of qualia, all of our knowledge exists through the same mechanisms: the patterns of connectivity that we are calling schema. I have proposed that our understanding of 'things' is an emergent property of knowledge about behaviours. I would extend this proposition to include facts, abstract concepts, theoretical knowledge and, well, our knowledge of everything. I shall come back to this idea in more detail in the next chapter when discussing forms of knowing, but the basic premise is that there is a single 'way of knowing' but a lot of different types of data that can be known. And much as Noë proposes in relation to qualia, it is the differences in the patterns of experiencing knowing that make them feel different.

The notion of a schema should be treated as an 'as if': as a schematic representation of a complex system which breaks it into simpler conceptual 'chunks'. There are no discrete physical structures within the brain that correspond to schema, there are only patterns of communication and expectation between neurons. While there may be a hierarchical nature to these patterns there is no reason to assume that requires a hierarchical structure. It is tempting to think of this as a modular system because of the analogy with computer code but there is also no reason to suppose that schema should be restricted to modules even though they are recursive. When I walk there will be a set of neurons which control the order and timing of the instructions that are sent to the muscles in my legs and these can be seen as a walking schema. Some of those neurons may well be included into other overlapping schema relating to running, kicking and swimming but it is easier to think of them as separate schema even if they comprise overlapping common physiological components. Similarly, some of those instructions may come from the same neurons regardless of whether I am moving my right or left leg and some may be included when I am walking uphill but excluded when I walk downhill. In short, they are virtual rather than real structures and the phenomenon of brain plasticity – of re-learning how to do something after brain damage in one area of the brain using brain cells from another area – suggests that they are not irrevocably tied to specific neural structures.

This discussion so far suggests that information travels in one direction in different 'types' of neuron. When signals are flowing into the brain from sensory systems (eyes, ears, proprioceptors, etc.), they are creating schema that relate to experience. When they are sending signals to control activity (to muscles) they are flowing out of the brain. However, given the notion of mirror systems (Iacoboni *et al.*, 2005), it would seem that a different visual input (e.g. the sight of someone else hitting a drum) can trigger me to cause some portion of the schema through which I would hit a drum, to be enacted. Mirror systems would seem to involve the triggering of the same schema from the brain outwards as well as from the sensory organs inwards. Of course, hypothetical thought involves a similar outward triggering process in a schema: we imagine what an experience would be like by voluntarily activating the schema. Interestingly, different individuals seem to experience sensory imagination in different levels and intensities – how vividly do you see an orange or hear a bell when I ask you to imagine them? It seems that some of us trigger more of the schema than others through this process of imagination but also, that we as individuals can trigger varying amounts of a schema at different times. Sometimes, I really 'hear' an 'imaginary sound' in my head and sometimes it is a much more abstract phenomenon.

This top-down and bottom-up complexity can also be seen in another of the ways that our theme of **convergence** and **divergence** manifests itself. I can use the same set of neurons over and over again to perform multiple steps when I'm walking but I can also calibrate details of each of those steps on the basis of what the terrain looks and feels like. My behaviour can be seen as convergent in the sense that each of the 'things' I do is still a step, and yet these continual minor adjustments to adjust to the terrain and maintain my balance are introducing divergence. Repetition changes the patterning of schema in two main ways. The similarities in each repetition reinforce the pathways that happen in the same way each time and as they become more reinforced they become more subconscious. And the differences in each repetition broaden the schema and make us more prepared to deal with variations and/or to 'decide' (i.e. not reinforce) that some aspects are irrelevant – that they are background noise rather than context. Once again the 'as if' caveat needs to be born in mind. In the actual neural pathways, there is nothing to differentiate convergent patterns from divergent ones. There is not a 'normal' or 'correct' way of taking a step and a series of variations, just a series of weightings in the neural pathways that reflect our experience of walking. The schema is a theoretical tool and not a physiological phenomenon.

But how is all this pontification about action, perception and schema supposed to be useful in a Practical Musicology? Can it tell us anything interesting, for example, about the notion of theme and variation, one of the primary forms of convergence and divergence in musical activity? Of course, if a theoretical explanation like this is going to be useful, then it has to help us think about things that were not totally obvious in the first place. There are four main takeaways from this discussion about the nature of schema. We need to think about knowledge in terms of process and behaviour instead of facts and this has various implications for this Practical Musicology. Secondly, the notion of a norm is dynamic and in a constant state of flux. We never stop learning how to walk because our experience of walking continues to affect the pathways of expectation in our brain. Thirdly, the notion that the vividness of our imagination is variable conjures up the intriguing prospect of developing strategies for learning how to control it better. And lastly, the theoretical construct of a schema provides a mechanism for exploring the notion of variation. Indeed, each of these four aspects of theory suggests mechanisms that would provide helpful strategies for both practice and pedagogy so I will discuss each of them in turn in a little more detail.

The idea of knowledge as process provokes a range of intriguing ideas. Reframing factual knowledge in terms of invariant properties and **affordances** for action or behaviour is one such strategy. In his book Song Means, Allan Moore (2012) explores the notion of analysis in terms of functional layers – of categorizing elements of a track as explicit beat, bass, melody and harmonic filler. He also goes on to discuss analysis through timbre, persona and space and place in terms of his Sound Box concept. For me these are all elements of an ecological perception-based approach to musical analysis: the aural imprint of *someone* (or several people) doing *something, somewhere.* This is further complicated by the fact that we hear and appreciate both an actual person (or persons) doing something and some musical metaphor. That metaphor is also perceived in terms of some imagined activity in some imagined space. In the last chapter, one of the musical examples I used was the immersive audio-visual recording of the *Muñequitos de Matanzas* – a well-known Cuban rumba group – that I worked on with Sara McGuinness and the El Alamacén collective. The interlocking rhythmic parts of the percussion ensemble are, on the one hand, quite clearly established and handed down from performing generation to performing generation and, on the other hand, subject to continual and creative variation within a set range of parameters. We can think of this in terms of two schema (once again with the 'as if' caveat). One is the schema for the actual performance of the sound – with conventions or habits for both usual and less usual patterns and/or ways of varying them. The second is the metaphorical schema – a schema that attributes the musical sound with an agency and a function: leading, following and 'behaving' with a perceived character in relation to other parts in the ensemble.

As we will see in Section 5.3, the notion of a schema is the basis for the process of categorization. Categories and facts rely on what we have described as **convergent** and **divergent** behaviours. That notion of converging and diverging is, in turn, determined by the structure and extent of schema. The schema can be narrowly defined by a relatively small range of experience and activity or it can be less definitively but more broadly defined. Our experience and activities are constantly either reinforcing or shifting the basis of our current definitions of these facts and categories. There are various important ramifications of this. Repeated behaviour and experience in a particular area cement our opinions and makes us more resistant to variation and flexibility about it. However, expertise is not only about learning and reinforcing 'the right way' but also of learning a broader range of nuance and problem-solving strategies. Expertise is, therefore, not only a process of reinforcing schema so that they become the **subconscious** second mode of thought mentioned in our themes. The arbitrary 10,000 hour rule, described as a 'provocative generalization' by its originator Ericsson (Ericsson, Krampe and Tesch-Römer, 1993) and popularized by Gladwell (2009) is a simplification. Recent developments in music education research (e.g. Reyes, 2017; McPherson, Miksza and Evans, 2018; Oliveira *et al.*, 2021) have explored more nuanced aspects of this such as community-based learning, self-regulated learning and motivation. Of course, in this version of the ecological approach, the musician's environment is crucial to their perception of **affordances**. Both Welch (2006) and Lehmann *et al.* (2018) provide summaries of the extensive research about these contextual factors. Practice and the reinforcement of a schema require the broadening process that both these contextual factors and a range of nuance can bring as well as the discipline of repetition in order to 'fix' certain pathways into the subconscious. This, in turn, requires the acquisition of 'meta-schema' – the habits of questioning, looking for alternatives and experimentation – which produce some of the socio-cultural fall-out associated with intelligence and expertise. These meta-schema introduce more instability, uncertainty and questioning of existing knowledge into our brains which are goal-driven towards solutions and certainty. Often, an individual who makes a partially informed but swift decision will be more successful than one who thinks through all the complexities. Indeed, the evolutionary explanation of emotions as short cuts to effective action which speed up decision making and bypass the slower process of reason (Damasio, 2000) is an example of this. Of course, as we see all around us in life, the individual success that comes from this avoidance of the complexities of wider ramifications and ethics is not conducive to optimizing outcomes for us on a collective level. Nonetheless, the perception of confidence in others along with the avoidance of complex thinking that causes stress has a long history of being a persuasive social combination. This was succinctly parodied by Paul Noth who produced a 2016 New Yorker cartoon of a billboard depicting a wolf in a suit with the caption 'I am going to eat you' surrounded by sheep, one of whom is saying 'He tells it like it is'. More germane to our particular argument, this mechanism is another aspect of the ongoing tension in the way we construct schema between our desire to 'solve' the world through completeness and accuracy in our interpretation and the constant process of alteration and adjustment. And, of course, visualization – the conscious and repeated imagining of a particular experience or activity – provides another process by which the structure of a schema can be influenced.

We are all aware that hypothetical thought and imagination can work on a range of levels of vividness. It seems that sometimes our imagination skims over the 'top' levels of a schema and at other times it can trigger the deeper levels that have a much stronger connection to perceptual experience. My musical imagination is sometimes quite conceptual and sometimes visceral – as if I have actually heard the sound. The question then arises of whether it is possible, and how important or useful it might be, to be able to increase this level of connection voluntarily. What kinds of strategies might there be for increasing the vividness of our aural imagination? I am someone who generally experiences a low level of perceptual 'realism' when it comes to imagining sounds but I know many people who report experiencing very powerful and vivid 'sounds'. However, I also know that in some circumstances the vividness of my aural imagination increases dramatically. While current research (e.g. Zatorre and Halpern, 2005; Grimshaw and Garner, 2014; Gelding, Thompson and Johnson, 2019) suggests both that musical imagination involves auditory and sensorimotor imagination and that aural training improves aural imagination, it is not clear how these are related to vividness. *A priori* it would seem likely that training would reinforce these types of schema, but it also seems likely that while improved sensorimotor imagination would improve performance, vividness of the imagined 'hearing' experience would be reliant on the auditory pathways. This brings us, though, to the second half of that question: how important or useful would it be to increase the vividness of aural imagination. Composing in one's head – either for the purpose of creating instructions for others or as a process of improvisation – seems to be an obvious candidate for a skill that would be enhanced by this kind of imagination. However, the question remains as to whether competences based on sensorimotor schema might be as important as aural imagination – or whether there are optimal types of inter-relationship and interaction between them.

Finally, the fourth aspect of these ideas about schema that has an impact on Practical Musicology is whether, how and to what extent the theoretical construct of a schema itself provides a mechanism for exploring the notion of variation. This notion of variation, of course, requires a theme or a norm that can be varied. As we have discussed, though, the very acts of doing, experiencing or even imagining an activity change our understanding of what it is and what the norms are. As each instance is different either in small or large ways, some detail about the probability or desirability of a particular neural pathway through a schema will be altered by the experience of it. Returning to the notion of a meta-schema which outlines those habits of questioning, looking for alternatives and experimentation, we all have these habits and strategies in various forms. From the most basic practice strategy of concentrating on the elements that are a problem to more advanced mechanisms to encourage lateral thinking, we are deliberately shaping our schema. Using the notion of the schema itself is simply another way of considering ways of altering it. Remembering that the schema is a theoretical construct rather than a physical entity, we can, nonetheless, use a variety of theoretical tools to plan how we can shape it to achieve our goals. Many of these tools exist already in the world of analysis. Gama *et al.* (2014) have used phase and network analysis to study collaborative behaviour in sport and Goffman (1956) pioneered the use of dramaturgical analysis of social interaction. Clark's (1996) Joint Action Theory (see also Kaastra, 2008), Csikszentmihalyi's (1988) Systems Approach to Creativity (see also McIntyre, 2012; Thompson and Lashua, 2016) and Actor Network Theory (Latour, 2005; Piekut, 2014; Zagorski-Thomas, 2016, 2018a) all provide ways of thinking, from a practical perspective, about the structure of the schema, finding the norms of variation and exploring 'less travelled roads' to increase creativity.

All of this also relates to the second type of aesthetic appreciation that I am proposing: the intentional and expert variation of a schema. Bearing in mind that the schema is based on probabilities drawn from previous experience, these types of variation are within the scope of previous experience but less frequent and therefore less expected. If we return to the Jo Beth Young example, there were five full takes of her vocal performance recorded in addition to the guide vocal which was discarded (see Video 5.5 on the website[3] for an audiovisual demonstration). Even with the 'wrong' rhythmic feel that was mentioned in her original demo recording of the song, there was a clear melody. A few aspects of this changed permanently during the rehearsal process and were manifest in the recording of the subsequent guides at the end of the rehearsal session and as the guide vocal during the rhythm section recordings. The vocal performance schema that developed during this process then became manifest in these five full vocal takes and a sixth take of the first verse only. Listening to them simultaneously, it is easy to discern that there are aspects of the performance that are virtually identical each time as well as moments where the rhythm, pitch and timbre of the voices vary quite substantially between performances. The majority of these variations occur at the start or end of phrases – either through slightly different rhythmic placing of the first or last word or syllable, or through the way pitch is explored in relation to the accompanying harmony (mostly in descending phrases at the ends of lines). Given her experience and expertise as a session singer, there is only one moment during all six of those takes where Jo's pitching is significantly off key. As she was constantly exploring these types of variation, the tacit knowledge about the harmonic structure of the song that is embodied in this ability is clear from that level of accuracy. Indeed, virtually all of the discussion about the choice of vocal takes between her and Mike was concerned with the aesthetics and quality of those minor variations in this song schema rather than the overall performance quality of the melody.

USEFUL QUESTIONS

Starting with the four 'takeaways' that emerged from the discussion of schema:

1. What difference does it make to think about your musical knowledge in terms of process and behaviour instead of facts?
2. Given that the notion of a norm is dynamic and in a constant state of flux, which aspects of your practice feel most stable and how do you think they might be changing?
3. Is it useful to control the vividness of our aural imagination?
4. Is this a useful mechanism for exploring the notion of variation?

---

[3] http://www.c21mp.org/practical-musicology/

Distinguishing between the aural imprint of *someone* (or several people) doing *something, somewhere* and the metaphors for activity that it might suggest e.g. hearing someone strumming a guitar and being reminded of a swaggering walk. What are the metaphors you want to suggest and how might the sound of physical activity suggest them?

Exploring the balance between the more expected and the less expected. Do certain forms of activity seem more 'normal' than others? Can you identify which aspects of the schema are invariant properties (the norms?) and which can be varied without disruption?

Stimulated recall of your own practice – get others to observe your practice and ask questions

Close observation of the practice of others – repeated watching, close-ups and slow motion

Hypothetical substitution – imagine how changing one thing might alter the whole

Exploring the vividness of our aural imagination: Cummings *et al.* (2017), working in sports science have developed a Layered Stimulus Response Training system for developing imagery ability – based on progressively building up layers of detail using stimulus propositions such as the details of the instrument or room, response propositions such as the physical feeling of performing the activity and meaning propositions such as our emotions or feelings about performing the activity.

How can you explore a schema so that you understand (and have unfettered / skilled access to) the potential variations?

The same processes of stimulated recall, observation of others and hypothetical substitution

Explore the possibilities for variation systematically and repeatedly and document your aesthetic responses – what works? And why do you think it works?

Bring ideas of metaphors from external sources to suggest other forms of variation – these might be the kinds of contextual ideas I discussed in Chapters 3 and 4, they might involve different emotional or semantic narratives, or they may be based on some more distantly related or even randomly connected idea like number theory.

5.3 Categories

Given that our experience from one moment to the next is always unique and new, the cognitive problem of how we decide that two different experiences are somehow the same or similar rather than different, and in what way, is difficult. On the very specific level, I have to be able to recognize that my wife in a red shirt and my wife in a blue shirt are the same person even though the sensory experience of seeing her is different. And I also have to recognize that the shapes that the light she reflects onto my retina when she is standing, sitting, kneeling or running are also all the same person. On a more general level, I can also recognize categories of people who are standing, people who are sitting, things that are blue, things that are red and things that are shirts – even though my sensory experience of each instance is different. Obviously, a category like a colour is purely a visual characteristic (although the 2015 blue and black/white and gold dress photograph, social media phenomenon adds a layer of complication) but a category like 'my wife' is multi-modal: we all have visual, aural and other sensory ideas of what a woman is like. Those of you who do not know my wife will probably use that general 'woman' category to conjure up some more or less specific hypothetical wife, while people who know her will use a more specific 'Natalia' category that they have stored away. That idea of using the same word – 'category' – to describe both a single person and a class of people, i.e. 'Natalia' or 'woman', may seem odd but, as I have alluded to above, I am using it to refer to a category of sensory experiences. However, before I discuss categories in terms of nouns like shirts and wives, I want to think about them in terms of the schema we have just been discussing.

I would suggest that a basic way schema are employed which is common to a great many living species is to categorize those schema based on goals – on what a particular combination of sensory experience and activity **affords** and whether that affordance is one of my goals or not. The type of activity/experience combination that will lead to food, the type that will lead to water, sex, warmth, the avoidance of danger, etc. In the 'Feeling of Being' theoretical interlude above, I mentioned three neural network types that neuroscientists have identified: the default-mode, the central-executive and the salience networks. The setting of goals is the substance of a salience network. What is important? What is pressing? We have basic goals like eating, drinking, sleeping and avoiding death which are existential, and others which are primal but not as crucial, such as the sex drive, pleasure and pain. When these goals are identified as pressing by the salience network, our central-executive network of brain function looks for actions (schema) that fall into the category of having achieved that goal in the past. And if, based on our current understanding of our circumstances, there is not a direct course of action that will achieve the goal, then we set ourselves the sub-goal of getting into a set of circumstances from which we have achieved that goal in the past (or a hypothetical situation from which it seems plausible we could achieve it). We can see, therefore, that step-by-step in an evolutionary manner, our ancestors must have progressed from a direct survival-based goal to the more indirect idea of setting the conditions for achieving success as a sub-goal. This has progressed still further to the point of setting the goal of the acquisition of the tools that will allow us to identify and establish those conditions (and to establish their stability). That is a rather convoluted way of saying that we have evolved into a species for whom understanding the nature of the world has become a goal. Unresolved interpretations of what is happening around us produce stress and resolving that stress through problem-solving has become a goal. It is a goal because, if we understand the nature of the world, then we can alter the nature of our environment and our behaviour within it to achieve those more basic goals. And one of the key ways in which we can understand the nature of the world is through this process of categorization which is also fundamental to the creation of social structures, language, science and the arts (and, of course, cheesecake and pornography).

The identification of similarities – our ability to put things into categories – is central to music and interpretation as well as to life in general. In musical terms these range from the relatively universal experience of activities and behaviours (and their associated sounds) that we might categorize as angry, happy or sad, to complex culturally constructed narratives such as the āvāz of Iranian classical music, the verse/chorus/seben structure of Congolese popular song or the intro/breakdown/build/drop structures of contemporary electronic dance music (EDM). As I will discuss in more detail in the next section, this process of categorization can be based on any or all of our **three types of thought**. It might be a relatively **automatic** process such as entrainment whereby we can synchronize our own activity with the same activity in others – clapping in time, for example. That might also be complemented by a **subconscious**, learned element such as particular dance steps or movements. In addition, there might be an additional **conscious** element such as listening for structural cues in a musical texture – such as hearing two sections in a song that have similar but slightly different melodies and different words as both being 'a verse'.

In each instance our knowledge is based on there being certain invariant properties as well as certain variable ones. Indeed, the whole process of categorization is based on the identification of invariant properties – of properties that recur in different instances of experience. The complexities of this issue are evidenced in the two main theoretical models of categories in psychology and linguistics – prototype-based and exemplar-based (Lakoff, 1990). This is also often referred to as *types* versus *tokens*. In the 1980s Nosofsky (1986) developed an exemplar-based generalization model which explores the ways in which *types* and *tokens* can be accommodated. This has become known as the Generalized Context Model (e.g. Habibi, Kemp and Xu, 2020) in which the process known as chaining is the model for how categories grow over time with new items being added on the basis of similarity. Similarly, in our model both *types* and *tokens* are embodied in schema. The really thorny question that psychologists and linguists are addressing is how we assess or compare similarity. In Gibson's (1979) model of ecological perception, invariant properties are objective, external phenomena and would therefore be recognized by all listeners similarly. I prefer to think of invariant properties as subjective, internal phenomena – some of which are the result of the physical properties of the environment we inhabit: gravity, the way light and sound propagate in air, etc. We may or may not perceive these in the same way as other listeners: think of optical or auditory illusions or the ways in which what we see affects what we hear and vice versa (e.g. McGurk and MacDonald, 1976). In addition, we will each have had a different range of experience and, therefore, the range of common invariant properties that have been marked into the various pathways and schema will vary from individual to individual. In essence, a schema records the existence of *tokens* or examples of a phenomenon by marking the neural pathways of experience – the 'neurons that fire together, wire together' axiom. However, that process of wiring together – the emergence of common invariant properties from multiple examples of experience – provides a framework of prototypical features that we can use to identify new examples or hypothesize imaginary examples. Some pathways are triggered in every instance and some are different. The pathways that recognize the presence of both a full drum pattern and a bass line within a certain range of tempos may be an invariant property of the drop section in EDM but the notes being played by the bass can vary from track to track. The category of a 'drop section' will have emerged from my repeated experiences of EDM and part of that experience may have involved learning the linguistic tag 'drop section' or it may only exist as tacit knowledge without verbal descriptions. And these invariant properties have meaning because of our expectations of what can, will, might or cannot happen next; the potential affordance of an invariant property. Our schema predict that a certain invariant property (familiar pattern of simultaneous stimuli) will afford one or more potential next steps in the schema (i.e. we will have expectations about what is going to happen). This notion of categories, then, is about classifying experiences as having invariant properties in common which will produce the same affordances.

It is worth returning again to linguistics for a description of the dual nature of categories in language: that they provide a stable representation system and have 'an open-ended "placeholder" structure that invites innovation' (Gelman and Roberts, 2017, p. 7900). The process of schema formation means that not only do we use existing schema to recognize new examples of experience that possess the same invariant properties, but that each new example also affects the 'wiring together' process and therefore alters our expectations for future experience and the types of invariance and variance that will be expected. Interestingly, Hacking (1996) coined the term Looping Effect for a specific instance of this phenomenon in which changing categories of 'human kinds' change the people thus categorized. If some experience changes my understanding of a category of which I consider myself to be a member, then I also change my understanding of myself. For example, if, having learned to play an instrument for many years, I consider myself to be a musician and then something happens that persuades me that the definition of being a 'proper' musician includes some invariant property that I do not possess (e.g. reading music, improvisation or familiarity with a particular technology), the Looping Effect is that my identity as a musician is undermined. Of course, the Looping Effect can be positive as well as negative – as a young girl I may have my schema of a sound engineer altered by seeing a woman doing the job (or by being told I might be good at it) and providing my schema with an example that would allow me to be included in that category.

Going back to the 'Fantasy Supervision League', if I were Björk's practice-based PhD supervisor and we were looking at the track 'Notget' from 2015, I would advise her to examine her approach to vocal performance by exploring the relationship between form and content. The very precise and exaggerated articulations and the deliberately fragmented narrative of the lyrical delivery draw attention away from the content and towards the form. Would a categorical analysis be useful in this regard? Is there a typology of mechanisms that she uses repeatedly? What are the similarities and differences between these mechanisms?

What are the invariant properties that define each of these mechanisms? What kinds of affordances for interpretation do these invariant properties produce and why does she think that they do? What other invariant properties of activity would produce similar affordances for interpretation? What other affordances for interpretation might the same invariant properties produce in others? What are the goals in this regard and how well are they being achieved by these invariant properties and the resultant affordances for interpretation? By deriving a set of research sub-questions such as this, there is a clear route towards a methodology and thence to specific methods. The methodology requires an approach that exposes and distinguishes between invariant properties of her vocal performance, the affordances for interpretation that they produce and the desirability of those affordances. Depending on the circumstances, the methods might include some or all of the following:

- the analysis of performances undertaken before the study began
  - critical reflection on a textual analysis (listening to the music)
  - retrospective interpretational phenomenological analysis through stimulated recall (remembering how you did it)
- the development of a new piece or pieces
  - reflective narrative about the development of techniques and aesthetics (noticing when things work and thinking about why)
  - using spatial or temporal tools to focus on some aspect and explore its potential for fulfilling the interpretative goals (watching and listening to yourself in unfamiliar ways)
  - deconstruction and re-representation of particular features to explore their potential for fulfilling the interpretative goals (watching and listening to yourself in unfamiliar ways)
- experiments designed to explore the possibilities of the process without necessarily completing a finished 'output'
  - the same set of methods as above but without the imperative to complete something

Of course, the typology of the mechanisms being used, explored and studied, would be up to Björk to identify and elucidate as part of the research process but they might include exaggerating and deconstructing consonant and diphthong sounds, breath and phrasing, timbral effects such as growls and rolled 'r's and sudden changes in energy expenditure. How does this typology of mechanisms relate to her established vocal style (or the ways in which it has evolved) and the specifics of this album project?

Before I move on to the next section, I want to consider the somewhat meta-idea of categories of category. What kinds of organizing invariant properties emerge as musical categorizing principles? Using the ecological approach, we have the notion of categorizing sounds in terms of somebody (an agent) doing something (an activity) somewhere (a place and time) but we also have the added dimension of the resultant sound (the output) being a metaphorical representation of something (an interpretation). This then, provides us with four categories of category:

1. Agent
2. Activity
3. Place and Time
4. Interpretation/Output

The first of these is based on our perception of the 'makers' of the music. As mentioned at the start of this section, all of these grouping principles are based on activity: on a type of activity/experience combination. They can also relate to both the general and the specific: from 'woman' to 'Natalia'. With the general, the categories are based on what they are likely to do and what they are likely to look or sound like: aspects of these that they all have in common. With the specific, we base our notion of that individual on the types of behaviour they are likely to engage in. As mentioned earlier, it may seem odd to describe a specific person as a category but we should think of a person as a category of experiences – the different experiences of seeing them from different angles, in different lights and in different contexts and similarly with our other senses. I categorize all those different experiences as 'Natalia'. There is a two-way street between the *types* and the *tokens* and the features that they exhibit – Natalia is a *token* when it comes to the *type* categorization of women and the *type* when it comes to the experiences (*tokens*) I categorize as Natalia. Of course, some features will have been more frequently reinforced by our experience and others less frequently so. Some of these features will become a defining characteristic for us – returning to musical examples, the level of expertise we expect from a person in order to be able to categorize them as a musician. Others will be optional such as their type of voice or instrument – but will require at least one of the options. And others still will be less important to their function – such as the types of clothes that a heavy metal or a classical musician might wear. I may have expectations but they are not a 'deal breaker' as to whether I can include a new example in the category.

It might also seem odd, having based the category of 'agent' on the type of activity/experience combination we can expect from them, to have 'activity' as the second type of category. Of course, there will be overlap in this regard, but the principle is to provide a greater range of nuance and subtlety than the over-arching features used for categorizing an 'agent'. An over-arching label such as 'musician' includes a wide range of potential activities. Each of those activities involves a wide range of possible variations. And again, some of these will be defining characteristics and others will be optional in various ways and to varying extents. There are a range of performance behaviours that involve stylistic forms of activity based on harmony, rhythm, timbre, etc. Some of these will produce generic categorizations – an operatic singer, a blues guitarist, etc. – and others will produce what Moore and others have called the idiolect (Moore, 2012, p. 120) – the individual 'voice' that marks Charlie Parker as different from John Coltrane or Mary J. Blige from Rihanna. In addition, we can also use this meta-category to distinguish the means from the end. Just as interactive digital maps can provide us with a range of options for getting from A to B and we can make a choice based on the mode of transport we would like to use or the aesthetics of the journey itself – do I prefer to walk through the park or down the high street? In the musical world, factors such as 'good technique' or 'authenticity' may influence musical decisions about how to 'get there' and I might sometimes make those decisions for musical reasons and sometimes for other reasons. I might, for example, record two imperfect takes of a piano part and decide that, rather than editing together a good version from what I have, that I would prefer to play it a few more times and get it right in a single performance. The result – an acceptable take of the piano part – is the same in both instances but my decision about which 'journey' to take was determined by other factors.

Our categories of place are also contingent on an activity/experience combination. They may be to do with physics or ergonomics – such as the way that sound propagates within a space to create resonance and reverberation or the way that good sight lines between musicians affect a performance – but they may also be to do with cultural meaning: a sung mass should involve the acoustics of a church or a singer-songwriter should sound intimately close. Indeed, there is evidence (e.g. Till, 2019) that the Spanish caves chosen as the sites for 40,000-year-old cave painting were selected for their acoustic properties – presumably sites for rituals that combine the acoustic and the cultural. And this pairing continues from natural phenomena into the world of built acoustics. Particular buildings are famed for their musical acoustics: the Gol Gumbaz Mausoleum in Karnataka, India, the Opera City Concert Hall in Tokyo or small venues and recording studios such as First Ave in Minneapolis, Muscle Shoals Studio in Alabama and even the echo chambers in the basement of the Capitol Records building in Los Angeles or the attic of Norman Petty's father's garage next door to his studio in Clovis, New Mexico where he recorded Buddy Holly. In some instances these are built to be special ritualistic places and in others their acoustic properties and the special events that happened there have contributed to or even created their status as iconic and even quasi-magical places – the recording studio at Abbey Road for example.

There are also aspects of hearing the 'when' in music as well as the 'where'. There are musical forms which are tied to a specific cultural event – from the singing of 'happy birthday' to the idea of singular events – the last night of the tour or a summer solstice gig. In recorded music and, of course, video, an historic moment can be re-enacted over and again: from the Beatles at Shea stadium in 1965 and Jacqueline du Pré playing Dvorak at the Albert Hall in 1968 to the Orquesta Osvaldo Pugliese at the Teatro Colón in 1985 or Beyoncé at Coachella in 2018. However, there is also a more generic set of time markers that can be used: the sound of historical instruments, the narrow frequency and dynamic range of early twentieth-century recordings or the crackle of vinyl from the 1960s and 1970s.

Fourthly there are musical categories that are based on the output of this musical activity and the kinds of symbolic or metaphorical meaning it might have for a listener. Whilst there may be categories of expression that fit into the 'activity' category of categories – such as the type of energy expenditure being characteristic of sad or happy behaviour – there are others that are musical metaphors rather than activity-based metaphors. I may, based on my learned experience, hear a particular chord progression or melody as strident or wistful almost regardless of how it is played. There may be some element of activity-based metaphor that is one or more steps removed from the immediate experience – a version of what Smalley (1997) terms 'surrogacy'. For example, I may hear a rising interval on a piano and associate it with the physical effort that singing an interval like that requires. It might therefore take on a metaphorical meaning related to reaching or striving that such an association might suggest and which the physical reality of playing different notes on the piano keyboard would not. Or the types of musical metaphors that a piece suggests to me might

USEFUL QUESTIONS

How can you explore ideas of similarity and difference in your musical practice? What are the invariant properties used to define similarity?

Can you identify the three types of invariant property in your practice? i.e. necessary, one of a list is required and common but not defining. As a reminder, our examples of invariant properties of musicians included: makes music (necessary), what type of instrument or voice (one of a list is required), how they look or dress (common but not defining).

What are the features of the various categories that are embedded in your musical practice?
What are the types of activity that define your practice?
Identifying both the invariant properties and the affordances that they offer
Can you use the same types of activity to produce difference sonic (or visual) results?
Explore the range of affordances produced by a single invariant property
Explore how the multiple invariant properties can suggest different affordances
Can you use different activities (or technologies) to produce the same sonic (or visual) results?
Explore the range of invariant properties that can produce a single affordance
Explore how multiple affordances can be suggested by different combinations of invariant properties

relate to activity other than that which caused this particular sound. I might hear patterns reminiscent of the sound of waves and water in Debussy's *La Mer* or the title of a piece might encourage me to hear something that would not otherwise have occurred to me such as a Chinese *pipa* (lute) performance entitled 'The King Takes Off His Armour'. I may also appreciate the structural integrity or complexity of a piece of music with metaphors based on circularity or some form of theme and variation.

5.4 Three forms of musical engagement

I will finish this chapter as I started it, using the pieces of music I created in 2020 with Kiamfu Kasongo a.k.a. Burkina Faso to explore the theme of **three types of thought**. My previous writing has built upon Middleton's tripartite explanation of musical interpretation (Middleton, 1993; Zagorski-Thomas, 2019a) – gesture, connotation and argument – to incorporate them into the cognitive model outlined above. This more general idea of three types of thought uses the categories of **automatic**, **subconscious** and **conscious** although these should be thought of as overlapping – almost as phases along a continuum.

Middleton's category of 'gesture' relates to the **automatic** in my model, to direct subconscious connections between musical sound and other forms of experience. We can think of empathy and entrainment as good examples of this form of engagement. The impulse to tap one's foot or nod one's head along to a sound is an interesting and complex phenomenon. Colleen Reichmuth (Cook *et al.*, 2013) famously training Ronan, a Californian sea lion, to 'dance' to Earth Wind and Fire and the internet phenomenon of Snowball, the sulphur-crested cockatoo, dancing to the Back Street Boys on YouTube[4] both drew attention to how unusual this capacity of entrainment is in animals. Although newborn humans do not have the physical coordination to be able to synchronize their actions to sound there is evidence that the cognitive capacity is inherent from birth (Háden *et al.*, 2015). Similarly with empathy, there are studies which suggest that it has developed more in humans for evolutionary advantage as well as the fact that it can vary between individuals based on the hormone balance in the brain (e.g. Preston and De Waal, 2002; Knickmeyer *et al.*, 2006). However, while there are physiological and chemical bases for both of these '**automatic**' phenomena, we can also learn in various ways to become better at them. In fact, in order to utilize them in musical ways requires quite extensive training and physical expertise. Playing in time and with emotional expression may be reliant on these brain functions but turning them into effective musical activity requires both muscle tone and control and the establishment of the right learned schema to complement and exploit these **automatic** types of thought. There is therefore a certain amount of cross-over into the second type of thought.

Middleton's 'Connotation' relates to **subconscious** forms of metaphorical connection – a feature of the pathways and schema mentioned above – that have become so engrained as to no longer require conscious control by the central-executive network. For example, in our everyday adult lives, we very rarely have to concentrate on how to walk despite the fact that it is quite a major feat of learning for us as infants. The informal musical education that we undertake simply by living in a world where we are continuously hearing

[4] https://www.youtube.com/watch?v=N7IZmRnAo6s

music means that we develop expectations about what is likely to happen in a piece of music: a complex set of tacit knowledge that we mostly take for granted. As we've mentioned in the section on categories above, some of these musical associations are to do with a relatively straight-forward and direct metaphorical connection between musical sound and types of human activity: the association of some types of musical shape with happiness or sadness for example. These relate to the types of action we expect people to engage in when they are happy or sad – perky and bouncy or lethargic and listless. For example, Gabrielsson and Juslin (1996) asked musicians to play the same melodies with different emotional 'intentions' and listeners were mostly successful at identifying the intended emotion. These types of schema are learned but are cross-modal – we learn to identify happy and sad behaviour in a general sense as infants and our ability to transfer that recognition to the world of music emerges out of that. While there may be significant cultural differences in some of the ways in which humans express emotion, there are also many species-specific (and often transspecies) features which are more universal. At the same time as we are learning about emotional expression, we are also learning much more culturally specific sets of expectations about music: the interval patterns we are likely to hear or use in a melody, common rhythms and their connections with movement, the contexts of musical habits and rituals and the formal structures they are likely to take. Most of us learn all these things as tacit knowledge – patterns that become embedded in the pathways of our brains without us acquiring the technical language musicians learn to describe them or any of the theoretical and structural relationships that can be extracted from them and used to enhance musical creativity and expression. And when musicians do learn these theoretical and structural relationships that a formal music education provides, they strive to embed that knowledge so thoroughly in their minds that they no longer have to consciously think about them. Similarly, when we learn to drive, we start by having to think about coordinating our hand and feet movements in relation to the sensory feedback – what we are seeing, hearing and feeling. However, our aim is to be able make all of that activity subconscious: to be able to think about the 'bigger picture' of how we are going to get where we want to be without worrying about the position of our hands on the wheel or thinking about the order of 'mirror, signal, manoeuvre'. Theorists such as Csikszentmihalyi (1997) and Sawyer (2006) discuss this in terms of 'flow' – the way that musical activity often exists on the boundary between the conscious and the unconscious. While we may occasionally get out of our car at the end of a frequently travelled commute and realize that we have little or no memory of driving, for musicians and sports men and women, the experience of a state of 'flow' involves something different. Rather than a feeling of absence from an activity, there is very often a very intense sense of presence in the experience accompanied by a kind of effortlessness: as if the instrument is playing itself. Indeed, even for those who aren't musicians or artists, the act of listening can often involve many of the characteristics of this sense of 'flow' – an effortless understanding of the music that often seems to exist outside of time and which somehow combines aspects of both conscious and subconscious forms of interpretation and engagement.

Middleton makes the point that his notion of 'Argument' (Middleton, 1993, p. 189) relates to the traditional subject matter of Western musicology – to the ways in which we can use our conscious powers of reasoning and pattern matching to map musical structures onto conceptual frameworks. Whilst he was clear that he thought any form of musical engagement involved all three of these forms of interpretation, he points to the fact that Western musicology is very rarely concerned with the visceral experience of entrainment or empathy or with the subconscious 'flow' involved in the joy of schema matching: the pleasures of the predictable or the appreciation of a musical job done effortlessly well and elegantly. This third **conscious** form of thinking constitutes the basis of his 'argument'-based engagement and is concerned with the ways we make sense of music when it somehow does not fit with our previous experience. This can be on a relatively simple level – such as hearing a melody we have never heard before. It does not exist as a previously experienced pathway in a schema and yet many aspects of it do. The potential for this experience exists within the schema in as much as many melodies that are like this one in several ways have been experienced before. In fact, it often feels as if we have or should have heard this melody before because it is made up of familiar 'component' experiences – invariant properties. Alternatively, the process can also require us to work harder at making sense of the experience. That 'harder work' might be in terms of complexity or unfamiliarity. Of course, something that is complex is also often unfamiliar as a result of that. The distinction I am trying to make is between music that explores existing 'rules' or expectations by applying them in more convoluted ways or in different contexts and music that seeks to create a new set of 'rules' or expectations. Most of musical history has been characterized by an overlapping push and pull between these two forms of innovation: 'rule' breaking is incremental and leads to a new set of explorations. The 'traditional' narratives of musicology have tended to focus on individual musicians or limited collaborative groups: the relatively limited set of musicians identified as leading the Tropicalia movement in Brazil for example or a 'family tree' of Congolese guitarists from Wendo through Dr Nico to Franco and beyond. It is the conscious decision making and creativity of these musicians who have driven the agenda by extending the 'rule' set or by becoming even more expert within the existing 'rule' set or, more usually, some combination of these two things.

Indeed, the concept of 'rules' (and the reason I keep putting them into inverted commas) is important in this regard because it relates to a variety of forms of theorizing and practical musical education. The theoretical modes of thinking about music that are used in many musical traditions often involve the implicit embodiment of that theory in a system of language or representation as much as, and in some instances more than, an explicit statement of that theory through educational practice. So the use of tablature notation when learning guitar parts embodies specific ideas about good technique and practice – about 'correct' fingering in particular. In many instances though, the ideas about what constitutes good practice are simply embodied in the actions of experts. For example, the formal and informal dissemination of knowledge in the world of record production and audio mixing is almost exclusively driven by accounts of expert professional practice both in the informal worlds of the trade press and YouTube and the formal world of university education. Just as in the eighteenth and nineteenth century worlds of Western art music composition the 'rules' of harmony and form were extended incrementally – with some small change in ideas of consonance and dissonance or the acceptable boundaries of sonata form being introduced and explored – the contemporary world of record production progresses in relatively conservative steps rather than radical leaps. Radical leaps such as the move to 12-tone serialism or free jazz may well be fêted for their bravery but are seldom popular. In general, we prefer our problem-solving activity to be embedded in a familiar, existing theoretical context and musicians such as Björk, Miles Davis, Claude Debussy or Joni Mitchell who push certain boundaries one at a time rather than breaking all the rules at once like John Cage, Yoko Ono or Ornette Coleman are more popular.

The ways in which the 'rules' are broken or stretched are not always down to the creative drive of individual musicians. Indeed, as many theoreticians of creativity have pointed out (e.g. Csikszentmihalyi, 1988; Boden, 1994), individual creativity should always be examined in its context and many examples are more interesting when they are understood in a broader context.

It is a common experience that listeners have more patience with music that is new to them when they have a 'way in'. Some of this is based on an internal logic – such as listening to new material by artists that we already like or which has been recommended by people we trust – and that logical process involves matching the new experience of this music onto some existing schema (the music we already like or the music we like that was recommended to us). This process does not convince us that we like this new music but it provides us with a motivation to continue looking for ways to make sense of it. Other examples are to do with acquiring some theoretical or contextual knowledge that makes sense of the unfamiliarity in some way. For example, while I have not been brought up with any experience of Persian classical music, an hour of reading about some of the structural features and approaches to improvisation provided me with a 'way in' to the listening experience. The **conscious**, problem-solving element of identifying these structures – albeit in a very inexpert manner – somehow made the **automatic** and **subconscious** elements that I did have work better as a musical experience: entrainment and the recognition of various types of expressive gesture and the materiality inherent in musical instrument timbres. The pleasure of making sense out of this unfamiliar sonic world takes us back to the notion mentioned earlier, that unresolved interpretations of what is happening around us can produce stress and resolving that stress through problem-solving has become a goal for humans. Achieving goals through problem-solving is a pleasurable experience, but so are the other elements of thought: the **automatic** processes of entrainment and empathy and the **subconscious** processes of matching experience to existing schema. The pleasure that comes from the problem-solving element encourages the creation of new schema as we listen more and some of the **conscious** elements become well-worn neural pathways – they 'fire together' and 'wire together' – and thereby create new **subconscious** schema. As we can see, therefore, the context in which an individual dwells (Ingold, 2011) – the individuals around them, the knowledge to which they have access – provide a system (Csikszentmihalyi, 1988; Thompson and Lashua, 2016), a network (Latour, 2005; Zagorski-Thomas, 2018a) or a community of practice (Chaiklin and Lave, 1996; Wenger, 2010) that influences and, indeed, is part of the problem-solving process.

These influences can also be more general and impersonal: trends and changes that affect whole cultures or communities. In Chapters 3 and 4 I discussed several of these, from the changing cultural attitudes to gender, sexuality, disability, class and race to developments in the technologies of musical practice. The ways in which these factors affect our perception of **restriction** and **affordance** are also, obviously, a key determinant in our approach to problem-solving. The way that changing social mores, beliefs, values and conventions affect our understanding of those **restrictions** and **affordances** constructs our sense of entitlement (or lack of it) to be a participant in various forms of activities and, therefore, the types of problem-solving strategies we will envisage as possible. In addition, the ways that technology of all sorts affects our environment and our bodies similarly affects our perception of what is possible. Likewise, factors such as migration (voluntary and forced) and cultural mixing through global media are continually expanding the extent and form of *intertextuality*. This can be found in the long history of economic and political *roma* migration from Northern India through the Persian Empire and the Middle East and North Africa into Southern and Central Europe and beyond. It can also, of course, be found in the extended legacy of colonial slavery and the many African musical traditions that were forced to collide with each other and with those of their colonial masters. In addition to ways in which these factors were discussed in Chapter 3 we can also look at how they also reflect various social constructions based on the value of different ways of thinking. McClary's (2002) analyses of the ways in which gender has been portrayed in the operatic works of Monteverdi and Bizet point to the Christian European prejudices about the rationality of the male and the irrationality of the female. That is not, I hasten to add, to suggest that subconscious learned behaviour is irrational or that conscious modes of thought are rational (and certainly not that they are related to gender!). Rather, that the ways in which these types of thought and musical engagement come together acquire ideological capital in various ways that are used to signify **convergence** and **divergence** from culturally established norms. It is not only the musical traditions and the people who make them that are valued differently, the modes of musical thought that are required to engage with them and produce them are valued differently as well.

All music uses all three of these mechanisms in various ways but we are much less practised in explaining the first two than we are with the third. I started this chapter with a short discussion of how the pieces I wrote with Kiamfu Kasongo reflected **automatic, subconscious** and **conscious** modes of thought and will finish by looking at how those ideas might be extended through the ideas outlined in this final section. We are not only less practised in explaining the first two than we are the third, but, as Middleton pointed out, Western musicology also values the third mode more highly. Any attempt at a kind of evolutionary justification for valuing conscious thought over other forms falls down pretty quickly – humans have extended capabilities in all three of these areas. The problem-solving prowess of squirrels is well known to anyone who attempted to design bird feeding mechanisms to exclude them and yet they, and most other animals, have not developed the capacity to closely entrain their movements to the rhythmic pulse of sound. We have also mentioned that entrainment is a capacity in which humans can develop higher and lower levels of skill with practice. Notions of accuracy, subtlety and nuance – in short, of skill and expertise – are applicable to all three of the modes of engagement.

There are a good many examples in both popular and art music forms where the authorship of a piece is attributed to the person who commissioned, organized, managed and edited the creative practice of others. Kiamfu is a highly skilled guitarist, arranger and composer whose creative practice is mostly channelled through the existing traditions and styles of Congolese popular music. In this instance he was acting as a session musician, using his skills in contexts that were not of his own volition. Of course, a piece like this, that is comprised of an edited recording, relies as much on Kiamfu's musical identity and expertise as on my ideas for how to edit them into something new and different. At the start of the chapter I talked about this piece in terms of the **automatic** level of entrainment to the pulse, the **subconscious** level of the shapes and gestures of Congolese guitar playing, and the **conscious** level of manipulating and subverting these tropes. For me, the piece is a way of drawing a different type of attention to the beauty of Kiamfu's playing and I see it completely as a collaborative piece. It is, of course, true that the impulse to create these pieces came from me and he would be unlikely to give a moment's thought to creating a piece like this. Not only that, but I do not think that Kiamfu likes the results very much – he finds them interesting, funny even, but, as he pointed out on first listen to one of the pieces, 'You can't dance to it'.

As a another example in the 'Fantasy Supervision League' model, if I were Ty's (the late Benedict Chijioke's) practice-based PhD supervisor and we were looking at the track *Eyes Open* from 2018 (also featuring OG Rootz, Deborah Jordan and Pumpkin), I would suggest we use these three modes of engagement as a starting point. There is clearly a very close and detailed inter-relationship between the rhythmic flow of his lyrics and the backing track. I would suggest he explores the way that this relationship develops through the song-writing process. How can he identify and tease out the three modes in this process? There's obviously a complex interplay between the lyric writing and some initial rhythmic template – was that an actual demo track or a kind of rhythmic proto-track that he had in his head? Could he find some examples from his lyric notebook and the demo recordings that demonstrate how sometimes the **automatic** mode rhythmic imperative drove decisions about the lyrics and sometimes the **subconscious** and **conscious** mode lyrical imperatives drove decisions about the rhythmic patterns? While the detail of what is being looked for is different to the Björk example, the methods of collecting 'data' would be the same – choosing between the three types of data: existing tracks for textual analysis or a retrospective IPA/stimulated recall, a new project or a series of explorative studies with no final output, both of which could be studied through reflective narrative, focused documentation, deconstruction or re-representation.

USEFUL QUESTIONS

Reflecting upon how the musical activities you engage in use each of these types of suggestion / interpretation.

Automatic: how do instinctive and reflexive responses play a part in your musical practice? (things such as entrainment, empathy and reflex). How could you become better at them?

Subconscious: these schema include both inductive and deductive elements – action/response patterns you are trained in and problem-solving/metaphor-building mechanisms. Can you identify one or more schema that are central to your practice? What are the inductive and deductive elements that you can identify? What should you be better at? Why? How? Do you engage in repetitive learning activity to improve?

Conscious: what are the most common types of problem-solving activities you engage in during your practice? How do they relate to the aesthetics of what you do?

Theoretical interlude 4:
Three modes of perception

The building blocks for the three modes of musical engagement mentioned in the previous chapter are three basic modes of perception: the automatic, the subconscious and the conscious. In this embodied cognition approach, the mechanisms of perception are inextricably enmeshed with the mechanisms of action as schema. And, as we have mentioned already, the structuring and functioning of schema are intricately enmeshed with the salience network: with value judgements, expectations and goals. While there certainly is not yet a clear understanding of how attention and consciousness manifest themselves in the brain, neuroscientists (e.g. Posner and Rothbart, 1998; Eastwood *et al.*, 2012) have identified three sub-networks of attention concerned with: (1) orienting – choosing where attention should be focused, (2) executive functions – deciding how 'vigilant' we should be and (3) alerting – concerning the level of arousal that our attention warrants. It is also not clear how much 'attention' is being paid by the default mode network (Bear, Connors and Paradiso, 2007, pp. 720–3). There is evidence that it maintains a series of passive or subconscious lookout mechanisms that have evolved to alert us to potential dangers. All of these features of attention reinforce the idea that perception is goal-oriented and that attention is one of the mechanisms through which those goals are embodied. This theoretical interlude will look at each of the three modes of perception and discuss not only how they work, but how these mechanisms of salience, focus and attention are embodied in them.

1. **Automatic** – the physical responses to stimulus. The instinctive or reflexive responses to a stimulus are the most basic types of pairing: pain to muscle flinching, turning towards a loud sound, flinching from rapid visual movement, face recognition, retching from stomach pain, etc. Are these responses themselves 'hard-wired' or are there some 'hard-wired' features of our brains that afford these types of thing (plus empathy and entrainment) *automatically* as soon as we start to perceive the normal world? Maybe rather than automatic they are implicit or 'hard to avoid' affordances that stem from a more general structuring principle in the brain. There are those who argue (e.g. Calì, 2013; Kim *et al.*, 2021) that the evolutionary development of the brain has involved the embodiment of structuring principles similar to those outlined in Gestalt psychology. In any event, our perceptual systems have evolved to take advantage of the inherent structure of the perceptual stimuli. Indeed, one important

example of this is the process known as exogenous attention in neuroscience (see for example Brosch *et al.*, 2011; Chica, Bartolomeo and Lupiáñez, 2013). These are mechanisms by which our attention is automatically drawn to certain types of perceptual stimulus. For example, our visual attention is drawn towards movement. Indeed, rapid change in any of our modes of perception stimulates this exogenous attention phenomenon – sudden changes in the amplitude of sound, intensity of taste or smell, etc. We have evolved for these to grab our attention automatically. Sloman (1990) and Damasio (2000, 2011) have pointed to the way that emotions act as a trigger from perception to action that works faster than reason and an important part of this is the way that they can focus attention on some feature of our current experience. Exogenous triggers of attention, as Brosch *et al.* (2011) point out, interact with emotional triggers and the conscious, voluntary endogenous attention I will discuss later in this section. One point that I think both 'conventional' and Practical Musicology could explore is how these exogenous or automatic triggers to attention (and to related actions) are identified and/or utilized in musical practices.

2. **Subconscious** – functional, constructed schema. It is worth a reminder about two features of schema: firstly that they are a theoretical construct rather than a physical reality. There are no such 'things' as schema in the brain, it is just a way of thinking about how the brain works. Secondly that they are multi-modal. Schema do not relate to a single mode of perception such as vision but they reflect the idea that we understand the world in a multi-modal manner – knowing that the feel of moving your hand and arm to press a piano key, the pressure sensation of touching a piano key, the sight of your finger on a piano key and the sound of the piano note, are 'the same thing'. These schema are the pathways – both parallel and serial – that are formed through repetition and reward on an unconscious level. That notion of reward takes us back to the salience network from neuroscience. Posner and Rothbart (1998) suggest that the development of attention in infants is a way of avoiding distress and Eastwood (2012) theorizes the negative sensations of boredom in terms of the inability to attend to something salient. This and other research on salience and boredom (e.g. Tabatabaie *et al.*, 2014; Mills and Christoff, 2018) lead me to the hypothesis that the notion of salience maps in neuroscience (Bear, Connors and Paradiso, 2007, pp. 723–42) – whereby salience is mapped onto patterns of experiential stimuli – transfer into this psychological model in terms of schema being constructed around links to particular forms of salience: both physiological needs, pleasures and pains and the socially constructed pleasures of problem-

solving that map onto physiological stresses from unresolved interpretations. These are built into schema through the value judgements, expectations and goals I mentioned earlier. I am suggesting that aesthetics are built upon a complex interaction between the pleasure of problem-solving (Canestrari *et al.*, 2018) and sensory pleasure (see for example Skov and Nadal, 2020), where 'pleasure' can also be defined in terms of the resolution of stress or anxiety that unsolved problems or interpretations of our surroundings create. If schema are mapped onto the salience network through the resolution of these types of stress and anxiety then the satisfaction derived from the efficient application of a schema and from its effective variation makes sense.

3. **Conscious** – the metaphorical and hypothetical. It may seem strange to talk of perception being conscious or deliberate but this relates to the way that our endogenous or top-down attention network can alter our perception through orientation and interpretation and can generate hypothetically 'possible' pathways based on the frequency and patterning of previous experiences. As many of the more bizarre features of recent political life attest to, it is possible for individuals to interpret events that happen around us in spectacularly different ways. Simply from a musical perspective, most of us have experience of someone describing a sonic event as music while others dismiss it as 'just noise'. While that may seem to be a disagreement about aesthetics, it can be, and often is, a disagreement about which sonic characteristics and structuring principles are necessary for sound to be music, i.e. it is a question of ontology. Going back to the notion of endogenous attention, those value judgements, expectations and goals that are embodied in schema provide a conscious, functional framework for us to focus our attention on features we agree are important. That might be a process based on orientation – of focusing our attention on a particular place – or it may be a process of interpretation – that our interpretation of a scene or event encourages us to see things in a particular light or from a particular angle. That notion of *subject position* (Clarke, 1999), of perceiving something from one perspective rather than another, affects what we are able to see. The *subject position* that we occupy affords some perceptions and makes us blind to others. There are three versions of this. The first is what Gibson (1979, p. 286) describes as a 'vantage point' in which the physicality of the environment and our position in it influence what we can see and what we cannot see. The second is the way in which we can consciously position ourselves in a way that determines what we will see. Of course, the way in which that conscious positioning process happens also determines whether or how much we know what we are missing. The third

involves the conscious influence from a third party to create either of the first two types of *subject position*. We can be influenced into a position or we can be influenced to consciously position ourselves.

When it comes to hypothetical forms of perception, I am talking about the conscious imagining of perception: the mind's eye or the mind's ear. In the last chapter, in the section on schema (5.2), I talked about the question of how vividly we perceive imagined sound by consciously (or sometimes unconsciously) 'running' a perceptual schema. In the same way that I distinguished between *tokens* and *types* in categories, we can imagine either a specific instance – a memory – or a more generic instance. The more generic instance involves only the invariant properties and not the specific variables that 'belong' to the specific instance of a memory. However, we can also imagine phenomena that have not occurred before but which seem as if they could if some condition were true. How likely it is that the condition will be met distinguishes potential solutions to problems or situations from the more fantastic imaginings – and, I would argue, forms the basis for arbitrary and seemingly irrational beliefs. Unresolved interpretations of what is going on in the world create stress through the salience network and resolving those interpretations relieves the stress and gives us pleasure. It is sometimes better for our mental health to adopt a relatively far-fetched interpretation than it is to maintain the stress of an unresolved interpretation.

6

Learning and knowing

There is a quotation which is frequently misattributed to Albert Einstein but which seems to come from 12 Step Addiction literature from the start of the 1980s: the definition of insanity is doing the same thing over and over again and expecting a different result. Surely that is also the definition of how, in the words of the old joke, I get to Carnegie Hall? 'Practice, Practice, Practice'. Repetition is one of the fundamental ways in which we learn. It is the 'bottom up' of **inductive** thought through which we learn from experience (and create schema) and can be contrasted, as we have seen, with the 'top down' of **deductive** thought: of finding connections between experiences which were previously unconnected.

In December 2019, as a follow-up to the Classical Music Hyper-Production project, I recorded Louise Cournarie, a PhD student at the Royal Academy of Music, playing Rameau's *l'Enharmonique* on the piano, the fifteenth piece in his harpsichord Suite in G. Part of Louise's research is to explore novel approaches to playing harpsichord repertoire on the piano and she is interested in the possibilities for both independence and synchronization between the hands. Relating this back to the discussion about the ecological approach and the 'real' and metaphorical forms of agency that we might perceive, Louise is trying to find ways to suggest independent voices within the music. As an aside to her main research focus, we decided to record the different voices separately, as multiple takes that were overdubbed. Although we made a short 'demo' in 2019, we were then held up by workloads and the pandemic and only managed to record a full version in October 2020, almost a year later, and I am only just mixing it now (in October 2021). We recorded three versions (see Video 6.1 on the website[1]):

---

[1] http://www.c21mp.org/practical-musicology/

- A 'normal' hands together version
- A version played to a click track with the left and right hands played separately
- A version played to a click track without ornamentation that was divided into three parts: the upper melodic line, the lower 'bass' melodic line and any middle lines or harmonic 'filler'

I then edited and processed the third version to create versions of the ornamentation through audio processing and the manipulation of electronic spatial effects. Video 6.2 on the website[2] documents and demonstrates some of the techniques that were used to do this and how the aesthetic of what 'worked' and what did not work emerged from the process. Both Louise and I have many years of experience and a high level of practical skill in what we do. She has played this piece many times before and has even, as part of her practice regime and experimentation with the voicings, played the hands separately. However, both of us found ourselves having to learn how to play, record and edit it in this particular way. Just as, when you approach a familiar landmark from an unfamiliar direction, it takes time and effort to rethink and re-orient oneself, we were both having to re-orient ourselves in relation to our normal practice: what Bourdieu (1993) called the *habitus*.

The potential affordances in any given situation are understood through prior experience (the pathways and schema mentioned earlier) and through experimentation or new experience (the combined sensations of bodily activity and our sensory receptors) which creates new pathways and new schema. It is not only true that we know things because we have learned them but we can learn things because we already know other things. Vygotsky's (1980) notion of the *zone of proximal development* is based on the idea that the current state of my existing knowledge both allows and limits (affords and restricts) the potential for successful new learning activity. All new knowledge is built on the foundations of existing knowledge. Vygotsky's *zone of proximal development* – an important part of current education theory – is a feature of a larger conceptual phenomenon: that any new experience not only contributes to our knowledge in the way that it affects the structure of existing schema, but it is also filtered through those existing schema. Our existing knowledge, in the form of our schema or neural pathways, includes value judgements about what is important in particular

---

[2] http://www.c21mp.org/practical-musicology/

contexts, it includes expectations about causality – about what *kinds* of invariant properties produce what *kinds* of affordances – and it includes a variable set of goals that are being flagged up by the salience network as important in any given context. In short, the way that new experience is going to be interpreted through the brain and, therefore, how it is going to contribute to new knowledge at any given moment, will be strongly affected by what we know already – by our existing schema. In the last chapter, when I was discussing the three forms of musical engagement (Section 5.4), I talked about the way in which, once we have learned how to drive, our responses become **subconscious** and we can sometimes arrive at a destination with very little memory of driving there. In these instances, our existing knowledge – the schema – is using familiar new experience **subconsciously** to trigger learned actions and responses. Any 'newness' in the experience is being ignored because of the value judgements, expectations and goals that have been baked into the schema during the learning process. That is not to say that we *cannot* learn anything new about driving but that there is an inertia in the 'system' – our schema – that requires something to trigger the salience network in the brain so that we engage the **conscious** process of the central-executive network. This is the cognitive basis of the process of *interpretive flexibility* from theories of the social construction of technology that I mentioned in Chapter 4 (Section 4.1) and of Bourdieu's *habitus*. When Louise and I made a conscious decision to work on the Rameau piece in the way that we did, the new goals about how we wanted to do it were enacted through our personal salience networks and our **conscious** problem-solving – our central-executive networks.

Before we continue with our discussion of learning and knowing, I want to reiterate the first two types of aesthetic appreciation that I introduced in the last chapter before I introduce the third and fourth in this chapter. Our first two aesthetic principles relate to the **inductive** process of schema acquisition and involve the appreciation of 'correct' or 'expert' action through a schema and the recognition of intentional and expert variation of a schema. These relate to the first two types of new knowledge that can emerge from Practical Musicology as outlined in Chapter 2. First of these was the relationship between problem-solving and technical skill and we have discussed how technical skill is based upon the expert application of a schema and that expert variation is based on **deductive**, top-down thinking: of finding connections between aspects of different schema that would afford the attainment of a particular goal or a sub-goal that might lead to it being solved subsequently. Second in our typology of new knowledge from Practical Musicology was the relationship between the development and emergence of quality judgements and methods. While the expert application of the inductive, learned schema is one thing, the criteria for how it can be varied in an expert way are an aspect that becomes embedded in the schema through a deductive process. This deductive process embodies a quality judgement in that it suggests some form of conceptual blending (Fauconnier and Turner, 2003) whereby a feature of some other schema is mapped onto the one that we are trying to vary. Thus, having learned some chord/scale relationships through a connection of aural, visual and haptic connections and being able to fluently play appropriate scalar patterns or fragments over the relevant harmony, I might, for instance, find that inflecting those movements with gestures related to particular feelings produces sounds that fit with my idea of good music. As I use it more and more, this deductive process also becomes embedded in the subconscious schema – the 'rules' of variation are not specific activities but are a 'tried and tested' way of creating a range of variations.

6.1 Forms of knowing

Models of human cognition have become infused with the metaphor of the brain as a computer. Perhaps the most problematic aspect of this metaphor is the conflation of knowledge and data. Human brains do not contain registers for data storage like the storage of numbers in a digital computer or hard disk. They 'store' the probability of particular patterns of pathways occurring in particular situations. In short, memory and knowledge are about activity rather than about 'things'. The perception (or rather cognition) of things is an emergent property of the perception of affordances or potential activity. My understanding of shape is an understanding of how my sensory input changes when I move – for example, of the different ways a round plate creates (mostly oval and only very rarely circular) patterns on my retina as I move in relation to it (Noë, 2004). In short, the basic building blocks of knowledge are not facts but a knowledge of how things change, how to do something or how something happens.

However, there is another form of knowing in addition to the creation of schema based on our previous experience and that is the ability to identify connections between different schema; to find features in two or more different schema that have categorical similarities that allow you to build a metaphorical connection between them. That provides the basis for the mix of the Rameau that I created with Louise Cournarie. I tried to find sonic features of the ornaments that she performed, based on the instructions in the notation, and replace the keyboard-based performance gestures that are normally used with electronic manipulations. They start out quite literal – replacing performed alternations between two pitches with electronic pitch alternation of a single sustained note. The only difference is that there is no re-triggering of the hammer attack on the string at the start of each new pitch. It is a relatively minor change but it makes clear how strongly our understanding of the affordances of sound production by the piano are embedded in our minds when it stands out as 'not possible' on the piano for most people. As the piece progresses, the mapping from the 'original' sound becomes less literal. For example, the performed pitch variations are mapped onto amplitude variations or changes in the ambience – the intensity or length of the echo or reverberation in the space. But metaphorical mappings are not simply the domain of conceptual pieces such as this. As we discussed in Chapter 5, a great deal of musical meaning in general is metaphorical in character.

As I mentioned in Chapter 1, the world of artistic research in the academic world is largely concerned with conceptual art – and in the world of sound, with musical practices where the metaphors are made explicit, where they lead or frame the musical activity (rather than *vice versa*), where they mostly or entirely fall into the third, 'problem-solving' category of musical engagement and where a language-based exegesis is the strongest and most appropriate way to share the new knowledge. I must stress that I have no 'beef' with this at all – quite a lot of my own Practical Musicology/practice research falls into this category – but it makes life difficult for the practice researcher exploring phenomena where the metaphors are implicit or embodied, where the sonic or embodied activity leads or frames the metaphor, where they utilize the automatic and subconscious modes of learning and knowing and where the new knowledge is best shared in an embodied and non-linguistic form. And, of course, there is no clear binary distinction whereby work always falls into one of these two categories either in the world of music or the broader world of artistic research. For example, Nimkulrat (2016) themed an issue of *Studies in Material Thinking* on learning through experimenting with materials where the strongly text-based format of the journal and the absence of materiality other than how it can be represented in two-dimensional visual images posed a problem which challenged the contributors to come up with creative solutions for sharing their research. Sider *et al.* (2017) utilized a group-based 'pass the parcel' approach to exploring an artistic research question – in this case 'what is the potential of silence in a performance context' (theatrical performance in this instance) – each participant adding to and editing a communal multimedia document. The format of the *Journal of Artistic Research* also provides a multi-media format that offers opportunities for sharing new knowledge that might be best represented, at least partially, in a medium other than language. Coppier (2021), for example, is exploring ideas through artistic experiments that suggest metaphorical interpretations: exploring the concept of silence by conducting sound experiments that encourage us to think about silence, noise and hearing, and exploring the 'sound of worms' through a variety of recording and sound manipulation processes. The types of new knowledge that stem from artistic research tend to be restricted to technical knowledge (the relationship between problem-solving and technical skill) or to the mechanisms for creating metaphors relating theory to artistic practice. For me, this is an incomplete set of goals for my research and, in particular, it misses the notion that we can explore the development of various types of aesthetic through practice as a research activity and that there are shareable forms of knowledge about the process of developing aesthetic judgements.

6.2 Representational systems

The representational system that is probably most commonly discussed is language. It is held up as the development that distinguishes us from other species. Language is one of the few representational systems that humans have developed where the connection between the thing being represented and the way it is represented is arbitrary: there is generally no 'reason' behind the sonic or written version of a word that connects it to the thing it is used to represent. However, the second type of knowledge mentioned above, finding connections between features of two different schema and using those similarities to produce a *conceptual blend* (Fauconnier and Turner, 2003) of the two as a mechanism for creating new knowledge, is the basis for most representational systems. Pictures stimulate the retina in ways that have features in common with the things they represent. While the sounds we use to represent numbers may be arbitrary, the concepts of two ducks and two chickens have features in common. That notion of number then affords the idea of using a scratch mark on a stick or a rock to represent the passing of a day and provides the basis of a calendar. And if we go back to the origins of language, there are two related features of language which probably pre-date the use of arbitrary sounds or signs. Firstly, there is tone of voice: that I can make sounds that emulate and therefore represent an emotional or energy-based narrative. In a similar vein,

I can create sounds that are onomatopoeic: that sound like water splashing or the wind whistling. And as I mentioned earlier, the idea of representing an emotional or energy-based narrative that we want others to synchronize to is a fundamental principle of music: indeed, it is the fundamental point of representational systems.

And representations can be more or less 'realistic'. The phenomenon that represents something can share many or few experiential features in common with the phenomenon it represents. Theatre and cinema are generally representing more features of 'life' than, for example, a watercolour painting or a song. But even within a single representational system we can experience different levels of 'realism' or, as Denis Smalley terms it in connection with his writing on spectromorphology, *surrogacy*. This also formed the basis of my notion of *sonic cartoons* in the study of record production: I can hear a recording that sounds very similar to the experience of being in a room with some musicians. I can hear one where the clarity and separation of the instruments have been artificially enhanced with equalization and compression – less realism but more clarity. Or I can hear one where my interpretation is being deliberately manipulated through the use of distortion or filtering. They are all representations but they also have different amounts of experiential features in common with the phenomenon being represented. And importantly, they can represent the real or the hypothetical. Just as I can paint something real or imaginary, a recording can be something that actually happened or something that has been constructed to sound as if it happened.

To give a further musical example, my understanding of melody relies on metaphor – pitch, rhythm, volume and duration are discernible as the phenomenon of separate sound-objects in a continuous narrative sonic stream. This can stand as a metaphor for different types of energy expenditure and, therefore, for different types of activity that have emotional or other connotations. Musical sound works as a metaphor for (mostly human) activity and our interpretation of the activity is therefore translated into 'musical meaning'. But there is, of course, more to it than that because these are not purely imitative sounds. They are filtered through a formal system that does two separate things: it decreases the realism of the experience by using a schematic formalism and it introduces an additional element to the experience that relates to the skilful use of the representational system. I can appreciate both the subtlety (or familiarity, intensity, etc.) of the emotional narrative and the skill with which the musician has used the representational system of scales, harmony, rhythm, etc. These are the third and fourth types of aesthetic appreciation and are concerned with the creation of metaphorical relationships between schema – a representational system. And we can appreciate both the intensity and the efficacy with which the metaphor transmits the intended narrative and the elegance of the metaphor and the skill with which it has been realized.

And finally, returning to the notion of the real and the hypothetical as well as to the perception of realism. Bearing in mind that I can create a realistic depiction of a hypothetical or imagined event – such as Carracci's 1596 painting of 'The Choice of Hercules' – or an unrealistic depiction of a real event – such as Picasso's 1937 painting of 'Guernica'. There are also two forms of interpretation that can be invoked by a representation which can be understood in relation to the *type* and the *token* I discussed in the section on categories. They can also be thought of as real or hypothetical. On the one hand, I can relate a representation to a specific, real *token* of my lived experience and thus it can invoke thoughts and feelings through a process of association (Gabrielsson and Juslin, 1996; Juslin and Sloboda, 2001). On the other, I can relate it to a general, hypothetical *type* of lived experience: a narrative that does not relate to a 'real' unresolved or stressful issue and which just provides the 'pleasure' of solving the interpretation.

USEFUL QUESTIONS

How does your practice explore or involve ways of representing an emotional narrative through sound? What kinds of emotion are most important to you in these representations? Who do you know that represents them better? What can you learn from them?

How does your practice explore or involve ways of representing an energy narrative through sound? What kinds of energy are most important to you in these representations? Who do you know that represents them better? What can you learn from them?

How does your musical practice relate to 'real' life? What are the mechanisms through which this relationship works?

What could you change about the way that this relationship works? How would that be reflected in a change to your practice?

6.3 Thinking as doing

We also need to include another feature of this approach to cognition which is that our understanding of activity in the world is grounded in our experience of being in our own body. Based on the idea of mirror neurons, embodied cognition explains our ability to understand any experience solely through metaphors with our own embodied experience. Starting with the original mirror neuron research, we understand the sight of someone else grasping something by using the same neural patterns that we would use to grasp – minus the actual instructions to move the muscles (Iacoboni *et al.*, 2005). Put bluntly, my understanding of your activity is constructed by subconsciously imagining doing the same or some similar activity. More than this, for any experience our way of generating an interpretation is to find some feature of what we are experiencing that we can map onto some feature of our previous experience. Thus, my interpretation of a trumpet melody might be constructed from my previous experience of making noises with similar pitches and rhythmic attributes. If I am not a musician that would probably relate to my voice but if I am a musician I have another set of experiences to draw upon. If we return to the notion of affordances, this all relies on my experience of what is possible with the physiology of the human body but also on the less universal experience of what is possible with different types of tools, instruments and technologies.

In Jamaica in the late 1960s and early 1970s, Osbourne Ruddick (aka King Tubby) was one of the key figures in the development of dub mixing and I will utilize the Fantasy Supervision League conceit again in relation to him. Dub is a performative mode of audio mixing that utilizes editing (by switching certain instruments on and off during playback), processing (altering the volume, using frequency equalization and filtering) and spatial effects (adding and removing reverberation and delay/echo). While these albums didn't translate into the huge international sales success of an artist like Bob Marley, they did have a disproportionate impact on recording practice and studio-based song writing. As a sound engineer working in the late 1980s and early 1990s I learned to use these techniques in both reggae and a range of electronic dance music genres. Dub mixing is an interesting form of musical practice in that it involves both 'in the moment' improvisation and the potential for reflection and repetition that creating a recorded artefact instead of a performance affords: I can improvise mixes over and over again until I am happy. Thus, if I were supervising

USEFUL QUESTIONS

What kinds of moment-to-moment decisions are you making in your musical practice?

What are the kinds of things in your practice that you would like to be able to instantly re-do if you could re-wind time?

What are the kinds of things that work better in your practice when you do them without thinking? Why?

Ruddick, I would want him to explore this notion of thinking as doing through this performative editing process. The creation of a narrative structure through repeated performances of the mix is founded on the dual process of experimenting and listening – hearing and taking note of 'happy accidents' but also of hearing potential in moments that nearly work or hint at how something could work. Documenting this 'in the moment' process poses some problems but identifying a problem is the first step towards a solution. How could a form of documentation mark those moments of salience – when an idea strikes?

6.4 Acquiring Knowledge

Given that we have identified two forms of knowing – the ability to construct schema from prior (or rather continuing) experience and the ability to construct metaphorical connections between them – we have also identified two potential forms of learning. On the one hand, we have what we might characterize as 'training' – the acquisition of pathways/schema through repeated experience that provide an understanding of the usual affordances in a particular situation and the most frequent types of variation – a kind of cognitive script or flow diagram. This relates to consciously acquired musical skills such as instrumental fluency or technique but also to unconsciously acquired skills such as a familiarity with cultural forms, tonality, harmony, etc. On the other hand, we have a kind of meta-script – a schema of ways of looking for metaphorical relationships between other schema. In musical terms this might equate to an ability to map emotional narratives onto instrumental technique. Acquiring this kind of knowledge seems to be much harder – or at least is less common. Both of these types of learning are happening to us all the time through the informal process of living but we have also developed a range of formal systems and processes of education.

Looping back to the idea of influence, which we can characterize as an informal and often unintentional learning process, it is important to consider how the notion of influence relates to these two forms of knowledge and learning. The first, or bottom-up, form of knowledge acquisition is the process of forming schema – of learning which aspects of experience repeat in certain circumstances and which aspects can vary. So, for example, the sounds that I hear when people blow into tubular instruments have different characteristics than those that I hear when people pluck, scrape or hit things. The major characteristics that blown things have in common are to do with the ways that different frequencies start up – slower than both hit and plucked sounds and with a slightly different shape than scraping. In addition, though, we can hear a lot about the materiality of different blown instruments: about their shape and what they are made of. We can also hear different mechanisms that are used in conjunction with our mouths to create the vibration – like a trumpet mouthpiece and that of a flute, or between a single reed like a clarinet or a saxophone and a double reed like an oboe or a shawm. So the categorization process is like a hierarchy of perceptual distinctions – we have learned that certain features of our aural experience are always associated with blown instruments and others can be variable. Of those variables, some features might define a sub-category of brass trumpets, some might define a category of clarinets – and some might not be associated with any instrument we've experienced before: I don't know what that is exactly, but I can tell that it is a blown instrument and the pitch is low so I can tell it is quite big. The neural pathway that gets triggered by a trumpet sound will be slightly different every time we hear one but there will be some bits of the pathway that are the same and others that are different. The ones that are the same get reinforced and, therefore, we expect them to be the same the next time. If they are, they get reinforced more and if they are different then the previous reinforcement gets weakened. This is the neural mechanism that creates expectations – expectations about the type of noise we will hear when we see a trumpet – and expectations about the type of object we will see when we hear a trumpet. Expectations about how the pitches are likely to change – how they will move in steps, how high or low in pitch they might go and how loud or quiet they might get. I may spend more time hanging around with trumpets than you do and, if I do, I am going to build up more complex, extensive and nuanced patterns of recognition and expectation than you do. I might, for example, be able to tell the difference between a recording of Lee Morgan playing a trumpet and Clifford Brown playing one.

If I learn to play the trumpet, I am going to be using these schema – these expectations of what a trumpet should sound like – to test my progress. When I start to learn, I will be more concerned with the general aspects of the schema – am I making a noise that has a constant pitch and tone or which sounds like a comical fart noise? As I get better, I will get into the finer detail and I may decide that I want to sound like Lee Morgan rather than Clifford Brown. Forgetting about the aesthetics that guides that choice for the moment, in order to be influenced by Lee Morgan, I need to have a finely detailed schema that can differentiate between Lee Morgan and other trumpeters. Of course, that way I can also distinguish between different features of Lee Morgan and decide that I want to emulate some and not others. Indeed, I may want some aspect of Lee Morgan's tone and some aspect of Clifford Brown's phrasing.

I shall discuss the term *flow* in more detail in Section 6.6 on Experimentation below, but it is also relevant in relation to the way that behaviour changes once a schema becomes more firmly established. Within the world of dance, Laban has explored the ways in which movement changes as our understanding of it does.

> Movements performed with a high degree of bound flow reveal the readiness of the moving person to stop at any moment in order to readjust the effort if it proves to be wrong, or endangers success … In movements done with fluent flow, a total lack of control or abandon becomes visible, in which the ability to stop is considered inessential …
>
> (Laban and McCaw, 2011, p. 220)

These two notions of bound flow and fluent flow are the embodiment of the cognitive processes that underlie them: the period during which a schema is forming and the period during which it become trusted and usable – when conscious monitoring is no longer necessary.

I have not yet discussed the second form of knowing and learning mentioned above: the ability to construct metaphorical connections between existing schema. In essence though, that is the process of being able to combine some aspect of Lee Morgan's tone and some aspect of Clifford Brown's phrasing. It is the possibility of imagining something that has not happened yet but which seems plausible based on our previous experience. While the potential for hypothetical thought is not exclusively human by any stretch of the imagination, the extent to which we can do it does seem to be one of the things that distinguishes us from other species – and in particular, the way in which we can voluntarily create arbitrary

USEFUL QUESTIONS

How can you develop a new meta-script? (a way of looking for metaphorical relationships between your musical practice and other features of your life)

What is the primary way in which you map emotional, structural and other narratives onto musical sound (or your ways of making sound)? Think of an alternative way?

Eno's *Oblique Strategies* involves a series of general axioms such as 'Humanize something that is free from error' or 'Faced with a choice, do both'. Come up with ten such axioms that you think would be useful in your practice.

---

connections between distant and even unrelated schema seems important to both hypothetical thought and representational systems (and therefore, ultimately, to language). It does add, therefore, an additional dimension to the notion of influence when we introduce the notion of deliberation and choice. This top-down element of deliberately constructing metaphorical connections between existing schema is therefore the link between influence and creativity.

6.5 Creativity

This ability to construct metaphorical connections between existing schema is also fundamental to the notion of creativity – the ability to create something new and in some way valuable. Creativity would, under this theoretical model, be defined as the process of discovering new metaphors; of making new connections between schema. Once again these new connections can be thought of as occurring through our three mechanisms of restriction, affordance and influence but also as occurring through the conscious deliberation of problem-solving or through subconscious schema. Thus, a songwriter might choose to try to write a song using a guitar rather than a piano because of the rhythmic affordances it provides. They may have a range of pre-determined features – lyrics or musical influences of various sorts – that are thought about in a deliberate and conscious manner in combination with a series of subconscious schema that – through being 'run' – produce output that is then subject to critical reflection, selection and variation. There is an additional element to this, which is that creativity is a collaborative activity – even when we are notionally doing it on our own.

We are using the knowledge of previous and current generations to create new knowledge or artefacts for ourselves or for future generations.

Bruford (2018) brings together ideas from various scholars of distributed creativity (Dewey, 1934; Burnard, 2012; Glăveanu, 2014) in his SDCA framework of selection, differentiation, communication and assessment. His continuum between functional and compositional forms of performance maps partially onto the **inductive** and **deductive** modes of thought and shines a light on the connection between that and the **convergent/divergent** dichotomy by pointing to the way that inductive learning is almost always a form of enculturation rather than autodidactic in an isolated, 'making it up from scratch' sense.

Returning to the Fantasy Supervision League, if I were supervising Janelle Monae in relation to her *ArchAndroid* album from 2010, I would suggest she clearly needs to explore this through the notion of intertextuality in her performance and vocal arrangement. She might break it down in terms of fragments of vocal styles that evoke different musical cultures – from 1950s jazz and hip hop to the Pearl and Dean cinema advert. But in addition to those forms of mode three intertextuality, I would also suggest she considers modes one and two – the automatic and the conscious. How do the subtle shifts in the groove of her vocal delivery relate to those larger cultural tropes and how do they help to maintain a larger structural coherence across this stylistic mosaic? And how do the timbral and register shifts that reflect and help to create the narrative contrasts also use subconscious energy-related metaphors to move between a more throw-away dilettante mood and emotional intensity? Why does she consider this kind of intertextuality works as creativity? Can she explore why some outputs might be considered creative and others to be derivative? Using various forms of audio representation, what are the invariant properties of creative or derivative narratives that can be isolated in this regard?

USEFUL QUESTIONS

How do you think we might be able to teach creativity?
What kinds of mechanism can we use to discover new metaphors? There are the two versions here:
  thinking about what we want to say and finding a metaphor that fits
  thinking about the normal ways in which we work and changing some aspect of it to see if we recognize new metaphors that we like.

6.6 Experimentation

During the course of a more detailed discussion about Miles Davis' *Bitches Brew* (Zagorski-Thomas, 2018a), I have written about the ways in which Davis explored structured forms of improvisation which, while they may not deserve the soubriquet 'free' in the way that Ornette Coleman and others did, move dramatically away from the established jazz format of using 'standard' song structures as the basis for improvisation. While these can be seen as starting to emerge on the part-written, part-improvised collaborations in the 1949 *Birth Of The Cool* recordings and developing more strongly on the 1959 *Kind Of Blue* album, it was during and after the 'Second Great Quintet' of Ron Carter, Herbie Hancock, Wayne Shorter and Tony Williams that the idea that has come to be known as 'time, no changes' – of modal, near-tonal or atonal improvisation over a steady pulse or groove – emerged. Davis also developed, particularly in his studio albums, the 'technique' of putting together ensembles who had little or no experience of playing together in order to stimulate energy and creativity. This, of course, relates to our third form of new knowledge that relates to practice research – exploring the relationship between the expected and the unexpected through experimentation.

While creativity is generally considered to be a deliberate act and, therefore, to involve a level of pre-planning, there is a counterbalancing notion of spontaneity and improvisation that exists in varying degrees in different musical traditions. While the processes of conscious deliberation and subconscious schema may similarly come together in various combinations, the key difference is in the absence of a subsequent stage of reflection, selection and variation. If we return to the interactive nature of experience that I mentioned in relation to Vygotsky's *zone of proximal development* at the start of this chapter, we can begin to understand the cognitive mechanisms for this. In addition to the fact that new experience alters and shapes our existing schema, we also have to remember that existing schema influence how new experience is processed and what affordances are recognized and acted upon. We mentioned Sloman's (1990) and Damasio's (2000, 2011) work on the idea that emotions are an evolutionary mechanism to bypass the time-consuming process of reason at moments of crisis. Many of the processes that we call instinctive or intuitive are, in fact, learned. The structure of a schema involves this kind of fast-tracking, of instantaneous **subconscious** responses to particular types of sensory stimulus that lead to what athletes call 'the zone' and what Hanin (1980) has termed the *zone of optimal functioning*.

Hanin and others (e.g. Robazza, 2006) point out that this 'optimal functioning' is highly affected by emotion and anxiety in both positive and negative ways and in ways that vary strongly from individual to individual. This notion of performance anxiety is, of course, very familiar in musical circles as well. This notion of *flow* (Csikszentmihalyi, 1997) has been applied in both sports science and music performance studies (Jackson, 1996; Custodero, 2005; Araújo and Hein, 2019), and Jackson (1996, p. 76) describes some of the key features that athletes identified as 'the autotelic experience of flow, total concentration on the task at hand, merging of action and awareness, and the paradox of control'.

Flow is a process whereby the central executive network is disabled or muted – the salience network has identified a single goal with a clear method: a schema that will achieve the goal. There are clear 'pathways' that deal with predictable incoming stimuli **subconsciously** and the situation is sufficiently familiar and 'safe' so that we do not have to be vigilant. There can be various levels of this whereby the central executive network functions with some clear goals – consciously looking for opportunities within a relatively limited context: looking for potential space to run into on a football field or the suggestion of a possible emotional or gestural narrative by other members of a musical ensemble that could be explored.

And much like any process of experimentation, the key to success is in the preparation – in making sure that the right circumstances are in place to restrict, afford and influence in the required manner. In the long term, of course, that relates to the right kind of training as a musician but it can also relate to having the right combination of people in the right room with the right set of instructions. In short, we need to move beyond the psychology of the individual towards the social psychology and sociology of groups.

USEFUL QUESTIONS

How are you most often spontaneous in:
    Your musical practice?
    Your life?
How do you prepare yourself to be spontaneous?
What do you think are the most important pre-conditions?

Theoretical interlude 5: *The mechanisms of influence*

Building on the three forms of engagement introduced in Section 5.4 – through the process of affording interpretations rather than the narrower notion of meaning that is normally associated with semiotics, the theoretical model seeks to provide a framework for understanding *musicking*. In the next chapter the focus is on what it is that music can share (and how) but, as I will argue later, the model also addresses the why. And, of course, the reasons and motivations behind communication are framed in terms of influence, restriction and affordance – the mechanisms by which we (and our environment) change other people's minds and behaviours.

Under the model as it stands so far, there are two ways in which we can change other people's minds and behaviours: altering the structure of their existing schema through an inductive process of 'doing' it differently or through a deductive process of making new and different connections. This process of persuading the person to modify their schema by either altering it or adding to it to make it more complex or nuanced can be a direct configuration by a co-present actor or indirect configuration through a medium. I have identified eight mechanisms of influence through which these types of schema alteration can occur:

1. Exert physical control

This could be between human actors or could involve the design/physical structure of an object configuring an actor's behaviour or altering some aspect of their schema. The occurrence between human actors has overtones of coercion but is quite common in the teaching of physical skills – placing a pupil's hands in the right position for a task, for example. In relation to the design/physical structure of an object, this, of course, relates to Gibson's (1979) original ideas about the physical affordances in the environment. Our perception of those affordances – as embodied in a schema – can be influenced by encountering some new object or form of environment. This might be something very direct such as the way that using a different gauge of guitar string influences a player's hand movements or something more indirect such as the influence a room's acoustics have on a performer's dynamics.

2. Instruct (or suggest)

This relates to giving an instruction that causes the recipient to alter some aspect of their existing schema. Obviously, telling someone to do something differently requires authority. The person who is instructed needs to recognize some authority in the person doing the instructing – otherwise we can characterize it as a suggestion. I will discuss authority in more detail in Chapter 9 and it is obviously a highly complicated phenomenon based on a broad range of social contracts ranging from employment and education to threats and intimidation. In musical activity, in addition to employment and education, creative ownership and leadership can often be a source of authority. This can range from a composer giving instructions about the dynamics of a piece to a performer setting a tempo through a count in. These levels and types of authority are where the grey area between instruction and suggestion exists. Of course, in many instances we have a choice about compliance, about ignoring an instruction or rebelling against or resisting a situation into which the actions of others have put you. Influence does not always work.

3. Contradict

In a situation where the influence is concerned with altering a schema rather than adding to or making it more complex, it may be necessary to contradict some aspect of the recipient's existing schema. This requires the influencer to recognize and be able to identify a feature that they would like to change. While there may be an overlap with instruction and suggestion here, the difference lies in identifying 'wrongness' in some way: that there is something that needs to be changed rather than simply that there is something I think you should do. Contradiction can just as easily take a more egalitarian form such as 'why don't we try it like this instead?' which is usually predicated on the idea of having shared goals and a collaborative negotiation process by which they might be achieved.

4. Reinforce

Very often, in both life and music, an inductive process of experimentation produces a 'happy accident' and one or more of the participants acts to reinforce a tentative or ambiguous aspect of the recipient's existing schema: 'Yes, that's it!'

Once again, this can be about shared goals and collaboration or as an affirmation from a position of authority. It may also be unconditional or, as above, require the influencer to recognize and be able to identify the feature that they want to reinforce. Indeed, as such, it can be used as a strategy for recruitment (see point 8) – to use the positive as a way of bonding and potentially introducing some contradiction: 'Yes, the phrasing is perfect, but how about … '

5. Demonstrate

In point 1, about exerting physical control, we were dealing with non-verbal forms of influence. Demonstrating can provide non-verbal forms of instruction/suggestion, contradiction or reinforcement. As such, in the world of music, it can avoid an additional level of 'translation' into language and communicate ideas directly as sound or gesture. This illustrates the ways that different schema have different levels of complexity and nuance embedded in them and how different levels of complexity and nuance in language may or may not also be embedded in the schema. We may all be familiar with the phrase 'a picture paints a thousand words' but that is only pertinent when what we want to share is inherently visual. The whole *raison d'être* for exploring different ways of representing knowledge about practice in this book is not to valorize one medium over another in a general sense, but to establish the criteria for choosing between them in different contexts.

6. Inform

The first five of these mechanisms have been concerned with direct engagement with an issue. The last three can be thought of as engaging with forms of contextual knowledge that might be embodied in schema. As such, they are focused more on a deductive approach: in this instance, providing information that encourages the recipient to make different connections with other schema, change existing ones or to change the recipient's perception of the invariant properties that lead to particular affordances. Thus, a composer might provide a performer with the information that a particular bar is intended to serve a particular harmonic function (e.g. in leading towards a modulation) which would not provide a specific instruction as such but might suggest a new set of affordances for improvisation in and around that bar. And, as with the earlier direct points, this does not have to be language-based, another performer might accentuate a particular musical feature in a way that provides a similar form of musical 'information' to encourage different types of behaviour.

7. Suggest a narrative

The discussion so far has centred on influence 'in the moment' or at least about a particular musical moment. A lot of musical communication is about the 'bigger picture' – about how something should develop over time. These may, of course, map directly onto real time (albeit with a small delay such as with a conductor) but they may also involve representational systems that telescope time (such as a two- or three-second gesture that suggests a dynamic structure for a much longer piece). And with both language-based and other forms of suggestion, the schematic representation may involve more complex or distant metaphors such as graphic scores or the narrative of the mythical sunken church of Debussy's 'La Cathédrale Engloutie' which is meant to guide and inform a performance.

8. Recruit

Finally, music is a social activity in both a literal and a metaphorical sense. This can be seen in the sub-grouping of musicians within an ensemble but can also be less formalized and subject to a more open process of influence and negotiation. In Chapter 5 I discussed the ways in which Jo Beth Young and her rhythm section decided to synchronize particular beats and notes and not others during a rehearsal. Some of those decisions were explicit and discussed and others were tacit. And in Chapter 6 we mentioned how Louise Cournarie worked to both synchronize and suggest independence between her hands (and between contrapuntal lines) in her piano playing. In a more general sense, this process is about identifying or creating commonality: about common goals or characteristics. The theme of **convergence** and **divergence** relates, in this instance, to the ways in which people who feel part of a group are more amenable to adopting the behaviour of that group. It relates back to the notion of identity through activity. If we perceive ourselves as similar to certain others because we act in similar ways, it is understandable that we might be influenced to act as they do in some new context because we have previously identified ourselves as similar.

7

Communication and influence

I have been using the term 'influence' in conjunction with restriction and affordance without any detailed exploration of what it is to 'influence'. One of the many definitions of the word is 'the capacity to have an effect on the character, development, or behaviour of someone or something' (Oxford Languages/Google) and, of course, within this theoretical model that is framed in terms of how we perceive restrictions and affordances: what is likely or possible in any given circumstances. The term 'communication' in relation to music is somewhat controversial because it has moved beyond its more generalized Latin meaning of 'sharing' to become more explicitly linked with language and therefore with semantic meaning. This chapter explores what it is that music can share but it also looks at how musical practitioners share knowledge and experience with each other. This process of sharing and influence can happen both directly and indirectly and across space and time. I can be influenced by what Gell (1998) terms the retentions and protentions of artwork through time – listening to music that came before me – or through space – listening to music that was created elsewhere. I can be influenced directly by experiencing the practices involved in making that music or indirectly by experiencing some 'stored' version (a recording or a score for example) or a recreation by a third party (a covers band or a modern orchestra playing a nineteenth-century symphony for example). In a rather ferocious critique, Bowden (2004) dismisses Gell's inference that features which connect a set of stylistically unified artworks are dynamic and unstable, saying 'when a set of objects which is closed, as in the case of a deceased artist, then absolute and not just provisional interpretations of the features … are possible' (Bowden, 2004, pp. 318–19). Of course, this criticism relies on the idea that only the artist and the physical nature of the artwork could be the source of this instability. It ignores the idea that the 'career' of the artwork after it has been created is affected and changed by its cultural and physical environment and the way that encourages and suggests new interpretations. Born (2005) points to this instability through the example of the *Rokeby Venus* by Velazquez which was slashed by Mary Richardson, a suffragette, in protest at the treatment of Emily Pankhurst and subsequently restored – a 'career' that changed both the painting and its meaning in history, politics and society. And, of course, we can find numerous examples of pieces of music whose meaning has changed for subsequent audience members – from Beethoven's *Ode to Joy* after its adoption as the anthem of the European Union to the adoption of Bruce Springsteen's 'Born in the USA' by Donald Trump supporters during his presidential campaigns. How a piece of music has influence is a dynamic and continuing process.

Between 2006 and 2009 I wrote and recorded a series of pieces for my PhD (Zagorski-Thomas, 2010b) and, after I had completed the doctorate, subsequently reworked those pieces into my Recorded Music Album in 2012 and into my Sound To Picture Album in 2019–20. The original idea behind the piece was to explore some of the ways in which the influence of certain ideas about what Moore (2002) might call the third person authenticity of various audio effects and processors has restricted or afforded their use in electroacoustic music and popular music styles. I aimed to utilize techniques and technologies that emerged within popular music and apply them in an electroacoustic context. In addition to this notion of influence as the 'external' ideas that helped to shape my conception of the affordances and restrictions involved in the project, there were also two additional forms of influence that were important. Firstly, there was the influence that I exerted on the seventeen musicians who played on the tracks and the corresponding influence that they exerted on me. Secondly, when I reworked the piece in 2019–20 to be a Sound To Picture Album, I deliberately created and edited the videos based on what might be considered the opposite of the 'normal' sound to picture process: I wanted the visuals to be reflecting and punctuating the music rather than vice versa. How did putting the sound and picture together influence our perception and interpretation of each of them in isolation? (The three versions of the album can be found in Videos 7.1, 7.2 and 7.3 on the website.[1])

While my original doctoral work was very much a practice research approach – and not at all uncommon in the world of composition PhDs – it is interesting to note in retrospect that the culture of composition in the university sector valorized a deductive rather than inductive approach. Composition is written

---

[1] http://www.c21mp.org/practical-musicology/

about as if, as Cook (2000, p. 64) writes, 'the conception of music is a purely ideal process, an achievement of the imagination untrammeled by the mechanical process of setting pen to paper' (or even of playing a musical instrument for that matter). And while Cook was writing to counter this mythology, the academic world of composition, and many of the practitioners themselves, continues to tacitly maintain it. This goes back to the heart of what I was saying in the first chapter about the way the stories are told being as important as the way the practice is carried out. In the worlds of electronic and electroacoustic music,[2] the descriptions of how technology is used in composition are primarily deductive – about the concepts and hypotheses that drove the practice – and in popular music record production, the narratives focus on the inductive process of experimentation. Of course, in both worlds practitioners (and academic practitioners) are doing both. I am sure that experiments, happy accidents and informative failures were just as much part of the process of John Chowning's composition of *Stria* (1977) as the conceptual drivers of frequency modulation synthesis and an understanding of the Stanford Artificial Intelligence Language (Clarke, Dufeu and Manning, 2015). Equally, Chris Thomas, Bill Price and Steve Jones' work on the guitar sound for the Sex Pistols' 'Anarchy in the UK' (1976) involved the conceptual starting point of a live, constantly shifting mix of multiple layers of different voicings of the same chords as well as the experimentation of actually doing it (Buskin, 2004).

Looking back, then, the influences that I chose to explore and write about in my PhD work were focused on the experimental processes of 'creative abuse' (Keep, 2005) or the 'anti-program' (Akrich and Latour, 1992). I was also focused on quite a conservative or traditional form of exegesis: a forty thousand-word written text that provided a cultural context for the finished audio works that constituted the creative output. Given that the initial creative impetus was about deliberately employing ideas and influences from the world of popular music in the world of art music, the new knowledge that emerged in the exegesis was far more about the historical and cultural basis of the practices being employed than about the knowledge types that I would now identify as the outputs of practice research. If I was supervising myself in retrospect, I would be aiming at two important differences:

---

[2] The term 'electroacoustic' in its literal sense should, of course, encompass all forms of popular music which combine electronic/electric instruments and processing with acoustic ones, i.e. the vast majority of popular music from the second half of the twentieth century onwards.

- That the practical, inductive element of the process was represented equally with the theoretical, deductive element through the inclusion of more examples of work-in-progress and informative failures.
- That this media-based element (rather than just text) was used more directly in the telling of the narrative rather than being a series of appendices.

Some examples of the deconstruction/substitution method of representation (see Chapter 2) illustrating what was done originally and how I would do it now can be found in Video 7.4 on the website.[3]

In terms of the second set of influences – the ways in which the character and experiences of myself and the musicians influenced the development of, and choices made in creating, the musical output – the original thesis only addresses one facet of this. This is in the use of individuality in performance as an aspect of composition/production (Zagorski-Thomas, 2010b, pp. 37–9). When the recording rather than a score is 'the work' then the micro-timing and timbral shaping of the performances become part of the compositional process. Mike Stoller of 1950s and 1960s songwriting/production duo Leiber and Stoller once said 'We don't write songs. We write records' (Zollo, 2011) and there are many examples when artists and producers have employed particular musicians in order to incorporate their performance characteristics in a recorded composition.[4] Documenting that within practice research, of course, is highly problematic: how do you show or explain what the piece did not sound like because of the influence of the person you did use? I could, for example, try to demonstrate or explain what was important and/or unique about John Hoare's trumpet performance on 'The Bell End Theory' (see Video 7.5 on the website) and the re-working of 'Vocal Staging' from the PhD submission into 'Tribal Goings On' from Recorded Music Album (where the original vocals were replaced by a trumpet processed through a vocoder). Given that the piece was inspired by sample-based hip hop from the early 1990s (hence the titular puns relating to A Tribe Called Quest and their 1991 Low End Theory album), I was looking for someone with a strong practical knowledge of classical, bebop and hip hop styles that I could sample and manipulate. We can then get into a world of intertextuality to explore the influence of John and my own common language about trumpet tones. The baroque trumpet piece and

---

[3] http://www.c21mp.org/practical-musicology/
[4] See for example Edmunds (2001, pp. 163–7) for a description of how Marvin Gaye chose particular musicians from the Funk Brothers 'stable' of players at Motown to play on the *What's Going On* (1971) sessions.

the bebop solo fragments were precisely what I was wanting and expecting but I remember coming away from the recording session and being unsure if I had exactly what I wanted in terms of the 'trumpet rap'. This was, I think because I had some relatively unrealistic expectations about what a trumpeter imitating a rap vocal might sound like. While, it 'grew on me' in the context of the 'Bell End Theory' piece, when I came to re-work 'Tribal Goings On' I decided to use the vocoder to make it more 'voicey'.

The other facet of this second set of influences was the way in which these performers were integrated into the creative process. The social structures of musical activity have always reflected, emulated and been influenced by the social structures of society in general. The divisions of labour and agency have also reflected divisions in society based on the perceived value of newness versus expertise or even virtuosity in an established existing field. This has led to mechanisms through which agency has been transferred from performers to 'leaders' of various sorts: such as composers, conductors, section leaders in orchestras and record producers and arrangers in popular music. A more recent example of this transfer of agency can be seen in the fragmented processes of contemporary record production where performances and sections of performances are edited and re-used in configurations and contexts in which the original performer not only often has no agency but frequently has no knowledge of. All of the musicians on Recorded Music Album performed alone in a room with me, having been given verbal instructions, in some cases notation, and listening to a soundtrack that bore very little resemblance to the final recordings.

The third set of influences reflects how the context and circumstances in which the audience encounters a piece have a powerful influence on how they interpret it and can even affect what they hear (McGurk and MacDonald, 1976). In the 2012 re-working of my PhD piece into Recorded Music Album, aside from removing the majority of the vocals,[5] I also replaced three of the sections with a series of short 'Due(di)ts': duets between myself as an editor and one of the players. They ended up being five pieces for bassoon, piano, cello, marimba and violin although the piano and marimba pieces were duets with myself. In 2019-20 I started work on creating videos for them as the Sound To Picture Album. On various trips to Cuba between 2016 and 2018 I had made videos of the passing countryside in several drives in the back of cars – both within

---

[5] The original vocals involved pastiches of popular music vocal styles performing texts derived from the academic content of the thesis and I decided to re-work the pieces to create versions without this 'doctoral' content.

and between cities. I had intended to use the rhythmic passing of trees, cars, lamp posts, fences, etc. as a temporal frame to write some new pieces. Purely as an act of curiosity, I tried playing the Bassoon Due(di)t as I watched some of this footage and was intrigued by the fact that my brain was continually trying to connect sound to picture and suggesting spurious but fascinating pairings between momentary sonic features and momentary visual ones. Video 7.6 on the website[6] pairs the same segment of the Bassoon Due(di)t with different fragments of the 'car videos' to demonstrate this phenomenon through the deconstruction/substitution method of representation (see Chapter 2).

Once I had created a series of random pairings between the 'car videos' and the Due(di)t pieces, I decided to create videos from my other Cuban footage where I would edit the video to accentuate certain rhythmic, gestural and larger structural features that reflected my compositional intentions but which listeners often missed. Thus the first piece, 'The Natural Order of Things', involves a series of vocal and instrumental two note loops – the notes in each loop are multiples of 1/16th notes at the same tempo ($2 \times 1/8$th notes, $2 \times$ dotted 1/8th notes, $2 \times 1/4$th notes, etc.). Each instrument is 'represented' in the video by short moving video loops which are the same length as the musical loops and which appear at different places on the screen when that instrumental loop plays in the piece. For example, there are four trombone loops matched with four video loops of 1950s Cuban cars, four piano loops paired with video loops of buses, four trumpet loops paired with Rumba dancers in folkloric costumes and so on. The vocal loops are paired with text syllables which appear as they are performed but which only come together to reveal a full sentence near the end of the piece. There are also a series of other video components which relate to various musical elements which come and go. The video is therefore an abstract schematic representation of the musical ideas which structure the piece and the intention is that they will influence the listener towards 'hearing' some elements of that structure. Video 7.7 on the website uses various modes of representation – temporal focus/structure; spatial focus/zooming-in/multi-perspectives; deconstruction/categories – to clarify this relationship between sound and picture.

Of course, these various forms of representation show some aspects of what I consider to be the mechanisms of influence: pointers to their existence rather than explanations of how they work. These, along with the examples discussed in Chapters 3 to 6 have used audio-visual materials to create representations that

---

[6] http://www.c21mp.org/practical-musicology/

are designed to signpost connections between these various forms of musical practice and the ideas being discussed. Thus far, though, it could be argued that the analytical 'meat' is still expressed through language. The majority of the rest of this chapter is about the ways in which we communicate – share and influence – through musical sound in addition to language. I have used the theoretical model to propose eight mechanisms of influence in the fifth theoretical interlude and then discuss types of influence: influencing others, seeking influences for oneself, and voluntary and involuntary influence. In the rest of this chapter I distinguish between the way that musical practice can influence a listener and the way that musical practitioners can influence each other through musical sound and finish by discussing the role of language and other representational systems (rather than musical sound itself) in these processes of influence.

7.1 Musical influence

The eight mechanisms mentioned in Theoretical Interlude 5 are all discussed in terms of an individual being influenced by someone or something external to them. These same processes relate to the act of learning that I discussed in the last chapter. We can actively seek out phenomena which will influence ourselves – sets of instructions, demonstrations, written narratives, etc. – and we can also come across them accidentally. And the comparison of deliberate versus accidental is a close corollary of voluntary and involuntary. Sometimes the process of influence can be accidental and sometimes it can even happen against our will. It is also true that influence can work on the two levels we discussed before: we can be influenced in our behaviour or activity and we can be influenced in the way we interpret a phenomenon. And we can be influenced by experience as well as through language: by the sights, sounds and other perceptual experiences of musical activity.

Thinking initially about how our interpretation of a phenomenon can be influenced, I would distinguish between direct and indirect influence and would explain those in relation to our three modes of perception and cognition. Indirect influence, the ways in which conscious problem-solving convinces us to change some schema or the metaphorical relationships we create between schema, is more thoroughly theorized in musicology than the notion of direct influence.

Direct influence is based on the other two modes of perception: **automatic** and **subconscious**. At its most basic level we have discussed the notions of entrainment and empathy. While both of these are inherent features of human behaviour, the process of influence takes some time to emerge despite being based on these primal behaviours. While the mimetic process of mirroring certain embodied characteristics of emotion and feeling – like smiling in response to a smile – is a very early development, we also develop more sophisticated versions of this kind of activity in childhood: hearing some types of performance as happy and others as sad or angry. This is predicated on a combination of both physiological and cultural connections between the sound of gestures and some emotional (or physical) meaning. This direct form of musical influence emerges into an understanding of the skills of acting, pretending and the ability to change one's mood through performance. An example of the kind of expert acting through song that requires the technical skill to shape a functional musical performance (i.e. 'correct' pitch, rhythm and timbre) with an emotional narrative is Idina Menzel's performance of 'Let It Go' from Disney's *Frozen*. Although it is a highly mediated performance that has been 'touched up' with dynamic processing and almost certainly also with fine-tuning, pitch adjustments, it is still obviously a highly skilled performance of the song's emotional roller-coaster narrative. While the steady increase in the dynamic energy of the song is inflected with many minor gestures (e.g. the pitch slide up to 'Here I stand' or the small timbral break on 'It's funny how some distance'), there are also many subtle editing features: most of the breaths in between lines have been removed except for the first verse (e.g. the first entry on 'the snow glows white' and before 'a kingdom of isolation') when the energy being expended on singing is lowest but the narrative is about the struggle.

The first two modes of meaning, the **automatic** and the **subconscious**, need to be examined in more technical detail so that different forms of sonic morphology can be mapped onto semantic descriptors. These will range from basic functional metaphors such as musical gestures that sound like walking, running and skipping or how simple/difficult an activity is (or humanly impossible with machine/computer music) to more subjective and emotive metaphorical morphologies such as happy, sad, wistful, heavy, swagger, etc. These types of meaning can be discussed in the analytical terms of conventional musicology – what was done – but they can also be fruitfully explored through the lens of Practical Musicology: how can they be done 'better'? What kinds of lines might be drawn in which circumstances between the first person authenticity of emotional expression and the third person authenticity of technique and control? Are there, for example, any health implications for young singers trying to emulate the sound of technologically mediated recordings?

The same kind of approach can be brought to bear on indirect forms of influence: the conventions of the representational systems that we learn both passively as participants in culture or society and actively through music education. This ranges from the simple (e.g. the adoption of a scale of recognizable pitches) to the highly complex (e.g. the conventions of sonata form or even serialism). Indeed, practices that combine the representational systems of two or more styles or traditions can be explored through notions of heteroglossia (e.g. Bakhtin, 1982; Monson, 1997) or intertextuality (e.g. Burns and Lacasse, 2018) through the methods of Practical Musicology. Staying in the world of musical theatre and using the 'Fantasy Supervision League' conceit again, I will use the example of Lin-Manuel Miranda's musical *Hamilton* and the way it combines rap, hip hop, RnB and musical theatre. Miranda might have examined the intertextuality of *Hamilton* through the workshopping process used in creating the musical. There were a range of songs and lyrics that didn't make the cut into the hit show. There were three iterations of the work: the *Hamilton Mixtapes* developed between 2009 and 2013, the Off-Broadway show in January 2015 and the revised Broadway show from July 2015 onwards as well as some aspects that retrospectively emerged through some of Miranda's *Hamildrops* in 2017–18. How were the decisions about what was right and wrong for the show made? Which criteria or characteristics of the various forms of 'textuality' – the musical styles – were identified in order to guide the original 'making' process? How did that process help to expose or identify things to add, subtract or change in those criteria?

In addition to this development of song writing and performance styles through this process of experimentation and refinement, there are a range of stylistic mechanisms that are used to suggest musical and dramatic metaphors. Miranda has written the songs 'Satisfied' and 'Helpless' in *Hamilton* to play with time by presenting the same events from two different perspectives. Angelica Schuyler remembers the first time she and her sister Elizabeth met Alexander Hamilton when singing 'Satisfied' as part of the scene where she toasts their marriage. This replays the events portrayed earlier in the songs 'A Winter's Ball' and 'Helpless' but musically it also uses various tropes taken from hip hop and RnB, not only using the lyrics 'rewind' but using reversed sound, echo and filtering to suggest other world-ness. It also uses the structural notion of a 'call back' which is very common in musical theatre, quoting the 'Helpless' song to suggest both the freezing of time at the wedding and going back in time to the original meeting. The same method of reviewing the workshop process along

USEFUL QUESTIONS

What do you think has most influenced you without realizing it?
What have you recently consciously emulated?
　Why did you choose it?
　Which features influenced you most and why?
　Which features influenced you least and why?

with any other documentation of versions and discarded ideas could be used to track this process of developing the intertextual language and aesthetic.

The three forms of engagement introduced earlier also take us back to the question of the uses of music. While we may well want both to learn and analyse performances/compositions/constructions in terms of expression and virtuosity, we may also want to think about them in terms of how well they perform their function. In particular, Miranda might want to explore the development of the piece through the lens of narrative dramatic function. As each of the pieces evolves in the different stages of workshopping, how do (or did) the various features of the intertextual influences contribute to that narrative structure in terms of the **automatic**, **subconscious** and **conscious** forms of engagement.

7.2 Influence, aesthetics and new knowledge

As discussed in Chapters 1 and 2, the question of what constitutes new knowledge in Practical Musicology is a vexed one. Many of the outputs of artistic research provide very specific solutions to very specific artistic problems in very specific contexts. In the world of 'traditional' research, case study (see Rowley, 2002; Yin, 2009) approaches are generally recommended where the phenomenon is tightly enmeshed with its context, where the study is of 'a contemporary set of events over which the investigator has little or no control' (Rowley, 2002, p. 17) and are mostly seen as less rigorous than other qualitative methods with larger sample sizes and/or control over the parameters under investigation. Now that I have 'laid out my stall' more extensively in relation to Practical Musicology, it makes sense to return to this vexed question of new knowledge and to the ways in which aesthetics can be incorporated. For practice research to communicate knowledge, it has to address this process of how the music that a practitioner makes influences a listener's interpretation. Obviously though, there is no single homogenous listener and no single 'correct' interpretation.

Nattiez (1990) suggested the subdivision between poeisis and esthesis which in many ways correlates to the difference between intention and interpretation. There are many pitfalls in trying to incorporate his third 'immanent' or 'neutral' category of the empirical nature of musical sound into a form of analysis but it does provide a way to bridge the gap between musicologies of making and those of experiencing. Indeed, as suggested earlier, the notion of *musicking* seeks to establish commonalities of active participation between poeisis and esthesis by thinking of the musical 'text' as a social activity rather than an object. Within my framework, the perception of affordance acts as a mechanism for both intention and interpretation but both Gibson's and Nattiez's focus on immanence and objectivity and I would suggest that ignores the potential variations in the embodied experience of the 'same' phenomenon. We all mostly experience gravity in the same way but there are also minor differences because our bodies and our experiences are all different. Given that our identities and our understanding are built on those embodied experiences, then our understanding of the immanent and objective is a distributed, communal 'as if' – a subjective theoretical construct which is only 'true' in as much as it is predictively useful in a variety of contexts. If we go back to the idea of case studies – and in particular, for Practical Musicology, of case studies which focus on the development of aesthetics and of elucidating tacit knowledge – we need to understand what kind of new knowledge they can produce which would be predictively useful in a variety of contexts. Of course, the mechanisms of influence outlined in Theoretical Interlude 5 are part of my attempt to do that.

Practical Musicology therefore has to make the subtle distinction between describing the music-maker's intention and describing the mechanisms through which they are intending to communicate and influence a listener's interpretation. We thus need to revisit the four types of new knowledge that practice research can produce (described in Chapter 2) and the four types of aesthetic appreciation (outlined in Chapters 5 and 6) and to look for ways of representing the mechanisms through which, and the areas where, this new knowledge is produced. To recap from Chapter 2, these four types of new knowledge relate to:

1. The relationship between problem-solving and technical skill
2. The relationship between the development and emergence of quality judgements and methods

3. The complex aesthetic relationship between the expected and the unexpected
4. The mechanisms for creating metaphors relating theory to artistic, pragmatic or activist practice

And the four types of aesthetic appreciation relate to **inductive** and **deductive** modes of thought – the bottom-up acquisition and execution of schema and the top-down process of making connections between certain aspects of them which Lakoff and Johnson (1999, 2003) describe as the metaphorical nature of thought and which Fauconnier and Turner (2003) describe as *conceptual blending*. The four types of aesthetic appreciation are:

1. The appreciation of 'correct' or 'expert' action through a schema
2. The intentional and expert variation of a schema
3. The intensity or efficacy with which a metaphor conveys an intended narrative
4. The appreciation of the elegance of the metaphor

They are, however, always culturally inflected: both by the technicalities of the musical culture but also by broader cultural tropes. The many ways in which the contributors to Nettl and Russell's (1998) collection on forms of improvisation have discussed how aesthetics are related to wider social practices is a case in point. I will briefly discuss each type of new knowledge, one by one:

7.2.1 The relationship between problem-solving and technical skill

There is a tension between the technical fluency of virtuosity – the inductive process of schema activation – and the disruption of that through deductive problem-solving. There is always not only a balance to be decided upon between these two types of activity but also decisions to be made about the approach to take. This can relate to any and all of the four types of aesthetic appreciation. Thus, to return to the *Hamilton* example, if Lin-Manuel Miranda was seeking to publish a practice research output on devising and staging the show, what was the conscious difference in style between his earlier show, *In The Heights*, which combined contemporary Latin styles with hip hop, and *Hamilton* which has a more formalized musical approach to this type of intertextuality? During the process of development, were particular artists and/or songs used as models for certain numbers? If so, was this about taking certain rhythmic features and vocal flourishes which were based around improvisation in their original popular music forms (e.g. cross rhythmic rapping and ad lib tracks from RnB) and through composing with them? This could then be discussed in terms of how necessary it was for Miranda and the other performers in the show to have extensive experience and expertise (a highly developed schema) in the various musical styles involved. How much did the deductive process of merging features from different traditions together disrupt the flow of any of those traditions?

By exploring the same phenomenon through a range of different examples in the same case study, we can see that Miranda and his fellow participants might use a series of experiments to explore what 'works'. Thinking through how various ways of combining aspects of the musical styles involved would have different impacts on the four types of aesthetic appreciation would hopefully allow an inductive process of 'extracting' some general principles. This might relate, for example, to how aspects of vocal technique in switches between musical theatre, RnB and rap voices during Renée Elise Goldsberry's performance of 'Satisfied' were negotiated – on the cast recording, the first rap section ('I remember that night, I just might regret that night … ') has an entirely different feel in terms of timbre, energy and flow than the later section ('So this is what it feels like to match wits with someone at your level. What the hell is the catch?'). The second section is much more authentic in terms of the conventions of expert delivery in rap while the first might be seen as an expert variation that blends more in the way of musical theatre acting skills into a rap context. And both sections of the performance can be appreciated differently in terms of the metaphorical meaning that giving an eighteenth-century woman these kinds of voices suggests – both in terms of the efficacy with which the metaphor suggests meaning and our appreciation of the elegance or aptness of the metaphor. The first is perhaps more effective and apt in driving along the historical narrative while second works better for the personal narrative of the woman and in driving the political subtext about race. But while insights such as these might aid our understanding and appreciation of the work, it is when we examine the mechanisms through which they work that we can glimpse sharable forms of knowledge. If Miranda and the other participants engaged in these kinds of experiments and analysis for the whole case study then we might be able to find some general principles about these mechanisms. There may be, for example, evidence to support the notion that a recognizably singular stylistic schema is better at suggesting particular types or intensities of emotional feeling than an intertextual blend.

7.2.2 The relationship between the development and emergence of quality judgements and methods

Generally, for people who have spent a long time immersed in a musical culture, we find it very easy to distinguish between variations in schema (of standard practice within that musical culture) that are deliberate and those that are accidental – or the result of a lack of expertise. There are exceptions. Comedians such as Les Dawson in the UK and Victor Borge more internationally have built portions of their comedy act around deliberately playing the piano 'badly' – but in ways that make it obvious that they actually can play. Much like a lot of humour, they undermine a schema that is well established. Alternatively, Thelonius Monk developed an aesthetic around his jazz piano style that was deliberately awkward – with hesitant, uneven rhythms, sharp variations of dynamics, unusual changes of melodic direction and discordant note clusters. Monk's idiolect was even misunderstood in some jazz circles to be the absence of 'good' technique rather than the cultivation of a unique one. Our expectations about our expectations are deeply ingrained in our psyche.

Some quality judgements are simply based on the perception of something difficult being done well. There are a lot of clues that are relatively cross-cultural that relate to expert rather than inexpert activity. Mostly they relate to evidence of a clearly formed schema such as:

- purposeful action (repeated consistently)
- actions or results that clearly fall into categories (i.e. repetition and expert variation – there seem to be rules of variation)
- action that is clearly not easy (the failure to find a mirror system in my own experience – I cannot do that but I know it is physically possible for me or someone like me to do that)
- action that appears impossible or superhuman (they are physically capable of something that I don't think I am capable of)

We can also, with a relatively small amount of information about a musical culture that we are not immersed in, start to recognize the features of expert activity that are important. Different musical cultures value different aspects of technical and problem-solving skill differently: technical accuracy over emotional expression, encouraging entrained movement versus encouraging problem-solving interpretation, large-scale structural metaphors versus small-scale improvisational variation of a theme or embellishment of a background tonality. And, of course, within a culture, individuals will differ and an individual's preferences may vary at different times according or mood or context.

How do we find our way through this minefield? As Ingold (2011, 2013) and Noë (2004) suggest, we understand through doing – in Ingold's term, 'wayfaring' or 'dwelling'. In quite a reductionist sense, **induction** is a necessary pre-condition for **deduction.** We cannot produce a hypothesis without previously having some experience or data. In some ways this negates the dichotomy of **induction/ deduction** and suggests a circular or iterative notion of schema formation followed by schema analysis (identifying patterns and connections). However, circularity suggests that it is sequential and they are continually happening simultaneously. This is my notion of what 'dwelling' or 'wayfaring' is in Ingold's work: a parallel process of living in and learning from my environment through an **inductive** process alongside a **deductive** process of making connections and asking questions such that the brain connectivity I describe 'as if' it were schema feels both continuous and ever-changing. And this is true of our quality judgements in music as well. They feel well-established and yet every new experience changes them and this is important in this context because when we are making new work we are also developing some new specific version of our aesthetics.

The notion of quality is based on the chemical reward system of positive and negative reinforcement. While we are clearly driven by the relatively basic chemical drives of hunger, thirst, avoiding pain and death, sex and bonding through empathy, there are also chemical rewards related to solving problems and identifying virtuosity; what neuroscience describes as the pleasures of the mind (Kubovy, 1999; Canestrari *et al.*, 2018). One of the key developments of the human brain is about developing a chemical reward system that is concerned with resolving any conflict about the interpretation of our current experience. Berridge and Kringelbach (2013, 2015) summarize research that distinguishes between objective and subjective markers of pleasure (e.g. neuro-imaging versus self-reporting), between liking, wanting and learning (i.e. habitual/learned associations – Pavlov) and which also suggests that there may be common neural 'circuitry' involved in a variety of types of pleasure. While I agree about the first and third of these distinctions, I would not distinguish between 'hardwired' forms of liking and wanting and 'learned' forms of liking and wanting but rather between the basic chemistry of liking and wanting and the ways they are embedded into the 'wiring' of schema. Liking is an **inductive** bottom-up process that flows from experience and wanting is a **deductive**, top-down process that relies on hypothesis. Both of them are based on homeostasis and the salience network – of deciding or feeling when we are hungry, thirsty, the wrong temperature, horny, or if there is an interpretative tension that needs to be resolved. I would characterize a lot of the chemical rewards of pleasure, and especially those of problem-solving, the other way round: that when the salience network identifies an unfulfilled goal, it generates a chemical displeasure through stress and tension until the goal is achieved. Jepma *et al.* (2012) have produced some evidence that when curiosity is roused brain regions sensitive to conflict and arousal are activated and when the curiosity is relieved, the reward processing regions are activated. Importantly for this argument, the example they used for perceptual curiosity was a visual ambiguity using clear and blurred pictures of the same image.

What I am suggesting then is that our notions of artistic and intellectual 'quality' – of whether we have successfully achieved our artistic goals – are based on exactly the same mechanisms of stress and pleasure. The goals in question may not only be perceptual but may be based on activity as well – a stress from not being able to do something as well as we want to. From an evolutionary perspective, we can see that it would make sense to associate pleasure with identifying and developing the ability for virtuosity – of learning how to do something by acquiring and developing a schema – and with the general process of problem-solving – of identifying connections between features of different schema and using that to hypothesize new pathways that would be possible but which have not been experienced previously.

Back to Lin-Manuel Miranda, it would be interesting to document the changing aesthetic from his earlier musical *In The Heights* through the various instantiations of *Hamilton* to explore how the more formal theatrical aesthetic developed. This can often involve difficult moments of wrestling with our identity – of who we thought we were and who we think we are becoming. After all, the judgements we make about when we are doing good or bad artistic work are about as personal as it can get. My instinct as a supervisor in this instance would be to get Miranda to look at his reflective journal and look for statements that relate to his identity: about when he considers himself to be more a performer than a composer, director or impresario using examples of **convergent** and **divergent** behaviour. This could then be mapped onto the documentation of the practice using 'data' gathered to identify or corroborate criteria – the characteristic features of 'good' and 'bad' work. This should range from the inductive perspective of factors like virtuosity to the deductive perspective of how the conceptual structure of the piece came together. Working through the four types of aesthetic, in addition to expert activity (schema) and expert variation of schema through problem-solving, the aesthetics of various metaphors used in the piece should be considered both in terms of their efficacy and their elegance. Once again, this should then be mapped onto some general principles – perhaps about the relationship between identity and aesthetics. And, of course, another necessary development in the world of Practical Musicology is to develop an archive of examples – of research that provides supporting (or contradictory) case studies. In this instance, Miranda might use Mani's (2021) work on creating intertextual operatic work that uses Indian Karnatic modes of ornamentation in Monteverdi's operatic work.

7.2.3 The aesthetic relationship between the expected and the unexpected

I have already discussed the nature of categories and how their 'members' have invariant properties and affordances in common with each other. The ideas of expectation are closely related to category. These can be quite large scale and persistent categories such as the types of features and activity (invariant properties and affordances) we expect to see in musical theatre or they can also be small scale and fleeting. By singing or playing the same 'thing' twice, I am setting up a temporary micro-category which then produces expectations of potentially more occurrences. Klotz (2017), while talking about the 'art of the mistake', alludes to the frequency mentioned aphorism in jazz: 'If you make a mistake, do it three times'. The repetition establishes it as a category and therefore not as a mistake – after the second iteration, we kind of expect the third. Creating aural 'examples' is an important part of the way music can be seen to communicate; from the structuring technique of call and response to the statement of a musical theme for subsequent variation. The demarcation and presentation of a musical phenomenon as being exemplary and therefore as more important than others that surround it is an essential technique in musical practice.

A lot of music theory is discussed in terms of tension and release, of establishing expectations and either fulfilling them or confounding them. In the period frequently described as the 'Common Practice Era' in western art music, these expectations are mostly explored through voice leading and harmony or large-scale thematic structures such as sonata form. With

Lin-Manuel Miranda's work we might distinguish between different types of expectation. The format of *In the Heights* in the tradition of musical theatre was a relatively unexpected one: obviously *West Side Story* set a precedent for using Latin music (pre-dated by appearances in musicals by artists like Carmen Miranda) but the rap element was more unusual. However, the writing of the songs and the story-line maintained less unexpected formats. *Hamilton* did almost the opposite. The expectation about the musical influences in Miranda's repertoire pointed towards another intertextual piece but, in addition to the inclusion of more hip hop and RnB and less Latin music, there is a lot more that plays with expectations: from the large scale features such as the 'colour-blind' casting of the Founding Fathers to the extended use of structural themes, variations and call-backs which play with those micro-category expectations. Once again, if Miranda was looking to place this work in the context of Practical Musicology then the new knowledge that concerns the relationship between the expected and the unexpected needs to be transferrable. Given the show's level of popularity, it would make sense to get Miranda to use this case study to discuss the tension between 'lowest common denominator' and elitism through the mechanism of expectations.

7.2.4 The mechanisms for creating metaphors relating theory to artistic, pragmatic or activist practice

This last category of new knowledge is where the majority of work in practice as research and artistic research has focused, although mostly from the perspective of an internal – 'emic' – analysis of the specific ways in which the work in question embodies or portrays theoretical ideas through some artistic metaphor. And this feature of the research does indeed often shed new light on the theoretical work by exploring how it can be embodied in creative practice. However, this is not the main focus of Practical Musicology. It is not about shedding new light on the theory, it is about shedding new light on the mechanisms through which theory can be applied and exploring when and why they 'work'. Thus, while a musicological analysis of Miranda's work might use the lenses of intertextuality and heteroglossia to explain how *In The Heights* and *Hamilton* reflect and interpret multiculturalism in contemporary US culture, a Practical Musicology approach would aim to understand why particular metaphors were chosen.

Miranda, in order to frame the work as this type of research, would need to explain what the aim of those multiple voices and influences is and not only that they exist. His work is very much about exploring both the energy and the problems of multi-culturalism: very explicitly in *In The Heights* and more metaphorically in *Hamilton* through the eighteenth century politician's position as an outsider. According to Noble (2021) there were six distinct drafts of *In The Heights* between the Wesleyan University student production in 2000 and the Broadway musical in 2007 and we have already discussed the similar developmental process for *Hamilton*. This type of documentation provides the potential for creating clear narratives about how the two works developed the musical and dramatic metaphors that embodied those ideas. Indeed, the existence of the 'documentation' in terms of the versions, provides the potential for a third person retrospective Practical Musicology study – although this type of study would still be better accomplished in collaboration with Miranda. This documentation (in either form), in turn provides the 'data' for an inductive process to hypothesize some general principles about that development. The development of characters as representatives of particular factions or ideas, for example, might be demonstrated through examples of changes made in various versions and then also discussed in terms of the different levels of freedom in this regard that a fictitious story like *In The Heights* provides in comparison to the fictional representation of history in *Hamilton*.

USEFUL QUESTIONS

What are the ways in which something can be flagged as an example and thus take on a symbolic meaning?

Thinking of the four types of aesthetic meaning:

Which type of expert musical activity do you most enjoy? Be quite specific – improvising over a blues, singing a torch song, mixing the rhythmic elements of a track, composing for string quartet, etc.

Which type of expert musical activity do you wish you were better at?

Which area of musical activity are you most spontaneous and creative in?

What is the most powerful piece of work you have created, performed or been involved in? Why was it so powerful and in what way?

What is the cleverest piece of work you have created, performed or been involved in? In what way was it clever?

7.3 Talking about music

Despite the notion of music as sharing, language is still an important aspect of all forms of musical activity both in the ways that it is incorporated into *musicking* itself and in the ways it is used to frame and structure musical activity – in introductions, descriptions, lessons, rehearsals, sales and marketing, etc. It is relatively unusual for musicians to incorporate verbal instructions into performance – although we do have the relatively high-profile exception of James Brown's 'Take It to the Bridge!' Despite that, lyrics do provide a map for non-singing musicians within a song structure and a good deal of the information on a score consists of the printed word. It can also, of course, be a gatekeeping tool which can be used to both include and exclude others through the use of technical language or jargon. Scholars such as Porcello (2004), Stepánek (2006) and Traube (2011) have looked at how musicians describe sound and others have looked at the way language is used during rehearsal and in discussions between composers and performers (e.g. Bayley, 2011; Bayley and Heyde, 2017; Kubiak, 2019; Kaastra, 2020). These are some of the areas where I would suggest there are cross-overs between these ethnographic and case study cases and Practical Musicology. Although Bayley, Heyde and Kubiak are all examining these types of discussion in terms of how they contributed to shaping an aesthetic through developing a performance strategy, and both Heyde and Kubiak were participant researchers, the research is less concerned with developing generalized strategies for doing it 'better' and more an analysis of how it was done in these instances. Thus, while the knowledge embodied in these outputs might allow practitioners to develop strategies for rehearsing new works, the research itself was not about experimenting with and testing such strategies.

One thing that should be clear from all the examples that I have been using throughout the book is that within Practical Musicology there is an important role for the written word as well as for multi-media representations. The frequently cited 'writing about music is like dancing about architecture' is probably a quote from American comedian Martin Mull in the 1970s but is both pre-dated and post-dated by many similar similes (singing about economics, knitting about football, etc). The argument is spurious in some ways as all uses of language are attempts to represent something that is 'other'. However, the idea that some forms of representation are more appropriate than others in some contexts is at the heart of this book. The conventions for storing knowledge in print were born out of technology and necessarily favoured the representation of knowledge through the written word and, to a lesser extent, in visual images or diagrams. Those technologies slowly changed during the twentieth century. In 1983, I bought John Pierce's book *The Science Of Musical Sound* (Pierce, 1983) which included two 33rpm 'flexi-discs' of musical and sonic examples. Within a few years this was superseded by CD, CD-R and DVD and more recently by the internet. As the academic publishing world moves increasingly towards open access and online publishing, the world of multi-media is simultaneously developing more potential for representing information and narratives through immersive audio-visual systems, tactile and haptic representations, and various forms of animation. While, of course technology innovators get much more excited about innovations that produce entirely new affordances, the academic world should be more excited about innovations that are making the production of existing and established complex media simpler. We are all becoming amateur film makers on our phones and many of us are becoming amateur editors and animators as well with various hobbyist and semi-professional software packages that are becoming more and more ubiquitous. This allows us to choose the mode of representation that is best suited to the information and narratives that we are trying to represent. During the various Covid lockdowns, many music academics were creating video lectures, teaching performance, composition and other practical skills online and generally having to find ways of representing knowledge in appropriate ways. That is also the future of research presentation. It is only a relatively short step from a PowerPoint conference presentation to a multimedia journal article and that step is already being taken.

Theoretical interlude 6: *Belonging and not belonging*

A key part of our lives and of the way we reflect and represent them through musical activity is the tension between dependence and independence, between acceptance and resistance – a social version of the first big lesson that a human has to learn about perception and experience, the differentiation between 'me' and 'not me'. If, as we discussed in Chapter 5, there is no difference between the feeling of a neuron that fires because light hits our retina and a neuron that fires because one of our muscles has moved, then learning the difference between 'me' moving and something that moves that is 'not me' is a crucial stage of development. This relates to the theme of **convergence** and **divergence** not just on a conceptual level but also because the neural basis of 'same' and 'different' becomes 'wired together' because they 'fired together'. Things are not 'the same' until their similarity and their difference to other things have been marked by some level of repetition: until the pathways become well-trodden and therefore marked and recognizable. This process of category formation provides the criteria for assessing **convergence** and **divergence**. And, as the categories get more sophisticated than 'me' and 'not me', the processes of doing something 'the same' or 'different' become the basis for feelings of dependence and independence, acceptance and resistance, and belonging and not belonging.

This idea of 'same' and 'different' or belonging and not belonging provides the foundation for various social theories about the development of music. Wallin *et al.* (2001) edited collection on the *Origins of Music* includes a broad selection of such theories and points to the fact that music is reliant on a broad range of disparate cognitive functions and therefore these theories may not be mutually exclusive. Social co-ordination can be seen in all of the primary theories about musical development – synchronizing mood by synchronizing behaviour (e.g. lullabies), establishing a sense of unified identity by synchronizing behaviour (e.g. communal singing), co-ordinating activity by synchronizing one activity to another (e.g. work songs). And then there is also the aspect of it that marks out individuality (e.g. the many theories about attracting mates and establishing dominance among peers) – that singing is saying something with a special voice to mark it as important, that music is an activity in which skill and/or physicality differentiates people and yet it provides no clear or obvious material benefits. Why would a singer be a more suitable mate or a more dominant character? Of course, all these evolutionary theories of music go back further than human culture but we can see in music – or, more primally, co-ordinated and structured sound-making – ways of marking and communicating **convergent** and **divergent** behaviour and activity to others and of reinforcing it in ourselves.

Of course, there are many ways in which musical practice can embody and represent **convergence** and **divergence.** It can be woven into complex narratives that both literally mimic or embody social activity and can suggest it through metaphor. Different members of any ensemble can synchronize in close or more distant ways, can demonstrate independence or originality in relation to the other members, and can configure into temporary or permanent sub-groupings within the larger ensemble. All these ways of being together or being apart, of belonging or not belonging – they can all suggest different types of interpersonal relationships. During a discussion with Mark Mynett about his PhD (Mynett, 2013) on contemporary metal music production he described his aim as creating the impression of 'a large creature moving very fast in a small space'. Many of the techniques that he uses are concerned with creating highly accurate synchronization so that the various players fuse into a single perceived agency. For me, this was highly reminiscent of the changes in the classical orchestra in the eighteenth and nineteenth centuries, reflecting socio-economic changes parallel to the Industrial Revolution. One metaphor for these changes would be a progression from a grouping of individuals in the eighteenth century into the nineteenth century when various instrumental sections were supposed to subsume their personality to create a single agency: from a crafts-based approach to a music 'factory' with a division of labour and large-scale, depersonalized production.

The social functions of music can also reflect these quite basic structuring principles of belonging and not-belonging. In many instances it produces a **convergent** process of ritualized emotion. This can involve allowing a group of people to act out or share an emotion without the 'real consequence': of sadness without bad things happening or happiness without good things. It can also formalize 'difficult' or embarrassing activities such as using dance as a courtship ritual. It can also be used for 'real' mood reinforcement or change. And on the other hand we have **divergent** processes such as formalized rebellion whereby the teeth can be removed from socially disruptive tendencies. If we look back at the history of the migratory Roma as outsider musicians, they moved from North India through the Persian empire and the Middle East into southern and central Europe. One of the traditional 'crafts' that travelled with them and provided employment for many was that of the musician: making themselves 'special' through music was one way of making their different status as immigrants into something more exotic than the norms of migrant labour. A similar trope can be seen in rock and roll and popular music as a place where extremes of behaviour are tolerated. There are glamorous and mundane ways of not belonging and if you can join the former you often become lionized as your audience live vicariously through their heroes.

8

Interaction and influence

Returning to the UK Arts and Humanities Research Council grant funded project on Classical Music Hyper Production mentioned in earlier chapters, I would like to discuss another two of its practice-based sub-projects: an electric version of Shostakovich's eighth string quartet and digital/electroacoustic versions of some Debussy piano preludes. Working with the Konvalia Quartet[1] who played electric violins, viola and cello on the Shostakovich, myself and Andrew Bourbon sent each instrument through a chain of guitar effects pedals. In live concerts at Kings Place and the University of West London, Andrew and I 'performed' the effects processing of two instruments each (I had viola and cello and he had the two violins). In the studio version we recorded the electric instruments without effects and added the processing afterwards. The Debussy piano pieces were also performed at the same concerts, with the parts divided between four pianists[2] on Roland digital pianos. Only the *Cathédrale Engloutie* prelude (Book 1, No.10) was recorded as a studio version but there were two versions: one with parts extracted from a single MIDI performance of the whole prelude and the other as a series of overdubbed piano performances of separated parts. They aimed to explore the creative possibilities of staging performances and recordings of the Western classical repertoire using techniques and technologies used in popular music. One of the key issues that we identified was the need for performers and/or technologists to adjust their *habitus* (Bourdieu, 1993) to accommodate the process. The differences between these two sub-projects and between the recording and concert hall contexts in each of them provided many points of discussion between the participants/researchers in regard to the norms of musical interaction in different contexts.

[1] Dorottya Szabados-Drótos (violin I), Agata Kubiak-Kenworthy (violin II), Marietta Szalóki (viola) and Andrea Derdak (cello)
[2] Dr Emilie Capulet and Nataša Šarčević of London College of Music, UWL with postgraduate students Trinh Lu, Sulhee Kim

A short video about the technical set-up and attendant problems that we faced in the live performance of the Shostakovich quartet can be found in Video 8.1 on the website.[3] A similar video about the studio version can be found in Video 8.2. Likewise, the technical and performative challenges faced by the four pianists in the live versions of the Debussy preludes (see Video 8.3 on the website) relate to playing the fragmented arrangements to facilitate the dub mixing process. The MIDI and studio versions of the *Cathédrale Engloutie* prelude (see Video 8.4 on the website) were described by Emilie, the pianist, as creating a 'rubato layer cake' (Capulet and Zagorski-Thomas, 2017). All of these pieces are discussed in more detail in the section on 'New Knowledge About Interaction' below.

In addition to the activities of communication and sharing that were discussed in the last chapter, there are other forms of interaction which are more about the near instantaneous triggering or synchronization of action in others rather than the more complex 'messages' mentioned earlier. These forms of triggering and synchronization – the patterns that people create when working together – can be both functional and expressive and can be either momentary or continuous. They are also, of course, about influence, restriction and affordance. The large-scale UK Arts and Humanities Research Council-funded Centre for Musical Performance as Creative Practice produced a set of five books about performance studies of which Clarke and Doffman's (2017) edited volume on *Distributed Creativity: Collaboration and improvisation in contemporary music* addressed some of these issues of understanding musical practices 'in the moment'. Toynbee's chapter (2017) takes us back to the notion of context by discussing the 'macrosocial structure ... having a deep causal impact, downward as it were, on to the level of the individual or group' (Toynbee, 2017, p. 37). He describes the labour of music and creativity as having both a concrete and abstract dimension: as a coded voice and changing through the two processes of translation and intensification. He describes 'translation' as a distorting process from one culture to another and 'intensification' as being a process internal to a culture. Linson and Clarke (2017) use an extended version of the ecological approach (Gibson, 1979) to talk about distributed creativity – distributed through the body, between multiple agents, between humans and 'tools' and distributed culturally (through time and space and thereby conflating Toynbee's translation and intensification). We can see this as two different 'as if' categorizations that may provide differently useful models for representing the

[3] http://www.c21mp.org/practical-musicology/

process of influence (itself a different type of 'as if') through communication and interaction. Toynbee provides a method for bringing the wider scope of contextual influences to bear on interaction while Linson and Clarke provide a typology for exploring the ways in which creativity can be distributed.

Returning to the issue of *Studies In Material Thinking* edited by Nimkulrat (2016), Shercliff and Twigger-Holroyd (2016) explored collaborative textile craft group activities as a way of understanding different types of tacit knowledge and conceptualizing similar tasks within a group. Although the study used an interactive process to explore these ways of conceptualizing rather than seeking a 'better' way, there are levels of quality implicit in the studies which could be described in terms of culturally constructed notions of quality found in pragmatic practice research. This provides an example of how the interaction in a project can be more for research purposes than as central to the creative purpose of the practice. Indeed, returning to the Hyper Production performances and recordings mentioned above, although we all wanted to produce musical outputs that were interesting and innovative, the point of the project was first and foremost to conduct the experiments. And this is also a reminder that while Practical Musicology, being driven by the pragmatic creation and negotiation of the aesthetics of 'better', is often best undertaken through practice research, it can also involve a non-participant researcher studying the development of such an aesthetic in the practice of others. It can also – and frequently will in studies involving the aesthetics of interaction – mean that only one (or some) of the participants in that interaction are researchers.

8.1 New knowledge about interaction

In order to discuss how Practical Musicology can produce new knowledge about interaction, I will outline the types of interaction that we are dealing with and then discuss the four types of new knowledge. One general distinction is what Burnard (2012) refers to as *temporal mediations* – the fact that they can each happen in real time or indirect time. Although Bruford (2018) is more interested in real-time activity, he makes similar distinctions based on his own experience and the interviews from his PhD (Bruford, 2015). Bearing this temporal distinction in mind, I would then identify four types of possible musical interaction between the types of participant that were outlined in Chapter 2:

1. Between an enabler (such as a designer or maker of technology / instruments) and an instigator (e.g. composer or producer) and/or creator (e.g. performer)
2. Between creators (e.g. two or more performers or programmers)
3. Between creators and/or editors and instigators and/or managers (e.g. between one or more people who make or manipulate sound and one or more people who influence the sounds that they make or manipulate – composer, producer, conductor, musical director)
4. Between a non-musician and a music maker

As I outlined in Chapter 2, there might not only be more than one person undertaking each of these roles but there also might be one person undertaking several of these roles. I might take the role of instigator, manager and creator in a project while also including several other creators.

8.1.1 The relationship between problem-solving and technical skill

One of the important aspects of musical interaction that relates back to our inductive and deductive modes of thought is that we can, and very often do, adjust our learned behaviour subconsciously in response to our current experience. To use an everyday and non-musical example, once we have an internalized schema for walking, we also develop some internalized and top-down subconscious 'rules' for adjusting our gait based on incoming visual cues: so that we do not fall over on uneven ground or that we can negotiate a staircase for example. I do not have to think consciously about how to adjust my gait but I do have to keep looking at the ground so that those subconscious 'rules' can be applied. I not only internalise the rules for how to do something but also some aspects of how to solve problems related to doing that something. When I become very adept at some form of musical practice (or any other skilled activity for that matter) it is not just because the bottom-up processes have become wired together through repeatedly firing together, it is also that some of the top-down problem-solving activities that require me to adjust my behaviour in particular circumstances have also become hard wired. This, I would suggest, is also the basis of what we call intuition. Mermikides (2010, pp. 100–105) has written about how both the primary pulse and the deviations from it in a performance are constructed in a collaborative but not equal process and that there are multiple ways of deviating – his SLW (Swing, Latency, Weighting) model being one way of thinking about this. Applying this model in a Practical Musicology context a researcher could, for example, use our various methods of documentation and representation to explore how an ensemble moved towards a particular rhythmic feel and whether there were discernible patterns relating those inequalities of agency and the balance of **inductive** and **deductive** (or **subconscious** and **conscious**) activity.

As another example, one relatively obvious aspect of the Shostakovich electric string quartet mentioned above was that the monitoring of intonation became much more problematic for a variety of reasons. Players of acoustic instruments get used to a particular volume balance of their own instrument next to their face (or torso with the cello) and the others in the quartet. The unamplified electric instruments hardly make any noise and so we experimented with headphones and speaker monitors. It was surprisingly difficult to find monitor balances – even with a different mix for each player – that worked. In the live concert this was compounded by the effects and processing which often made it hard to tell 'whose sound was whose' and that slowed down the players' instinctive responses to intonation. This very specific problem in a specific situation can be explored in terms of how best these four players could work in this context on this piece. It can also provide more general understanding about how monitoring and effects or processing affect the norms of performance schema for electric instruments and why some performers find it easier to develop a satisfactory balance between their sense of expressive agency and the required alterations to their performance *habitus*.

8.1.2 The relationship between the development and emergence of quality judgements and methods

Although many of the music psychology publications that suggest that there are generalised skills relating to 'flow' and musical skill, they are still mostly based on studies of western classical musicians (e.g. Custodero, 2005; Araújo and Hein, 2019). Witek *et al.* (2020) did a study of listener entrainment to syncopation that pointed to differences between the responses by Ghanaian and US students. Crawford (2020) has also looked at how children from different cultures responded to Australian music education. Scholars such as Blacking (1974) and Spitzer (2021) have argued about the nature of human musicality and, as mentioned in the first chapter, recent arguments about the viability of comparative musicology (e.g. Born, 2010; Clayton, 2012) propose that, despite the dangers, there are benefits to be had. On a pragmatic note, the London

College of Music Examinations' Ensemble Syllabus[4] embodies this notion that there are some elements of expertise that might be cross cultural by allowing those being examined to explain the aesthetics of their musical culture to the examiner before an examined performance. However, while there may be certain general characteristics of skilful 'flow', entrainment and synchronisation skills, their precise details are often being negotiated on a case-to-case basis: from the extent to which uniformity and homogeneity are relevant in a specific context to the range of contrast that might be necessary throughout the timeline of a piece. One of the exciting potentials of Practical Musicology for me is the possibility that by exploring the specifics of how musical aesthetics grow in different contexts, we may start to uncover general principles of similarity and difference: of belonging and not belonging. Whether, for example, traditions, styles or contexts that involve similar types of interaction (as outlined at the start of this section) also have commonalities relating to the development of their aesthetics.

Given that each of the pieces in the Hyper Production project was meant to sound different to the 'normal' rendition, we had to develop a new aesthetic for each of the pieces which accommodated some of the required changes in performance practice but which also stayed 'true to the work' in a way that we all felt maintained the important aspects of the piece while changing others. For example, by separating the Debussy piano pieces out onto eight hands/four people, the gestural flow of the lines necessarily changed. The pianists spent several hours acclimatizing themselves to this fragmented and distributed version of their normal performance practice before we introduced any of the dub mixing techniques that were going to be used in the concert. Even with this rehearsal time, the physicality of eight hands and four brains meant that the gestural shapes and phrasing of the performance was going to be different – just as, for example, there is a difference in the gestures and phrasing between Mussorgsky's piano suite, *Pictures At An Exhibition*, and Ravel's orchestration of it. While this was discussed, it was not a primary focus of the research and therefore not documented. If it had been, we would have had to triangulate an analysis of how the performed output changed during the rehearsal process with some representations of the Internal Narrative – the participants' subjective assessment of when it was and was not 'working'. There were two inter-related factors in the development of this aesthetic. The first was concerned with making

---

[4] https://lcme.uwl.ac.uk/media/1520/ensemble-syllabus.pdf [accessed 7 September 2021]

sure that we all felt that the version we played 'worked' musically even if it had a different 'shape' to the solo piano versions. The second was about audience expectations and which leads us on to the third form of new knowledge.

8.1.3 The complex aesthetic relationship between the expected and the unexpected

There are generally well-established relationships built into the structure of musical traditions and cultures. We are used to hearing different types of interactions and some of them grow out of the specifics of the music – the instruments, ensembles and rules and conventions of the musical activities – while others are reflections of the social, political and economic environment from which it emerged: gender roles, class structures, access to Bourdieu's (1986) different forms of capital (financial, cultural, social and symbolic), etc. The expectations about which instruments or voices are likely to synchronise and/or accompany others, the pitch ranges of various components and the functions that they perform, or the way that certain instruments accentuate metric structure while others may play 'against' it; these are all simultaneously well established and constantly being disrupted – although going back to the point I made earlier about learned behaviour, there are also more and less established ways of disrupting these conventions. Vygotsky's (1980) *zone of proximal development* also relates to these expected and unexpected forms of interaction. Obviously, the notions of expected and unexpected are a direct consequence of the process of category building that we have described as underpinning our sense of belonging and not belonging.

Working in the world of firmly established repertoire such as the Debussy and Shostakovich pieces, audiences generally have very strong expectations about what they are going to hear. The Hyper Production performances and recordings not only took these pieces into new spatial and timbral sound worlds, they also, as mentioned above, shifted aspects of the phrasing and intonation. The different relationships between the participants that these methods required – how they heard their instruments, what kinds of synchronization they had to achieve, etc. – made an audible difference to the micro-timing of various parts, the linear dynamic shaping and the relative dynamics of various components. As mentioned earlier, in the developmental process we were continually negotiating the 'rightness' of these audible differences and deciding where we needed to meet certain expectations and where we should challenge them. Generally, we decided to take the approach that there was not much to be gained from subtlety but that we needed to feel sure of the reasoning and consistency of the ideas: that although the pieces may sound shockingly different in some ways, that it was clear to those who listened that there was a narrative – albeit an unexpected one – that could be identified and followed. In some ways, our approach to expectations was the corollary of the previously mentioned jazz aphorism 'if you make a mistake, do it three times' (Klotz, 2017) and something that I will discuss again in Chapter 9: authority is a social contract. Subtlety is often more appropriate in the context of the expected or it may simply be interpreted as a mistake. By embracing and making a feature of those types of audible difference in timing, phrasing and dynamics – alongside the perhaps more radical unexpectedness of the timbral and spatial changes in the dub mix – we hopefully made it clear that everything was deliberate, planned and thought through. However, we also knew that challenging listeners of classical repertoire with an aesthetic that was based on the meaningfully unexpected was going to divide an audience. Although we got a strongly favourable response from the audience at King's Place in London, some of the readers on Norman Lebrecht's *Slipped Disc* blog, for example, felt that there was no excuse for butchering the classics in this way.

8.1.4 The mechanisms for creating metaphors relating theory to artistic, pragmatic or activist practice

Monson (1997) uses the theoretical lens of heteroglossia (Bakhtin, 1982) from literary theory to discuss the way that musicians create conversations and interactions based on their personal 'voices' – what Moore (2012) and others describe as the idiolect. Goffman's micro-sociology of dramaturgy (1956, 1979) is one of the primary drivers behind theories of performed identity and includes work on non-verbal activity and musical performance (see for example Wallis, 2011; Auslander, 2016). Once again, we need to think back to a fundamental difference between the ethnographic and Practical Musicology: that we are concerned with identifying new strategies for employing these kinds of metaphor rather than highlighting and indicating where it has happened. Practical Musicology is not concerned with 'that it has happened', it is about exploring the mechanisms by which new metaphors can be tried out and about establishing the criteria by which the researcher thinks they should be judged and explaining why. In Theoretical Interlude 5, I discussed how various forms of musical interaction can produce sounds that mimic social activity or suggest it through metaphor. An ensemble can sound disciplined, nervous, relaxed or chaotic through the way that they interact in the same way that a solitary player can mimic individual's emotions through intonation, dynamics and phrasing.

As mentioned above, we aimed to have clear reasons for the treatments in the Hyper Production sub-projects. Part of the reason for choosing these Debussy pieces was the potential for metaphorical narratives that their impressionistic – in some ways almost musically figurative – nature provided. The *Minstrels* prelude is generally considered to be a response to Debussy witnessing some (slightly unstable?) acrobats on a walk on the promenade in Bournemouth during a visit to the UK. There are several theoretical frameworks through which these ideas of musical mimesis, imitation and caricature can be examined. The ecological approach (Clarke, 2005; Windsor and De Bézenac, 2012), Smalley's notion of spectromorphology (Smalley, 1986, 1997; Zagorski-Thomas, 2018b) and affect theory (Thompson and Biddle, 2013) are all concerned with exploring the ways in which musical activity suggests meaning through conjuring up some kind of embodied or social activity that brings along some meaningful contextual baggage: and that the conjuring process relies on the two phenomena (musical and 'other') having some sort of experiential commonality. There were four ways in which the metaphors for movement, instability and clumsiness were drawn out in the performance and they were all based on the types of interactions we have mentioned above. The first, as we have already discussed in a more general sense, was about fragmenting the performances into an arrangement, and working on the phrasing and timing of how the performers were going to bring them together. These combine both interactions between performers and between performers and instigator/managers and the metaphor suggested by this fragmentation aims at separating the agency of the *Minstrels* into separate characters. The second is about using audio processing on the various different lines from the four pianos to further suggest instability through tremolo, vibrato and other modulating effects. The third is about the spatial processing which was moving the individual audio parts around in a multi-speaker array to further suggest the multiple agencies of the *Minstrels* tumbling around. Finally, the fourth is the pairing with the video projection which consisted of a video by Natalia Zagorska-Thomas, called *Pale Girl's Dream,* of two embroidered paper children's dresses blowing around in the wind. The obvious connection being that the tossing and turning of the dresses paralleled the tumbling acrobats. These examples demonstrate how all of these different types of interaction can suggest metaphorical connections between the original composition, the scene for which it was designed to call up an impression (The *Minstrels*) and these additional interactions that the Hyper-Production performance introduced.

USEFUL QUESTIONS

What kind of new knowledge about interaction would be most useful to you in your practice and how does it fit into these categories? It might be interaction between people or between you and an instrument or other form of technology. Which skill do you wish you could acquire? Is it a skill that requires thinking and reflection or is it something you wish was automatic/subconscious?
What are the most important quality judgements you make in your work and how do you make them? What are the criteria for good or bad?
What kind of interaction in your practice is good when it is expected and what kind is good when it is unexpected?
What has been the most useful piece of theoretical knowledge you have acquired?

8.2 Signals and signs

From the 'count in' for a band to the conductor's baton for an orchestra and from a momentary glance as a cue across stage to the visual representation of sound on the computer screen, signals and signs are used everywhere to synchronize and structure performances and other forms of musical sound making. In addition, the vast range of notational forms from around the world sit somewhere in between the function of instructions – of triggering a performance from the trained musician – and the function of data storage – of a representational system that allows the communication of musical knowledge across time and space. In Theoretical Interlude 5 I discussed various forms of influence. Signals and signs that I am including as interaction work under the same principles as 'demonstrations' did in that typology but I would distinguish between them as being direct moment to moment or instantaneous triggers (or 'suggestions'). And these signals and signs are not only sound but visual and tactile influences as well – not only hearing the drummer but seeing the arc of their gestures and feeling the tactile impact of the sound. The ways in which they express complex multi-modal knowledge are essential to musical communication aside from the obvious pedagogical applications of signalling to inexperienced musicians during performance. These kinds of signals can be functional or aesthetic. On either the functional or the aesthetic level they may involve signalling a desire or intention for something technical or expressive to change – or to remain the same – or signalling a point of synchronization or a shape through gesture.

However, given that the majority of the things described here are the subject of well-established conventions, how would Practical Musicology fit into this picture? What aspects of interacting through signals and signs are complicated enough to warrant research into how it could be done better? In the world of classical music one can imagine that new works might throw up challenges relating to conducting or instructions in the form of graphic scores or the types of game-based pieces that John Zorn has created (e.g. *Cobra*; Hathut Records; 1987) with signals for triggering improvised responses or strategies. In the world of popular music, during the online Performance in the Studio conference in 2012,[5] Anne Danielsen and Paul Théberge discussed click tracks and guide tracks and talked about the way that interactions with a click track can 'produce entirely new feels that would have been very difficult to create with musicians [alone]'. Similarly, the visual displays that technologies of electronic dance music such as Abelton's Push or Eurorack Modular Synthesis systems provide might be explored in terms of the way that they trigger interactions with the technology.

8.3 Entraining

Much like other forms of musical interaction that we have described so far, entrainment can be literal, functional or metaphorical. Musicians entrain themselves together in order to perform ensemble musical activities and, on the literal level, two or more people entrain by singing or performing in unison, i.e. they do exactly the same as each other and, as far as possible, entrain the movements that are relevant to the activity completely. On the functional level performers entrain certain elements of their own performance to certain elements of someone else's – such as a bass player ensuring that certain notes of their part coincide with certain notes of the drummer's part. Functional entrainment, of the type that was so difficult to train in the Californian sea lion dancing to Earth Wind And Fire (Cook *et al.*, 2013), is clearly a basic human faculty and a necessary condition for any musical activity that involves more than one person (or people and machines). However, functional entrainment is

---

[5] https://www.artofrecordproduction.com/aorpjoom/component/easyblog/categories/rhythm-sections?Itemid=228

not simply a matter of deciding to do it. There are an inordinately large number of decisions to be made about how to do it: the number of coincident activities and the accuracy of the coincidence (temporal, pitch, timbre similarity), etc. Keil and Feld (2005) discuss participatory discrepancies in relation to groove and temporal coincidence but there are also the elements of variation, hocket and partial synchronization. By not copying or adopting something exactly I am claiming both a **convergent** and **divergent** relationship simultaneously – either as different components in the same social 'machine' or as two aligned but independent actors.

In addition, reiteration and repetition involve a similar process of entrainment. These are processes of non-synchronous entrainment where a musical activity (and the sound it makes) is copied after it has happened. You always have to know what is coming in order to entrain – an example has to be set and made clear that it is to be followed. The followers then have to consent, to be willing and interested in the process, and then, obviously, they need to be able to do it. While many species can copy action as part of a learning process, the ability to do it in time and to accurately synchronize our actions to an externally set time frame seems to be a more human specialism. McNeill (1995) makes very strong claims about the importance of synchronized muscular activity in the development and maintenance of human culture. He cites a broad range of activities from army drill, traditions of mass calisthenics in the far east, music-driven aerobic activity in gyms and fitness classes, simply being part of a communal musical activity (dancing but also simply swaying or clapping in time), contributing to a broader social event (religious service, football game) or helping to synchronize some non-musical activity (work song, wedding or funeral march). Furthermore, Thaut and others (e.g. Thaut, McIntosh and Hoemberg, 2015) have demonstrated in the period since the 1990s that synchronization to an audio pulse can provide therapeutic benefits to patients with movement disorders and within sports science (e.g. Karageorghis *et al.*, 2017) the use of music to improve performance is well established. What is less well established and to which Practical Musicology can contribute usefully is the question of how the musical mechanisms of synchronous and non-synchronous musical entrainment work, whether the accuracy, the particular types, or the levels of synchronization make particular forms of music 'work' better. And, when we talk about the ways in which **convergent** and **divergent** relationships in interaction can suggest other forms of social (and mechanized) activity, we can also explore the metaphorical forms of entrainment.

On the metaphorical level there are a great many ways in which entrainment can suggest features of other forms of activity. There are physical and gestural similarities that can involve the type of literal mimesis of some *musique concrete* or examples such as the tape loop of sound effects that forms the rhythmic basis of Pink Floyd's 'Money' (1973). This can become less literal but retain a strong mimetic element such as the ways that musicians can interact to produce sonic textures that share attributes with other phenomena: moving water, horses galloping, etc. Entrainment between players can also suggest cultural phenomena such as soldiers marching, church bells chiming, chanting on a demonstration – phenomena that suggest both a physical activity and some ideological or emotional resonance in some audiences as well. And, as I discussed in the previous chapter, the cross-modal entrainment might be metaphorical as well as in the way that the video of the passing Cuban countryside became perceptually fused with some features of the sound in my Due(di)ts.

8.4 Responding and not responding

In Chapter 7 (Section 7.1), the ways in which an individual can share their musical ideas were examined in terms of the three forms of engagement: **automatic, subconscious** and **conscious**. In Theoretical Interlude 6 I discussed how groups of individuals can suggest meaning through the way they interact – in particular, they can suggest belonging and not belonging to some category. Ensemble performances can represent metaphors for social activities by demonstrating the types of relationships that are being enacted – loose/tight, homogenous/individual, working in the same or different direction, all doing the same thing, creating a coherent whole out of individual parts, etc. As we have just discussed, this requires ensemble players to create intricate narratives of interactive response by entraining to each other, and non-synchronous entrainment – or copying something after it has been presented as an example – is an important part of that. Indeed, this notion of 'call and response' in music is a very widespread, if not ubiquitous, structuring principle. However, a response does not have to copy the 'call'. I can use the opportunity for either **convergent** or **divergent** behaviour, but even a **divergent** response is an acknowledgement of the existence of the 'call' – a kind of belonging. The response is also an activity that has been influenced by either another musical participant (direct) or by the context in which the activity is happening (indirect). And the response itself – the activity and the musical contribution it makes – can relate to some behaviour by the other participants or to the musical sound, and can be literal or metaphorical. This gives us several dimensions in which to categorize responsive interaction: synchronous and non-synchronous, convergent and divergent, direct and indirect, behavioural or sonic, and literal or metaphorical.

By the same token, the perceived absence of response can be used to create a similar range of meanings. On the one hand, it can be used as a metaphor for disconnection, for being above, separate, random or excluded. This can range from the simple rhythmic or tonal disconnection of a lead line from its accompaniment to more complex and jarring metaphors such as Charles Ives' metaphorical superimposition of two unrelated marching bands passing in the street. On the other hand, it can be a sign of leadership, of knowing that it is the job of others to respond. This takes us back to the idea of call and response or theme and variation and the idea of there being an agency which others imitate but which does not itself respond. In addition, the introduction of machines that make sound of various types in the history of music has introduced a third form of non-responsive metaphors of interaction; of humans having to respond to an unchanging and unresponsive machine. Thus, in addition to these several dimensions of responsive interaction, we must also consider the level or extent of the response and how that level or extent is being used to suggest affordances for interpretation.

For example, there are several examples in the Shostakovich where thematic material gets repeated and varied on different instruments in the quartet. Sometimes the thematic statements are synchronous and sometimes sequential or overlapping. Sometimes they are note-for-note reiterations (**convergent**) and sometimes they are transposed or rhythmically varied (**divergent**). Sometimes various voices in the quartet are strongly responsive and one or more are detached and independent. Andrew and I used some of these forms of interaction to create a map of how we applied the various effects and processors – although this map was more of a guide for improvisation rather than a score (see Videos 8.1 and 8.2 on the website[6]). Sometimes we were aiming to accentuate convergence and sometimes the opposite, etc. The ways in which we did this ranged from, for example, emphasizing the shape of a gesture with distortion (direct), to exploiting the cultural resonance of particular technologies (indirect) such as the association of phasing with psychedelia and disorientation. Sometimes we were working to use similar processing to accentuate (or disrupt) voice

[6] http://www.c21mp.org/practical-musicology/

USEFUL QUESTIONS

What is the most important kind of 'responding' that you do in your practice?
  When you respond to some feature of the music?
  When you respond to some aspect of your instrument or other technology?
  When you respond to another musician or practitioner?
When is it important in your practice not to respond to something?

groupings (behavioural) and at other times we were concerned with creating a particular timbral texture (sonic). These could relate to highlighting a particular kind of physical gesture (literal) or some more metaphorical connection such as Shostakovich's tormented state of mind at the time he was writing it or the devastation of the Dresden bombing (the city in which he wrote it).

These are all parameters which relate directly to my theoretical framework but there are a whole gamut of theoretical 'as if's that could be used to represent interactive musical responses. We could use the micro-sociologies of Goffman's (1956, 1979) dramaturgical approach or Bakhtin's heteroglossia (1982). We could use any of the context-focused approaches to tradition, identity, technology, use and value that were outlined in Chapter 4 to suggest strategies for creative (or functional) interaction. The 'language' or aesthetic framework of interactive responses that we use in a piece might be developed through an inductive experimental process where the data or output of the experiments are then examined to look for general principles that will make the work fully coherent. Or we might start with a deductive process of discussing how some theoretical ideas might provide a metaphorical framework that can then be tested and refined.

8.5 Distributed Creativity

Returning to Clarke and Doffman's (2017) title of *Distributed Creativity*, we have discussed that the notion of interaction involves several dimensions of potential responses that range from the **convergence** of mimesis to a broad range of potentially **divergent** responses. Different types of interaction will combine the literal embodied activities and the metaphorical interactions of the **representational system**. The next chapter considers creativity in the context of systems and networks, however, before that, I want to briefly discuss it in this smaller context of interaction and more immediate forms of response. Weinstein (2004) and Behr (2010, 2015) discuss band dynamics in rock music: discussing technique, innovation, originality, personality and dynamics as creative competitions within a micro-field. This can be thought about in terms of authority and judgement, which is the subject of the next chapter, but we can also see these more micro-levels of creative interaction in the moment-to-moment processes of performance, composition, improvisation, recording, etc. Nooshin (2017) and Heyde *et al.* (2017) are two of the contributors to the *Distributed Creativity* book who discuss improvisation both as a label and as a concept. They illustrate the problems inherent in the usage of the word. The two discussions also point to two related forms of creative interaction that might be considered 'as if' they lie at opposite ends of a continuum. At one end we have the notion of using some pre-existing materials as the basis for various types of 'rule'-based response and this can be seen in the various Iranian examples that Nooshin discusses. At the other end is the notion of free improvisation, the kind that Heyde, Redgate, Redgate and Wright are discussing, which relies on a kind of idealized idiolect: a 'pure' expressive voice which avoids the 'rules' and conventions of traditions and yet somehow has a characteristic sound. In another form of distinction, Negus (1992, pp. 54–5) differentiates between *organic* and *synthetic* 'ideologies of creativity' which might be defined as closed-system and open-system or self-sufficient and dependent. Except, of course, that there is a difference between ideology and pragmatics and none of these systems are closed or self-sufficient. Indeed, Nooshin's chapter references the continuing streams of intertextual influence in Iranian music through what she terms 'the imaginary family of improvisation' (Nooshin, 2017, p. 224). She mentions the ways that Iranian musicians have embraced intertextuality through 'world fusion' and jazz but also how the influence of Western classical notions of composition have influenced a 'new wave' of Iranian classical music.

For me, another exciting route for Practical Musicology is to explore the ways in which the 'rules' and conventions which musical practitioners all have for both **convergent** and **divergent** behaviour, i.e. for both their musical tradition(s) and their idiolect, work together and do not work together when different individuals interact musically. Why do some combinations 'work better' than others? We can ask this question both in regard to the way that individuals gel and how different musical fusions work. This was nicely summed up when Neil Heyde wrote about an improvising concert he'd participated in 'many years ago where I hardly played … I just thought I can't find a space, and I'm not going to play'

(Heyde *et al.*, 2017, p. 316). It is also apparent in several fusion albums (which I am much too polite to mention) where the players have done the musical equivalent of bumping into each and falling over rather than 'fusing'. And this does bring me back to the idea that Practical Musicology, practice research or artistic research do not have to produce good art to produce new knowledge. It might seem as if it would take a brave practice researcher to put something that blatantly has not worked into the public domain but I think that is because we have yet to establish the right platforms and the right narratives. As I have mentioned, a good deal of the experiments we conducted for the Classical Music Hyper-Production project did not produce a professional polished output. They were experiments, and the exploration and the new knowledge was about the processes and ways of thinking: a proof of concept or prototype rather than the 'production line model'.

Theoretical interlude 7: *Authority*

We can think of Bourdieu's (1986) notions of financial, cultural, social and symbolic capital in terms of the invariant properties that afford various types of power or authority. In this instance, there has to be a social contract where all the participants recognize invariant properties that afford power but they will not necessarily be the same properties for each of the participants. To use a very blunt feudal example, I may believe that my right to reign over you is ordained by God while you may ascribe the same affordance to the fact that I have an army who will kill you if you do not accept my authority. The authority that is afforded to me is the same while the invariant properties that each of us perceives as affording that authority are very different. In addition, different participants may perceive different affordances of power in different people. If, as an audience member, I go to see an ensemble perform, I may well attribute power to the most prominent or energetic performer. Within the ensemble itself, there might be several conflicting perceptions about who has authority over what.

The word 'authority' has two slightly different meanings. It can be used to describe the ownership of power over others but it can also be used to describe someone who is an expert in a field. In both instances it requires someone to have a belief in their own rightness. It is not enough to possess the ability to solve a problem or to explain and understand it better than others. Authority also requires two other conditions to be fulfilled. It requires the ability to influence others such that:

1. They believe you have the answer to some shared problem or that they could be in some way harmed or disadvantaged if they do not accept that authority

2. They believe that you 'own' that answer – that you are qualified to give it and that it came from you – or that you have the capacity to harm or disadvantage them.

Duncan's *Punch* cartoon from 8 January 1988 portrays the chair of a business meeting saying 'That's an excellent suggestion Miss Trigg. Perhaps one of the men here would like to make it'. It provides a darkly comic example of what can happen if the first condition is met without the second. If I don't believe in your authority I will imagine you have stumbled across something you don't understand properly that allows me to solve the problem. And, indeed, that is sometimes the case, although obviously not in Miss Trigg's case. This goes back to the idea of identity being defined in terms of you being the 'kind of person who does …' – knowledge that is based on action. Of the many schema that we develop throughout our lives, authority figures – people who tell people what to do – figure in a great many of them. And that category of authority figures, as we discussed in Chapter 5, is an aggregation of the invariant properties of our experience of people who have exerted authority. In the case of the men in Duncan's cartoon, having ovaries is not one of those invariant properties. Although, of course, the creation of categories is not always purely an inductive process, I may well use a deductive process of examining the validity of those invariant properties by, for example, drawing on other experiential schema to consider how relevant the ownership of ovaries might be in these circumstances.

Establishing authority is, therefore, reliant on the creation of a social contract. You need to learn how to perform your role in a network not just so that you know what to do but also so that other people can recognize what your role is; you will need to act like the 'thing' you are meant to be. The primary form of knowledge representation in the brain is action-based: 'things' are defined in terms of what they do and what they are believed to be capable of doing. Therefore, defining Bourdieu's various forms of capital in a more functional manner, a manner that is more suitable for a Practical Musicology, we should explore the way that it is perceived and ascribed by the various participants through their respective perceptions of the invariant properties and the specifics of what they afford in terms of authority. How does the kind of specialist knowledge, that is often described as cultural capital, manifest itself in different contexts and what are the results that those manifestations produce? And that, of course, leads to the question of how those results are judged by the various participants and why some judgements are more influential than others.

However, as we have already discussed, in addition to different participants having different perceptions of what affords power, they are likely to have different perceptions of who has power over what. And, in addition, those perceptions are also in a state of flux. We are also constantly changing our identity through what we do and what affordances are perceived or inferred, and the nature of 'the network' also changes around us – the other participants are all constantly changing their identity through the same mechanisms. In a context like a musical ensemble, where there are established communal goals, there is also a continual process whereby an established *habitus* (which embodies existing perceptions of authority) comes up against the need for innovation and variation of that *habitus* to achieve those goals. This is causing stress that needs to be resolved – we need to either change what we think of you or you have to change what you do. This works both in terms of networks engaged in musical practice and in the types of music they produce: the social roles and activities that are metaphorically embodied in sound.

9

Systems and networks

Understanding music practices purely in terms of the way that people come together and make various types of noises is one thing, but I have already mentioned the importance of various aspects of the context in which it happens. While some of these aspects of context may be understood from the perspective of the types of metaphors that the participants utilize (based on their cultural background), I have also mentioned the ways in which various forms of power and influence exist and are exerted as part of the processes of making music. It is also therefore important to think about music practices 'as if' they emerge within systems or networks which can be used to model the power and influence relationships between the participants, their tools/instruments and their environment. Once again, this will be undertaken within the theoretical framework utilizing influence, restriction and affordance.

Both I and others have written in the past about the systems approach to creativity (Csikszentmihalyi, 1988; McIntyre, 2011; Zagorski-Thomas, 2014b) and the use of Actor Network Theory in musicology (Piekut, 2014; Zagorski-Thomas, 2016, 2018a) but this has mainly focused on analyses of how the musical outputs of others have been affected by the functioning of a system or network – or 'as if' there were a system or network functioning. Applying these ideas to Practical Musicology involves understanding how these metaphors can be explored and exploited in creative practice. I have explained how the ecological approach and embodied cognition can be embedded into these theoretical models in ways that let us use theories about individual cognition to explain collaborative social behaviour. Notions of influence, restriction and affordance can be viewed as both individual and interpersonal. In my 2018 article about the making of Miles Davis' 1969 album *Bitches Brew* I explored both the physical phenomena that influenced Davis' perception of the affordances for making an album in such a radically different way (new technologies, etc.) and psychological and cultural phenomena as well (his recent working experience and the work of other musicians around him). Davis acquired new knowledge about the affordances of his circumstances through the twin learning processes discussed in Chapter 6: the bottom-up process of patterns emerging from repeated experience and the top-down process of making connections between existing schema that suggest new affordances for interpretation and action. He had already developed a *habitus* of stimulating novelty in his live ensembles by constantly changing personnel and deliberately putting musicians into situations that required them to go beyond their normal and familiar practice, and in the latter part of the 1960s he extended this to include changing their normal recording practices as well. Davis combined these strategies for putting musicians into situations where they had to respond to the unexpected with his emerging understanding of the new creative recording practices being used in rock, pop and soul. Rather than the slow and deliberate process of constructing a multi-track recording that artists such as The Beatles, Jimi Hendrix, Marvin Gaye and the Beach Boys in the world of popular music were moving into, Davis, in collaboration with producer Teo Macero, fragmented the improvisation process in a way that used the affordances of the technology in a more jazz inflected way. In the *Bitches Brew* sessions he got the ensemble to improvise multiple short fragments while he spontaneously made arranging decisions about what he wanted them to play and edited them all together. Some of these fragments were large enough to constitute sections but others were shorter and were spliced together 'on the fly' by editing the multi-track tapes as the session progressed. He then got Teo Macero, the producer, to undertake a second process of editing and splicing while mixing the multi-tracks down to stereo, to create more considered arrangements out of these rapidly constructed, multi-take collages. On the one hand, this is an example of inspired creative leadership – Davis shaping and influencing the performance and production processes. On the other, it is an intensely collaborative process that exploits the emergent properties of the existing individual expressive voices of both the musicians and the producer. This distributed creative process on the *Bitches Brew* sessions provided the inspiration for my working methods on an album I am currently working on and which I hope will be released roughly simultaneously with the book. This album, *Failing Upwards,* was described briefly in the introduction: a set of my songs which have been arranged through a contemporary re-imagination of the process used on *Bitches Brew.*

This chapter explores the ways in which systems and networks can be used in Practical Musicology to stimulate creative practice and I will provide some examples from *Failing Upwards*. In a process that is analogous to the twin bottom-up and top-down processes of cognition, we can also explore the potential for bottom-up and top-down processes in communal activity. The bottom-up approach involves the learned *habitus* – the line of least resistance – and can be thought of as the emergent property of a group where each individual simply responds to what is going on around them. They play according to their *habitus*. The top-down approach requires the notion of influence – where one or more individuals in the group exercise influence over the behaviour of one or more others. And this process is itself determined by a meta-level of influence – the process that determines the context in which the phenomenon occurs. In the Miles Davis example, there is the broader economic and cultural system in which decisions about which records should be made and there is the more personal negotiation between artists, producers and record executives about what kind of record it should be and who is going to have creative, technical and financial decision-making powers. Both Davis and the record company were concerned about the economic implications of the rising popularity of popular music over jazz and those broader influences also had an impact on the musical approach that was taken.

In the process that I chose for the making of the *Failing Upwards* album, there are echoes of the methods found in the history of record production that I would characterize as creating the affordances for a process of bricolage through distributed creativity. This is not a mainstream of practice in that history, but it can be traced through producer/artists such as Miles Davis, Paul Simon (e.g. the *Gracelands* album) and Roni Size. There are five key features that I would identify as:

1. Exploring the chosen players' responses to some given starting materials in a way that utilizes their *habitus* and/or idiolect as a key component of the compositional material. In Miles Davis' case, he gave musicians small fragments or ideas. With Paul Simon and Roni Size, the focus was about creating grooves with a specific cultural feel. *Failing Upwards* was based on pre-written song structures.
2. In all of the examples there is a clear 'big picture' ownership by a single 'leader' but the agency of the performers is the primary source for part writing.

3. The recorded parts were seen as a starting point for a process of editing and selection: the aim was always to use bricolage to construct a form of 'audio collage'. The mix was also part of the creative process. The songs weren't finished and then mixed, mixing was the last part of the song writing process.
4. The musicians were given relatively minimal 'priming' and the process relied on their musical judgement with relatively unspecific or generic prompting about which directions to take. The 'big picture' process was meant to be driven inductively – that what was played would trigger creative ideas about what to do with it.
5. The recordings were relatively 'quick and dirty', allowing the process to progress smoothly and quickly without much stopping and starting to get the 'right' take or to experiment with recording techniques. The focus was on making space for the musicians to explore their performative creativity.

As far as the process of documenting the making of the album and the videos for research requirements, as it has not been a funded project, it has been a patchy process. I have relatively low-quality videos of the drums, guitar and keyboards sessions but only some still photographs of the bass, strings, vocals and horn sessions. I have the full session files in a series of dated versions that go back to the first demos and I annotated most of the edits on the session files so that I could track the decision-making process. I have also kept quite a detailed production diary that details both technical and aesthetic thoughts about the way the project was progressing. The main gap in the documentation is that I have not interviewed the participants and do not have the resources for intensive discussions but I can follow up informally with targeted questions about specific issues. Despite this, I believe that it gives me sufficient resources to produce research materials utilizing all four of the methods outlined in Chapter 2. I can use the various audio-visual materials and the date-stamped file versions to create materials with a Temporal Focus. There is plenty of scope to utilize a Spatial Focus in a range of contexts through zooming in and out, creating schematic representations of tasks and processes and featuring multiple perspectives on the same phenomena. There are also opportunities for various forms of deconstruction of the process and for representing my Internal Narrative. Although a great many of the factors that have already been mentioned in this book could form part of the research narrative, I see the notions of distributed creativity and ownership as two of the central themes. Each of the participants in this network of activity has contributed to the album and yet, of course, its existence is entirely reliant on my impetus. The notion of influence therefore needs to be explored in parallel to the question of authority and power.

9.1 Shared and unshared knowledge

One of the key problems relating to the notion of affordances is whether they should be considered as individual or universal. There are two aspects of this. Firstly, there is the question of whether an affordance is a subjective or objective phenomenon. Gibson (1979) speaks mostly of them as objective but also argues that an organism will perceive what is afforded to it, given its physiological make-up, vantage, etc. This allows for the subjectivity of ignorance – that I may not be privy to some objective affordance – but is less clear about the subjectivity of bias – that I may have a different perception of a situation's affordances than you based on opinion rather than fact. I mentioned Clarke's (1999, 2005) treatment of this through the notion of *subject position* in Chapter 6. While Clarke utilizes *subject position* in relation to an analytical 'ecological approach to the perception of musical meaning' (Clarke, 2005, pp. 91–125), he does so 'to steer a middle course between … the idea that perceivers construct their own utterly individual and unpredictable meanings from an aesthetic object … and the determinism … of rigid structuralism – the idea that meaning is entirely contained within the objective structures of the work itself.' (Clarke, 2005, p. 93).

The second aspect is the difference between specific and general affordances. This works on a variety of levels of specificity and generality. A particular affordance may be specific to me as an individual or a category to which I belong – the affordance to improvise a musical performance for example is general to the category of improvising musicians but specific to that category in the whole population. Of course, there is the more literal or extreme version of both. For something to be truly specific it would only be an affordance for a particular individual, in a particular place, at a particular time and for it to be truly general it would have to be an affordance for any individual, at any place, and at any time. These are once again 'as if' assumptions but we can find examples that feel universal in the general sense – such as the affordances for physical movement that the law of gravity allows. However, setting aside that there might be some universal examples of affordance, if we think of knowledge as an individual's awareness of an affordance in a given situation then it also becomes clear that this kind of awareness can give an individual an advantage or power over someone without that awareness. It therefore also becomes clear that in any model of a system or network that for any given participant there are different types of knowledge:

1. Knowledge that is a (more or less) ubiquitous part of human experience – such as how to make a noise with one's vocal cords
2. Knowledge that is theoretically accessible to any member of the network but which requires work and effort – such as various levels of instrumental virtuosity
3. Knowledge that is somehow restricted to some sub-set of the members of the network – and that might be a physical restriction (e.g. vocal pitch/timbre and gender) or a cultural one (e.g. theoretical knowledge imparted only in certain institutions)

In short, the question of whether knowledge is power needs to be considered through the question of how readily available that knowledge is – primarily through the notion of restriction. Knowledge is only power if it is in short supply. This is, of course, an extension of the economic principle of resource scarcity – of a gap between demand and supply.

The *Failing Upwards* album project, which is still a work in progress, is built around a musical narrative of improvised and quite varied responses to groove-based ideas. The majority of the players are from a jazz background,[1] and, in addition, Jimmy Martinez (one of the two bass players) is a Latin/Cuban music player and guitarist, and Kiamfu Kasongo is a Congolese guitarist. Agata Kubiak-Kenworthy, who played the violin and viola parts, works in both the classical 'new music' and jazz worlds. The shared knowledge in this case is an approach to performing that involves this type of improvisation and variation of a given schematic 'kernel'. However, each of the players was recruited because of some 'less shared' characteristics in their playing – aspects of their playing which I liked and which also relate more to the third category above – something unique to them. Indeed this musical 'character', the idiolect mentioned in the last chapter, is a feature that gives them some authority in the musical worlds that they inhabit. In any given context, music practitioners in general and not only performers, will need to demonstrate and utilize **convergent** skills –

---

[1] Winston Clifford and Jasmine Kayser (drums), Wells Gordon (bass), Janette Mason (piano and keys), Claude Depper (trumpet and flugel) and Clare Hirst (tenor and soprano saxes)

shared knowledge – and **divergent** skills – their own unique idiolect. Bruford (2018) characterizes this difference in his study of expert drummers as being a continuum between 'functional' and 'compositional' practices. While I feel that these terms come with quite a lot of baggage which I hope that **convergent** and **divergent** avoid at least to some extent, they also flag up the inter-related nature of several of this book's themes. The experiential conditioning or learning of the **inductive** process is often **convergent** because it is frequently a social process by which many practitioners gain the same shared knowledge. And, as we have seen earlier, this **inductive** process is about acquiring the second, **subconscious** forms of knowledge in the **three modes of thought**. However, the opposite notion of the **divergent** idiolect as being necessarily **deductive** and **conscious** is much more problematic and highlights the problem of thinking of musical creativity as somehow isolated from the rest of our identity. The **inductive** processes of acquiring and shaping musical experience and skill are themselves influenced by our broader character traits – by how much, for example, our genetics and experience have encouraged us to be more or less adventurous or methodical in different contexts. Thus, as any music teacher knows, pupils who utilize the same curriculum, the same exercises and the same practice regime will not only develop different levels of skill but also different approaches to performance: their own idiolect.

Burnard (2012) uses a synthesis of Csikszentmihalyi (1988) and Bourdieu (1993) in her discussion of musical creativities and identifies 'six different ways in which musicians … generate distinct musical creativities' (Burnard, 2012, p. 229): self-social and socio-cultural *forms of authorship*, temporal and technological *mediating modalities*, and implicit and explicit *practice principles*. The two *forms of authorship* map onto **divergent** (the self-social idiolect) and **convergent** (the collective socio-cultural) modes of behaviour. Her *mediating modalities* relate to some of the contextual issues that affect practice. Temporal *modalities* refer to the structure of the working practices – whether they work in 'real-time' like live performance and improvisation or whether there is a process of reflection and revision of the creative output before it meets an audience (as with score-based composition and the creation of recorded music). Technological *modalities* relate to complexities of the technological context that I discussed in Chapter 4. This draws a different kind of dividing line between practice and context than I do but is, as we have seen several times, only concerned with creating a different theoretical 'as if' through which to suggest some possibilities for interpretation. In my 'as if' the temporal *modalities* would emerge from the context of the musical tradition(s) in which the creative practitioner established their work. In addition, the other contextual factors which I discussed in Chapters 3 and 4 – identity, uses and value as well as tradition and technology – are spread between Burnard's 'six different ways'. The implicit and explicit *practice principles* relate to **subconscious** and **conscious** modes of thought and knowledge in my model but also embody other aspects of these contextual factors. I see these approaches as different ways of 'slicing the cake' rather than a fundamental disagreement about what the cake is.

Relating these ideas of shared and unshared, or **convergent** and **divergent**, knowledge to the two over-arching drivers of Practical Musicology – developing quality judgements and representing tacit knowledge – can be done through many of these theoretical frames. If I consider the ways in which quality judgements of this type emerged in the *Failing Upwards* project, there are two intersecting notions – the quality of the experience or process and the quality of the musical results. How would (or hopefully will) I make these narratives of an emerging aesthetic apparent through a research publication? The Internal Narrative is obviously a key focus on the development of an aesthetic and looking back at my diary reflections (and using that and the question as the basis for stimulated recall) I would examine the editing process after each of the sessions for evidence of decisions made on the basis of four criteria: my personal goals for the project based on whether I feel it is (1) **convergent** or stylistically appropriate or (2) **divergent** or about individual originality; whether I feel that what the performer I am editing is doing is (3) **convergent** or stylistically appropriate or (4) **divergent** or about their individual originality. In addition, I would look at coding the types of edit being made into categories such as: creating structure/form, adding textural variety, producing momentary 'ornaments' or 'fills' in the arrangement, altering rhythm or groove, altering the harmony, creating or enhancing melodic hooks, etc. Using this to conduct a thematic analysis, I might employ a technique such as a Repertory Grid (Fransella, Bell and Bannister, 2004) to map those four criteria onto the categories and look for patterns. And while I would be extremely wary of translating quantitative results such as this into a 'map' of my aesthetics, they can produce a stimulus that lies somewhere between data visualization techniques (Tufte and Graves-Morris, 1983) and Rogerian psychoanalysis (Rogers, 2003) whereby the answers that you give are presented back to you in a different structure or context. This semi-inductive approach of looking for patterns in data by presenting it in different ways would hopefully produce some insights into this process of developing an aesthetic.

USEFUL QUESTIONS

What is your unique selling point as a practitioner?
What do you think is the most important piece of knowledge in your work that is commonly shared with other expert practitioners?

9.2 Judgement

In the earlier section on The Value of Music (4.3) the notion of judgement as power was discussed. However, we all have the capacity and the inclination to judge but we do not all have power such that our judgements have an effect on the world. As Allan Moore (2002) has argued about the notion of authenticity, judgements about subjective attributes such as value and authenticity should be understood as ascribed rather than inscribed – and that the number, function and vociferousness of the 'ascribers' will determine the power of the judgement: the influence which it has.

I will also reiterate the distinction that is important to the idea of Practical Musicology – research into how things can be done 'better' – as opposed to the musicology of how were or are things done. On the one hand, there are judgements that I referred to in the last section about the quality and originality of the musical 'output' compared to the quality and originality of the practices that produced it. There is also a larger and perhaps more philosophical question about the nature of newness which flows from our cultural obsession with distinguishing between that which is new to an individual or group and that which is new to the world. To use the rather hackneyed example of the Beatles, the newness of what they did can be described as having a magpie-like approach to influence: drawing on African-American rock and roll/rhythm and blues, Indian music, Western classical music, British music hall, European folk and cabaret. This is also made more problematic by the question of who writes the history books: Ms Trigg in the *Punch* cartoon mentioned above, was obviously not going to either write the history book or be included. The Beatles, in comparison, have been credited with a great many innovations for which we can often find examples that pre-date them. My wife and I own a drawing by the *Guardian* cartoonist Steven Appleby which has a series of images of solitary characters leading up to the fourth where a man is being fêted by an adoring crowd with the caption 'The man who had the concept fourth (that people who have ideas first, second or third don't always get the credit)'. Now obviously The Beatles were an extraordinarily creative and innovative group but how do we step away from the idea that they invented everything? This is important in regard to Practical Musicology because, while current streams in artistic research are focused on conceptual novelty, the vast majority of innovation in musical practice relates to more incremental and adaptive change. In Chapter 3 we discussed the notions of intertextuality (see for example Burns and Lacasse, 2018) and heteroglossia (Bakhtin, 1982) and in the section above we discussed shared and unshared knowledge – **convergent** and **divergent**. We need to become much more nuanced in our discussions about the newness in new knowledge. The four categories that I have proposed for new knowledge in Practical Musicology have already been explored in earlier chapters and these form the basis for judgements about the quality of the research. The quality of the musical output is a separate thing. The research aspect of quality judgements is how they are developed and made rather than whether the work turns out in retrospect to have been culturally significant.

Figure 9.1 'I Had the Idea First' by Steven Applebey

The terms Big-C and Little-c creativity have become popular in recent years and are used to distinguish between large cultural shifts in practice and the small, everyday changes. It seems as if creativity studies borrowed the terms Big-C and Little-c from cultural theory (Merrotsy, 2013) and Stein (1953, 1987) pointed to both the positive and negative implications of this categorical simplification and also suggested differentiating between objective and subjective creativity to distinguish between creativity in the output and creativity in the process. Others (e.g. Kaufman and Beghetto, 2009) have tried to subdivide into further categories to add nuance and Boden (2004) distinguished between historical and psychological creativity. With research into 'what happened' or 'how it is done' we can see that retrospective judgements about the impact of creativity are highly relevant, but as Practical Musicology is concerned with the prospective – 'how to do it better' – rather than the retrospective, we only need to concern ourselves with psychological creativity. Whether it turns out to be Big-C or Little-c in retrospect is not part of the process – although it is, of course, of huge interest to all the practitioners concerned.

Going back to the question of judgement in the world of Practical Musicology, while we may be concerned with both the output and the process of creation, the reception or after-life of the output is only of concern in as much as it might be part of the process – for example, if we want to include how it was marketed in the research process. In a collaborative process, we can consider our five types of participants mentioned in Chapter 2: enablers, instigators, creators, managers and editors. As mentioned earlier, those are roles not individuals and one person may take on several roles and several people may take on the same role. Each of these roles involves making judgements and, just as we talked about **convergent** and **divergent** skills in the discussion of knowledge, there are similarly **convergent** and **divergent** forms of judgement. In addition to Moore's (2002) ascribed forms of authenticity being second or third person – i.e. they are believed to be **convergent** with some socially constructed consensus – or first person – i.e. they are believed to be **divergent** in some way that demonstrates individuality – we also ascribe similar forms of aesthetic judgement. A performance might be expertly performed jazz without being particularly original. At any given moment in any given project, the participants, whatever their role, will have an opinion about how the project is going to turn out. However, as Ingold (2013, 2016) points out when discussing 'making' and 'drawing', that kind of opinion is both schematic and altered through and by the process: our idea of what we are making changes as the artefact or the performance emerges from our activity. As Dewey (1934) and pragmatists such as the contributors to Brooks' (2021) collection for the Orpheus Institute book series on artistic research would have it, our experience is a combination of 'doing' and 'undergoing'. And the response that our judgement elicits is also a combined process of 'doing' and 'undergoing' in that the urge to correct, edit or redo based on our judgement is driven by our three pillars of affordance, restriction and influence. What can or cannot be done in the current circumstances and what should be done given our experience of similar circumstances. In a practice context, we might keep playing the phrase we tripped up on until we get it right but that would not be 'right' in a performance context – although this brings us back to what Klotz (2017) says, the commonly quoted aphorism in jazz improvisation is 'if you make a mistake, do it again'.

In the *Failing Upwards* album, the instigator role was initially me but in several of the phases of activity, the idea to instigate something came from other participants based on their judgement that something was wrong or missing. Thus, for example, Claude Depper came up with an idea for a horn line for 'Mr Punch's Stick' rather than swapping solos with Clare Hirst. While the impetus for the idea came from a judgement about what was stylistically appropriate for the song (**convergent**), the actual line emerged from Claude's and Clare's combined ideolects (**divergent**). The judgements about the creator roles were also strongly distributed – although there were chord charts and some sequenced patterns, the instructions to each of the players was to make it their own. Although there were some instances where I asked them to try something with a different direction, the judgements about when we had something that was 'right' was mutual. The role of managing the sessions was generally in my hands and that required judgement about how to keep to schedule – which in itself has creative and aesthetic implications related to how quickly the process has to move on. Finally, the editing process has been very important so far – with key judgements about the arrangement being made in the editing process – and further decisions will be made in the mix process, some of which will be done by me and some by others (see Video 9.1 on the website[2] for a video about the making of Failing Upwards).

USEFUL QUESTIONS

Whose opinion about your work is most important to you? Why?
What is your blind spot? What do you think you most often make a wrong judgement call about in terms of the quality of your practice?

---

[2] http://www.c21mp.org/practical-musicology/

9.3 Power

Bourdieu (1986) describes power in terms of capital, using the metaphor of a valuable possession that can be traded for something else, to account for the leverage that knowledge, connections and status can provide (in addition to money and/or physical resources). As discussed earlier, this allows us to think of power in terms of affordances: of the opportunities or privilege that our circumstances afford. I also discussed the idea that power is not necessarily a 'zero-sum' game. Of course, there is a transactional and coercive element to power but it can also be about collaboration, persuasion, reducing other people's options (or making them less attractive) and making the options that we favour seem more attractive. In short, potential affordances are affected by the other two pillars of the model: influence and restriction. In addition, all of Bourdieu's forms of capital should be considered in light of how their 'owners' are also aware of the affordances that they offer. There is no point in owning financial, cultural, social or symbolic capital if one is unaware of how it can be used to one's advantage. This lies at the heart of Long Lingo and O'Mahoney's (2010) work on brokerage: of the power that can accrue from the 'meta-capital' of understanding how two unconnected people can be put together to combine their cultural capital for mutual benefit. Another feature of affordances as power is that the other parties involved in the process have to believe in your ownership of the capital. This is only irrelevant when there is actual force involved in the exercise of power. Otherwise, in the other multifaceted ways in which power can manifest itself through a 'social contract' rather than through physical coercion, those at the receiving end have to believe that they will be better off in some way by acquiescing rather than resisting. This relates back to the notion of shared and unshared knowledge. If knowledge is only power when that knowledge is in short supply and a good deal of knowledge lies in our second category, of knowledge that is theoretically accessible to any member of the network but which requires work and effort, then the maintenance of this power differential relies on the judgement that the benefits of this affordance are not worth the required work and effort of acquiring that knowledge oneself. This type of power takes many forms: from something as simple as a guitarist being able to exert some economic power over me (i.e. I am willing to pay for their skill) because I consider the value of their skill (and of not having to acquire it myself) to be equal to or higher than the amount they are asking to be paid. Alternatively, it may be some more complicated form of transaction like an apprenticeship where the apprentice willingly cedes power to the expert – they accept the power differential of acquiescing to being told what to do in exchange for some combination of a low wage (or even none in many internships) and a gradual learning process by which they hope to become a similar expert with similar power.

A further complication in this process is the notion that power is mostly shared rather than absolute because most tasks require multiple specialisms. They require teamwork and teamwork very rarely involves an equitable or even share of power and responsibilities. We have already encountered the way that authority is distributed through a network in our discussion of judgement. In musical examples, ensemble players will have different roles and those roles generally require them to exert some kind of power or influence over others at some points and in some ways as well as requiring them to cede power to others at other points and in other ways. At some points they may be setting the tempo or the dynamic level and at others they might be following. At some points they may be following suggestions (or even instructions) during a rehearsal and at some points they may be making them. At some point the technology they are using (from acoustic instruments to digital audio workstations) may provide exactly the right affordance for what they want to do and at others its design and materiality may force them into some kind of 'work-around'. The creative power in the development of a piece or a performance may be skewed towards one individual but is nearly always collaborative and collaborations very rarely involve an equal distribution of power. Even when working alone, the technologies of musical sound making and distribution exert influence or power over our decision making and we are, in essence, collaborating with the designers of those technologies. Indeed, Bourdieu's (1986) distinctions between money, knowledge, connections and status as the four forms of capital (financial, cultural, social and symbolic capital) very often form the basis for negotiations, collaborations and conflicts between participants in musical activity. The world of popular music in the second half of the twentieth century saw a constantly changing industry structure caused by shifts in the balance between participants with financial capital and those with cultural, symbolic, and social capital. Record companies were continually finding different ways of using money to get access to the specialist knowledge and people that they thought better allowed them to predict trends in the market. Sometimes they were licensing recordings from, and even buying up, small labels that were closer to understanding the grass roots than they were. Sometimes they were employing musicians and DJs in their artist and repertoire departments and signing acts directly. Sometimes they were confident about leading demand because they had signed particular star 'brands' and 'owned' the cultural capital, and at other times they were caught out by market changes and found themselves having to follow new patterns of demand. Thus, sometimes they felt there was knowledge required that they could acquire with work and effort (or money to pay others to expend the effort) and sometimes they felt that the knowledge was in the third category – that it was somehow restricted to some sub-set of the members of the network that they did not have access to.

As mentioned in relation to brokerage earlier, understanding the power structures of a particular musical moment provides a kind of 'meta-capital'. If you can understand the structures and how the participants work within them you can better understand how to collaborate with, manipulate or influence them. So while it may not always be useful or advantageous to explicitly discuss all aspects of the power structure in a given situation with all the participants, it is always useful and important to understand them. Many of the times in which conflicts emerge between participants it is because roles and responsibilities were not clearly enough delineated before a project began but at the same time, there are also many conflicts about appearances that can be avoided by leaving them unspecified. Perhaps more importantly, projects can become bogged down in lengthy discussions about process because no one individual has sufficient capital (of any sort) to command the authority to resolve intractable disputes.

In the *Failing Upwards* album, I was paying the musicians from my own pocket and the power relationships relating to that kind of 'session player' social contract are pretty well established for professional musicians. That contract is really about paying the musician to relinquish creative control over their performance: to allow me to edit freely. It is a complicated negotiation that involves the musician giving up some of their power over which performances (or fragments of performances) enter the public domain but also, more and more frequently with contemporary editing techniques, it can involve the musician allowing the timing, dynamics and pitch of their performance to be altered and yet still be presented to the public as theirs. Even back in 1969 when these editing techniques were much less powerful, after the original *Bitches Brew* sessions, Joe Zawinal failed to recognize his own playing on the record:

'I didn't really like the sessions at the time', Zawinul reminisced. 'I didn't think they were exciting enough. But a short while later I was at the CBS offices, and a secretary was playing this incredible music. It was really smoking. So I asked her, "Who the hell is this?" And she replied, "It's that Bitches Brew thing." I thought, Damn, that's great'.

(Tingen, 2001)

But what happens when the response is 'Damn, that's terrible' and your name is on it?

9.4 Translation and distortion

The notion of gatekeepers was mentioned earlier in relation to communication and the transmission of knowledge in the form of an awareness of affordances is central to the ideas of learning and influence in this model. Each set of experiences through which the schema in which an understanding of affordances is embodied is unique and, as such, the schema is slightly different in the 'new' individual than in the 'old'. In short, as Callon (1986) says in relation to the translation of knowledge between participants in actor network theory, the very process of transmission necessarily changes and distorts the knowledge. The translation of information to a new actor from one or more existing actors is, through this process of change and distortion, also one of the drivers for creativity and novelty. As Moore (2012, pp. 215–58) discusses in relation to semiotics, there is not a binary distinction between the idea of a particular form of meaning being encoded into a musical sign and the idea that meaning is therefore arbitrary and could be different for every listener. The model of embodied cognition and ecological perception that I have been employing, suggests that the nature and commonality of the human body will encourage many similar forms of interpretation from people who are embodied in similar physical forms. It also suggests that none will be exactly the same: that every process of communication is also a process of distortion. However, those distortions are not random and, as the term used in Actor Network Theory – 'translation' – suggests, they are actively created through interaction with existing schema and that process of translation involves both bottom-up or **inductive** connections being made between this new experience and similar existing experience, and top-down or **deductive** associations made between this new experience and existing schema that share some characteristics and not others. The active nature of this process of translation will produce some connections that are **automatic** and **subconscious** and others that are the **conscious** creation of new metaphors or conceptual blending.

In the *Failing Upwards* album, one of the key ways in which I can document and represent these processes of translation and distortion is to map my intentions and the way that I communicated them to the musicians – by using my production diary and the videos that I have – onto the sonic outputs – both their raw responses from the recording session files and the ways in which I have decided to edit them afterwards. There is, then, a dual process of translation: how the musicians turned my instructions / comments and the influence of the guide tracks into a performance, and how I then responded to those performances in the editing process. This, in turn, can be used to discuss how the quality judgements leading to the aesthetic choices in each of the pieces emerged from the process.

Both of the terms, translation and distortion, imply that there is some kind of original message or signal that is translated or distorted and, therefore, that the translation or distortion is in some way 'lesser' than the original. Interpretation would probably be a more suitable term for these types of process but it is a word that is loaded with baggage in musical practice. Indeed, to 'interpret' also carries the connotation of something subsidiary that emerges from an original text. Thus, before moving on to the last chapter and attempting to draw some general conclusions, it does make sense that the last point to be made is that we have to remember that words are merely tools in our research. They are a part of our theoretical 'as if' which was the starting point of the book. This is even more important in a world of research about making music: wherever we can, we should be using representations of music and musical practice to make our arguments rather than language.

10

Some conclusions

As we have seen, Practical Musicology is based on two defining principles that are separate from the theoretical model I have outlined in this book. Firstly, if we are researching how we can 'do music better' and we recognize that 'better' is a jointly individual and cultural construct, the research needs to include the question of how those judgements are made. That requires that we study how they emerge out of the creative process and what kinds of principles they are founded on. Secondly, musical practices involve a lot of tacit knowledge – not least about quality judgements – and the process of effectively sharing the research results should reflect that. There is no guarantee that language is going to be the most effective medium for the communication of that knowledge. The development of appropriate tools for the documentation and representation of that knowledge is going to be part of the ongoing research process. However, returning to the theoretical model, I am proposing it because I believe it provides a useful set of tools relating to conducting research based on those two defining principles. This concluding chapter starts with some reflections on these two defining principles. Drawing together some of the themes from the book, the rest of this chapter discusses what the cognitive mechanisms necessary for *musicking* are and how they might have developed. It will also examine how the same types of thought processes can be used across a broad range of musical traditions and be expressed through a broad range of technologies and cultures.

10.1 Aesthetics and new knowledge

The four types of new knowledge that were outlined in Chapter 2 and the four modes of aesthetic appreciation which emerged throughout the rest of the book are central to the idea of Practical Musicology because they embody the goal of studying how to 'do music better' which is at its core. By way of a reminder:

Four types of new knowledge:

1. The relationship between problem-solving and technical skill
2. The relationship between the development and emergence of quality judgements and methods
3. The complex aesthetic relationship between the expected and the unexpected
4. The mechanisms for creating metaphors relating theory to artistic, pragmatic or activist practice

Four modes of aesthetic appreciation:

1. The appreciation of 'correct' or 'expert' action through a schema
2. The intentional and expert variation of a schema
3. The intensity or efficacy with which a metaphor conveys an intended narrative
4. The appreciation of the elegance of the metaphor

I realize that the reduction of aesthetics to these seemingly mundane criteria might seem to belittle or ignore the feelings of wonder, joy, beauty and awe (and a whole gamut of others) that we can experience through music. I see these as the mechanisms through which those feelings can be triggered. The reasons why these mechanisms trigger these feelings are, I would venture to suggest, the remit of both musicology and Practical Musicology. The question of how an audience has responded is, as I have stated, a question for the 'what happened?' approach of musicology while the question of how the practitioner was trying to make it happen is a question for Practical Musicology. Of course, there is common ground and a blurred boundary and one can imagine a Practical Musicology study by an audience member that explores the potential for 'better' listening experiences. The important point, and the reason I embarked on the project, is that music research is not sufficiently covering the subject areas that are currently encountered in music pedagogy. It is not only Ewell's (2019) point that we need music theory that encompasses the whole range of music traditions and styles but also that we need to recognize that the 'performative turn' (Cook, 2002) in music theory needs to embrace aesthetics in both a practical and inclusive manner.

Returning to the Fantasy Supervision League, if I was supervising Japanese Dubstep DJ and producer, Takeaki Maruyama aka Goth-Trad, I would suggest exploring the interface between those two roles and the ways in which exclusivity acts as part of the aesthetic. For example, if there are six DJs playing a Back to Chill party in Tokyo, how is your set structured and why? What is the importance of dropping your own tracks and tracks that are not available publicly? How does the aesthetic narrative of your DJ set work and how can you use documentation to extract some features that afford sharable new knowledge about how it works? Using a process of hypothetical or real substitution, can you identify a range of functions that can be performed by tracks and which features are important in those functions?

10.2 Methodology and methods

A vital feature of our defining question – how to 'do music better' – is the issue of representing and explaining something which is substantially non-verbal. When we stick with conventional text-based publishing platforms we are indeed faced with the problems of 'dancing about architecture' or 'knitting about football'. As I outlined in Chapter 2 and, hopefully, have elucidated throughout the book, our methodology is determined by our research question and the type of answers we expect to receive. Answers about how to do something non-verbal are likely to be best presented non-verbally. Clearly, then, as academic publishing moves into a 'post-printing' phase, we have to develop publishing formats that balance text with other ways of representing information and narrative. We also have to take on the challenge of learning how to express ideas through these media. The technicalities are being made more transparent as production and post-production software and website design software take the 'heavy lifting' off the user's shoulders. We do, however, have to understand how the structure of arguments and narratives can be made effectively through these media. And they have to be not just usable but also searchable. How do you index a video or website presentation of practice research where the content might be mostly visual? In addition, electronic content with hyperlinks takes us into the realms of non-linear formats and it is only a short hop, step and a jump to computer game architecture and interactive and 'intelligent' forms of data and research presentation. Of course, these are problems for the academic world as a whole but, given the nature of the discipline, studies of and through practice – including Practical Musicology – are going to be at the forefront of these changes and need to be involved in these questions of research governance and administration. We need to be able to represent the physical attributes of phenomena in time and space in various different ways but we also need to represent relationships, connectivity, causality and our subjective internal narratives.

10.3 The four themes

Now, having talked through those two defining principles of Practical Musicology, I want to turn to the theoretical model that I have outlined through this book. How can we draw together the four themes mentioned in the Chapter 2 after all this discussion? Rather than simply trying to summarize the various points that have been made throughout the book, I want to discuss each of the themes in turn in a broader context of how they fit into Practical Musicology. As a reminder, they are:

1. The importance of **convergence** and **divergence** as a basic structuring concept in human thought and culture
2. The way that our perception and interpretation of **restriction** and **affordance** shape our activity in and understanding of the world
3. A categorical distinction between three types of thought: **automatic** activity like empathy, learned **subconscious** activity, and calculated **conscious** activity
4. Our capacity for the **schematic representation** of phenomena by re-casting something complex in a simplified or distilled form based on a limited set of categories, features or activities

All of these themes are based on the concept of thought processes as an iterative and interactive process of perception and action. Light hits my eye and stimulates a neural response (perception) but my eye also moves (action) and the light changes again – but when I move my eye I also perceive the feeling of moving the muscles. In time, as an infant, I learn to distinguish aspects of perception that are the feeling of moving and those which are environmental. I learn, for example how a person's shape changes on my retina as they move and how their shape changes when I move and they stay still (because of perspective). That learning process is driven by the goals that are embodied in the salience network – both basic physiological motivations such as hunger and thirst and the more complex human motivations involved in relieving the stress that comes from an unresolved interpretation about our current experience. The complex patterns of perception and action experience in the brain slowly resolve into schema in which repeated common features of experience (perception and action) become flagged as likely to achieve some goal. This is the inductive process I have discussed extensively throughout the book whereby repeated and rewarded patterns produce the *habitus* of our behaviour.

In situations where our immediate experience suggests that we cannot achieve a particular goal, we also have the deductive process driven by the central executive network whereby we can explore schema from the 'top' – working backwards from the goal. There are several ways this can work. We can look at schema associated with the goal we want to achieve and identify a context which led to its achievement in the past. Then we can look for schema which have led from something like our current experience to something like that context in which the goal was achievable. This is the idea of carving out a sequence of sub-goals which will eventually achieve the main goal. We can also look for versions of this in ways that are further removed from this process. We can look for schema which involve fewer characteristics than those we have previously experienced as necessary or which have achieved a context in which fewer characteristics than those that are desirable. For example, I usually go home by bus but there are no buses running. I could travel that bus route by some other means and achieve that goal. I could try walking but it would take me a long time. If that is not an acceptable solution I might look for other solutions that share some characteristics with the bus – take a taxi? No money. Steal a bicycle? My mother taught me not to steal stuff. Try to hitch hike? This is the world of the conceptual blend (Fauconnier and Turner, 2003) – of mapping features from one schema onto features of another to create a temporary hybrid schema that has the potential to achieve a goal. A temporary hybrid that might get tagged as successful and become permanent or might get tagged as highly unpleasant and stressful.

As the deductive process gets further removed from the original goal, we get further into the realm of lateral thinking. While being a similar process of conceptual blending, the features that the schema have in common become fewer or the achievement of the goal has to be reconceptualized. Thus, I might realize that it would be necessary for me to stay the night in the place where the buses are not running and the goal of getting home is subdivided between a temporary alternative place to sleep and a delayed journey until the morning when the buses will be running again. Then I have a new problem to solve: finding places that fit into the category of places to sleep and deciding which is the best option. And the notion of category is defined in terms of what a phenomenon affords. We put things in categories because they have features in common which afford something similar enough in each instance to be classified as 'the same'. Remembering back to our definition of a schema as a complex pattern of perception and action experiences, even if a category is something as seemingly disconnected from affording action as, for example, shape or colour, our perception of its properties is determined by our experience of how those perceptions change as we move or as it moves. Something that is circular very rarely projects a circular image on my retina and my understanding of circles is mostly made up of how the oval shapes they project on my retina change shape and size as I move.

In order to scale up this model from the individual to the social, we have to think about commonalities of perception, action and interpretation. Social constructions arise from agreements about interpretation and shared activity. In Douglas Hofstadter's *Gödel, Escher and Bach* (Hofstadter, 1979) he imagines an erudite anteater having complex philosophical conversations with an ants' nest while simultaneously eating individual ants. This metaphor of a complex system made of simple components producing the appearance of a large-scale intelligence might be a little disturbing when it is used as a metaphor for the brain but is a familiar metaphor on the social level: the United States is addicted to low gasoline prices, the middle classes are rebelling about the tax system, women are not prepared to put up with this any longer. We can discuss the social using metaphors based on these same cognitive features using the idea that we can identify consensus and commonality. Of course, general statements such as those above suggest unanimous agreement while being based on assumptions about statistical majorities – more of the 'as if'. Generalizations are useful but they also have to be justifiable and evidence-based.

This provides us with a way of thinking about problems – musical or otherwise – based on the theoretical 'as if' of embodied and ecological cognition and a metaphorical extension to the social level. We can create a schematic representation of a musical 'problem' or challenge in terms of goals and sub-goals, the schema that achieve them, the features (or invariant properties) of the schema that afford particular goals or sub-goals. We can also then engage in various levels of deductive thought that can suggest connections between schema, invariant properties, affordances and goals and we can extrapolate that out to the interpersonal level. This can then be built into strategies. Given that as a general model for thinking about how we might 'do music better', let us now discuss those themes in more detail.

10.3.1 Convergence and divergence

If we do think about a musical challenge through this form of schematic representation, then we can also discuss our experience in terms of how it converges with or diverges from these goals, schema, perceptions, activities, categories, invariant properties and affordances. This has obvious connections with the theory of cognitive dissonance (Festinger, 1957; McGrath, 2017) whereby individuals seek to deal with conflicting or 'dissonant' thoughts by changing their mind to remove the dissonance or by minimizing the importance of it. We can see how this relates to the goal of resolving interpretations. From an individual psychological perspective it relates to how new experience relates to previous experience and can, as mentioned above, relate to goals, schema, perceptions, activities, categories, invariant properties and affordances. On the social level it can relate to how one diverges from or converges with social norms – agreed similarities in a social grouping. This convergence and divergence can be voluntary or involuntary, inscribed or ascribed and temporary or permanent.

The two related topics of shared/unshared knowledge and belonging/not belonging are a starting point for ideas about convergence and divergence from which many sub-themes emerge. These can relate to our position in the contextual areas of tradition/style, various forms of identity, the use of technology, the value of music and the uses of music. They can relate to how our creativity relates to existing musical activity and the way we work with expectations. They can relate to the micro-levels of musical activity – from repetition and entrainment to theme and variation. As evidenced by many of the examples on the website,[1] this structuring principle works simultaneously as a way of representing research 'data' and as an analytical tool.

I have discussed categories in terms of schema. Certain aspects or invariant properties of a phenomenon are experienced as 'the same' or convergent and are therefore categorized together. When we are exploring highly complex categorical connectivity such as forms of expression that use intertextuality, the ways in which various features converge and diverge are an important tool for parallel processes of representing knowledge and analysing it. It can also be used in analyses that are focused on the ways in which categories can be diverged from. Thus, practices might be explored in terms of how they balance the use of skill in an existing field against innovation and change or how roles

---

[1] http://www.c21mp.org/practical-musicology/

and identities might be performed in terms of convergence and divergence with categories – the type of person who … Similarly on a group level our research might be concerned with convergence and divergence from group norms – types of entrainment denoting discipline and/or conformity, types of composition or arrangement denoting relationships and hierarchies, etc. I discussed how belonging and not belonging can be represented in various ways through musical practices and these obviously can produce the potential for metaphorical interpretations as well. Responding and not responding provide similar representational and analytical potential for researchers. One final example is the way that convergence and divergence can be used to examine power, authority and judgement. Expressions of power and authority are mostly based on social contracts rather than physical coercion. Participants in such a contract align themselves in relation to some notional authority because of the positive or negative affordances of convergence or divergence.

10.3.2 Restriction and affordance

Gibson's ecological approach (1979) is built upon the notion of affordance and its corollary, restriction. Otto von Bismarck called politics 'the art of the possible'[2] to distinguish it from idealism and that is one way we can think about affordances. At any given moment we perceive the world in terms of our immediate affordances for action and interpretation based on our previous experience. That, in itself, is a process of hypothetical thought, albeit one in which the hypothesis is usually well supported by the evidence of our life. I walk around, for example, based on the hypothesis that the ground in front of me is going to support my weight – usually a pretty good hypothesis but not always. However, we also continuously make less well-supported hypotheses about the affordances of certain actions – trusting politicians for example. Goals that are important to us or dangers that we really want to avoid can make us more reckless – basing decisions on flimsier evidence. So whilst all thought is essentially hypothetical, the affordances that we consider available to ourselves at any given moment are based on the inductive and deductive processes we mentioned above: looking for the invariant properties that have afforded our goals in the past and using them as a guide to behaviour.

---

[2] Bismarck is reported to have made the observation in conversation with Meyer von Waldeck on 11 August 1867. See for example: https://www.oxfordreference.com/view/10.1093/acref/9780191826719.001.0001/q-oro-ed4-00008442 [accessed 10 October 2021]

I have explored in Chapters 3 and 4 how framing the context of musical practices in terms of affordances can provide connections between quite disparate theoretical frameworks. We can think of musical traditions, styles and minoritarian cultures or communities as patterns of affordance and restriction. Obviously this provides quite a pragmatic approach for studies focused on how to do something – framing it in terms of what is possible at any given moment in any given situation – but also provides potential for questioning the authority of social construction. Social construction and ideologies of research and practice questions are notions of 'the possible' but quite often that notion of the possible is based on convention and habits rather than what is actually possible. It thus also provides a way of developing a systematic aesthetic of resistance to a set of socially constructed affordances that reside in a particular context or, conversely, a systematic aesthetic of newly constructed affordances that relate to a particular ideology. Similarly, studies that aim to look at the ergonomics of authority – of what constitutes effective leadership in various contexts – might also use notions of affordance, perhaps in relation to the three types of thought.

Returning to the Fantasy Supervision League, if I were supervising a practice PhD by conductor, Marin Alsop (despite her Honorary Doctorate from Yale), she could explore this notion of the ergonomics of leadership. This could work from an experimental exploration of the authority of particular gestures and demeanours, through the connection between the development of particular schema for the phrasing of dynamics over time, to the psychology of establishing leadership in a short-term guest conductor role. Of course, this embodied knowledge is exactly the sort of thing that she conveys through her work in education with masterclasses already.[3]

Indeed, thinking of schema as probabilistic maps of affordance for both action and interpretation is a useful avenue for investigation. Those types of probabilistic maps also provide a basis for thinking about intuition and spontaneity. The more well-established the pathways of a schema become, the less need is there for the central executive network of the brain to get involved. In some ways that feels like the definition of the difference between subconscious and conscious thought but it is not clear what the difference might be between control and awareness. There do seem to be a range of monitoring systems in the default mode network that border on the definition of consciousness. By describing schema in terms of both action and interpretation we can also bring in

---

[3] For example, this online Q&A session with students from the Royal Northern College of Music in the UK: https://www.youtube.com/watch?v=QzNeOB-ofpk [accessed 14 October 2021]

the concept of judgement. The notion of salience – of how important or relevant something is in a particular context – is, as I have described, based on goals which are, in turn, based on the positive and negative reward system. While there are clear ways in which many goals – such as hunger, thirst, temperature, sex drive – can be embodied in schema, but I have also discussed the mechanism by which unresolved interpretations create stress (Jepma et al., 2012; Canestrari et al., 2018). Discussing curiosity and creativity in terms of matching current invariant properties relating to our situation with potential affordances for interpretation provides a mechanism for talking about judgement as well. But, of course, in a social context, judgement and value require communal 'critical mass' of some sort so that the judgement has some impact in the world. We can discuss the authority or power of particular judgements in terms of their potential for inhibiting or affording actions and interpretations.

10.3.3 Three types of thought

Although it is tempting to think of the automatic, subconscious and conscious modes of thought as a hierarchy of sophistication, life is not as simple as that. Forms of musical entrainment that use both automatic and subconscious learned schema can be highly sophisticated, and conscious modes of thought can be making very simple and banal connections between and within existing schema. For the most part, Practical Musicology is going to be concerned with producing new knowledge about the sophisticated, difficult to acquire or achieve aspects of all three modes.

As I have discussed, a phenomenon like rhythmic entrainment, when studied empirically, is often reduced to some simple, idealized version – like studying our ability to tap our hands or feet in time with a click. Knowledge like that may be useful in some contexts for musicians but there is also a lot of practical knowledge that we can gain from studies about the nuances of different types of musical engagement and how, for example, rhythmic entrainment can be complicated by phenomena like syncopation and hocket or by an intention to suggest an attitude or feeling through entrained activity. It is important, therefore, that Practical Musicology extends beyond exploring conscious, conceptual structuring principles through creative practice (e.g. Impett, 2019) and engages with musical problems that embrace Ewell's (2019) challenge to broaden its scope. This requires Practical Musicology to include features such as groove, flow, improvisation, ornamentation, virtuosity and heteroglossia or intertextuality and these require us to represent all three modes of thought.

Val Del Prete, an Italian living in London, already has a PhD in neuroscience but has carved out a different career as a songwriter – topliner and vocal producer – for a range of K-Pop artists including Astro, Aespa and Twice. If, in the Fantasy Supervision League, I were supervising a second, practice PhD, I would suggest exploring the functionality of the song and the ways in which it contributes to the broader multimedia context of a Korean idol narrative. In interview,[4] she says:

> K-Pop leaves a lot of space for … experimentation blending different styles. I also love the fact that, when writing, I have to take into account the choreographies, incorporating musical elements that have their own 'visual counterpart' to create a multi-sensory experience for the listener. Sometimes, when I write a k-pop song I feel like creating a whole mini-opera with several sections intertwined.

The aesthetic of song writing, therefore, could be explored through all three types of thought and musical engagement through the prism of functionality: through its relationship to the broader career trajectory of the artist it is aimed at.

There is a body of work, particularly driven by academics working in popular music practice and music technology, where the need to teach 'how to' is being addressed. However, this sector – in universities, private vocational educators and the informal YouTube or LinkedIn Learning-style of provider – focuses overwhelmingly on a kind of detached apprenticeship approach. Practitioners whose expertise lies in producing (hopefully) excellent examples of practice and much more rarely lies in educating have created a training-based industry reliant 'how to do what I do' rather than 'how to understand what I do' so that you can do it better. This, of course, is also the model upon which the classical conservatoire system was predicated for both performance and composition: a classical musician's CV usually mentions who they studied with as well as where. On the other hand, higher-level jazz education has been accused of being a sausage factory process where dozens of musicians who have learned the same 'rules' emerge from college all sounding the same (Collier, 1994). My argument is that this process of producing 'clones' of particular forms of practice, whether individual or generic, and trusting that the musicians will develop their own 'voice' once they have this grounding, is not the best way to approach music education. We need to think creatively about how we ask students to approach

---

[4] https://www.panorama.it/italian-kpop-val-dal-prete-2655249307 [accessed 14 October 2021]

schema formation – the bottom-up acquisition of technical skill – and the top-down process of conceptual blending and problem-solving. And in order to think creatively about this we need a body of relevant research. Schema acquisition can be approached as a strategic and/or aesthetic process by getting the student to consider it as such. Creativity can also be top-down or bottom-up: the conscious creation of new metaphorical connections between schema or the recognition of a 'good' connection that emerges unplanned.

10.3.4 Schematic representation

The Cambridge dictionary definition of schematic is 'showing the main form and features of something' while the Oxford dictionary is more succinct: 'symbolic and simplified'. Using the term 'schema' to describe the patterns of neural activity in which knowledge is embodied reflects the notion that only the pathways that are repeatedly present or necessary are reinforced and therefore included in a schema. Representational systems are, in this sense, constructs that allow a schema to exist outside the brain. They are mirror images of the way we think. They provide us with ways of representing these patterns of invariant properties and affordances. And because they exist as separate entities as well as representing patterns of thought, we can judge them in the two different ways outlined above in the modes of aesthetic appreciation. We can judge the knowledge embodied and represented and we can judge the form of the representation.

We should also bear in mind that musicology uses schematic representations to analyse something that is itself a schematic representation. We can consider theory as a way of representing some knowledge about experience 'as if' a symbolic and simplified version were the truth. But at the same time, the musical activity that we are seeking to understand is representing some aspect of life and experience 'as if' the symbolic and simplified aural experience were 'the truth' about some emotional or energy-based narrative. There may be times when the musical representation itself can be more powerful than a theoretical, language-based representation but, in order for us to see this as research, we will need to reframe that musical representation in ways that illustrate the ways it can suggest interpretation. As I have discussed in relation to the methods of Practical Musicology, those methods might involve changing the subject-position in relation to time or space, comparing it with other examples or deconstructing it in some way. In addition to the processes of reflection or inflection of the practitioner's internal narrative, these forms of schematic representation allow both documentation and analysis.

If we consider music as a representational system then it represents through an audio or audiovisual metaphor. Types of activity (and the sound of that activity) act as a cipher for some other activity which in turn suggests alternate possible interpretations of that sound or activity. Embodied cognition suggests that we think of music as the sound of somebody (or some bodies) doing something (with or without some material tools) somewhere. That produces the affordance of some literal interpretation – from the energy of the activity or the shape of the gesture for instance – and some metaphorical interpretation – some individual or cultural resonance with your life for example. And, as I have mentioned, we appreciate the aesthetics of the representation as well as of that which is represented. Another aspect of embodied cognition that I mentioned earlier is that my understanding of a representation is based on my previous experience. People who paint understand painting differently to those who do not, people who play music extensively experience music differently from those who do not and people who play the trumpet hear trumpet music differently than those who do not. This is an extension of the idea that although we humans all have a great deal in common because of the shared experience of inhabiting the human form, we all have slightly different schema that language labels as 'the same'. When I hear the sound of bagpipes, it will conjure up certain images in my mind that are similar to yours and others which are different.

I will end this section with three examples of the ways in which we can explore practice through ideas about schematic representation. For many of us, a particular piece of music takes on an additional dimension of meaning by being associated with some important aspect of our life. For the most part, though musical representation is hypothetical, the emotional narrative does not relate to a 'real' unresolved issue in our lives. Indeed, some researchers have suggested that various forms of art allow us to rehearse our emotions and feelings (see Juslin and Sloboda, 2001): there is no 'real' stress, just the pleasure of solving the interpretation. Referring back to the Tony Sheldon example in Chapter 3, we can also see that performing a metaphor for an emotional narrative can be done with various levels of reference to 'real life'. Sheldon was 'tearing himself apart' emotionally night after night and Pender's (2016) response is that he should not be doing that with the right training. That, of course, leads us to the question of what is the right extent or form of emotional connection between a musical representation of such a narrative and the performer's own experience?

Another important question about representational systems in music – in particular, the formal language that is used to represent – relates to questions of innovation, expertise and creativity. While there is no hard and fast line, we can distinguish between the aesthetics of a newly created metaphor or representational system rather than simply a new representation in an existing system. Even innovators who can be seen as having produced seismic shifts in practice like Arnold Schoenberg, Ornette Coleman or Public Enemy retained some elements of earlier practices: Schoenberg and Coleman retained the instrumental timbres and ensemble formations of their established traditions and changed the rules of tonality and form. Public Enemy used sampling to change some of the ways that influence and quotation were used, and to change some of the traditions of vocal performance while maintaining many other features of rap and popular music.

Finally, techniques that demarcate some aspect of a musical performance as being exemplary in some way – a theme that is to be varied, a call that is to be responded to – require it to be understood schematically. Some features become invariant properties and others become variable. The invariant properties become the simplified frame around which variations and ornaments can be explored. In many instances, the ways in which variation happens are determined by affordances embodied in the 'rules' of the schema. They become intuitive or spontaneous pathways that seem to explore themselves rather than requiring constant decisions. Other performers – Thelonius Monk in relation to jazz improvisation or Joni Mitchell in relation to song writing, for example – deliberately seek out ways of re-shaping the representational system. Both Monk and Mitchell play with the 'rules' of melodic shape and phrasing while maintaining the integrity of other parts of the representational systems of music in which they worked.

10.4 Influence

The four themes discussed above have woven themselves throughout this book and each of them relates to the mechanisms of influence in important ways. Influence is an essential part of musical practice and works on a whole range of levels from the micro to the macro. My actions can influence or be influenced by the moment-to-moment actions of other musicians but my whole philosophy of music making can be influenced by people, things or ideas in ways that can be traced through my whole career. The mechanisms of influence and the ways in which they propagate through practice suggest the potential for studies of musical Butterfly Effects (Lorenz, 2000) as well as of more direct and immediate forms of influence. And, as I discussed in Chapter 7 and elsewhere, the people, things and ideas that influence us do not have to be musical or even arts related. Indeed, the types of influence that relate to character traits probably have at least as much if not more weight in determining our musical character than the more straightforward influence of our musical training.

The typology of eight mechanisms of influence in Theoretical Interlude 5 all relate to the ways in which schema can be altered – by physical force, by argument, by demonstration and by creating a context in which the person being influenced would choose to change their schema. In essence, influence is about causing someone (or choosing yourself in response to some stimulus) to make some feature of a schema convergent with someone else's or divergent from what it currently is. I can be influenced to adopt some practice or interpretation that is new to me or I can be influenced to abandon some existing practice or interpretation. We can also think of that as seeking to acquaint someone or be made acquainted with a new set of restrictions or affordances such that they adopt them. And influence can work through any of the three forms of thought. Finally, given that we have equated the schema of cognitive activity with the notion of schematic representation, influence certainly relates to that fourth theme.

If Alex Camargo, the vocalist and bass player from Brazilian thrash metal band Krisian, were to join the ranks of the Fantasy Supervision League, the connection between external influence and quality judgements would be a clear direction in which to go. His thirty-year career in a band with his two brothers, their original influences of German and American bands Sodom, Kreator, Morbid Angel and Slayer, and the influence of touring with American, Swedish, Austrian, Greek. Polish and Danish bands in the intervening years provide plenty of scope for this. One fan wrote on the YouTube comments for the 2018 track 'Scourge of the Enthroned' that 'What's truly impressive about Krisiun is how they're managed to keep the same sound all these years but every album still manages to sound fresh!' I would therefore ask Camargo to reflect on that notion of continuity by experimenting with what would not sound 'right' as well as producing experiments that were pastiches of the most important bands that have influenced him. Can we start to identify markers of both quality and style? And what kinds of generalization can we extract from that?

10.5 Practical Musicology

How then should I summarize Practical Musicology?

Firstly, I will return to the motivation for writing this book. Musicology is living in 'interesting times' just as we all are. The study of and through practice has been reflected in the 'performative turn' (Cook, 2002) and the development of practice research, artistic research and autoethnography (Borgdorff, 2012; Adams, Holman Jones and Ellis, 2015; Bulley and Sahin, 2021). At the same time we have heard Ewell's (2019) provocation that musicology cannot become more inclusive simply by including a wider variety of repertoire, it also has to adopt and develop a theoretical frame that is similarly inclusive. When Middleton (1993) was writing about his tripartite model of musical gesture, he concluded:

> What I would suggest is that these three areas - gesture, connotation, argument - operate in different repertories in diverse ratios and interrelationships; and analysis needs to reflect that. Within musicology, gestural analysis is the poor relation. For historical and cultural reasons, popular songs offer ideal material for starting to put that neglect to rights.
>
> (Middleton, 1993, p. 189)

Within this theoretical framework I have re-jigged gesture, connotation and argument as the automatic, subconscious and conscious modes of musical engagement. The precise terminology of our theoretical 'as if' is less important than the fact that the toolbox of 'classical' musicology is skewed towards understanding explicit, conceptual aspects of musical structure. Of course, that was more appropriate when the music being examined had been created using those kinds of 'design principles'. I would certainly not claim that the theoretical model I have outlined here provides an unproblematic 'solution' in the quest for an un-skewed theoretical frame but I do think it provides a 'way in' for thinking critically about a broad range of musical styles and traditions.

A second factor in the argument for Practical Musicology relates to the point I made in the section on *Three Types of Thought* above about the relationship between current research and 'how to do music'. When I started teaching music technology and popular music practice in the late 1990s and early 2000s, the reading lists were still relatively threadbare. With a few important exceptions, popular music studies was mostly focused on sociology, history and cultural theory. Scholars who did write musical analyses – such as Richard Middleton, Allan Moore, Philip Tagg and Walter Everett – did so from an audience perspective. In music technology, the choice was mostly between historical accounts and technical descriptions of the technology. Will Moylan (1992) provided one of the few theoretically rigorous texts on how to 'do' mixing but that, and the majority of the texts that followed focused on either a craft-style aesthetic of industry 'good practice' (e.g. Case, 2007; Izhaki, 2008) or descriptions of the techniques used by particular iconic individuals (e.g. Owsinski, 1999; Massey, 2000). While, particularly in the world of music technology but also in popular music performance and song writing, there is more research and writing that explores creative practice emerging all the time, theorizing aesthetics is rarely addressed explicitly.

This relates very closely with the academic and research world's long and complicated dance with the notion of subjectivity. Subjectivity is often considered a dirty word within research circles but it is a vital component of all research, not just the arts and humanities. The most basic question of what to study is always a subjective value judgement. Which of the world's problems are more important than others? Which are more solvable? How much would the research cost and what would the balance between costs and benefits be? How do we balance between, expense and value for money, importance and solvability? These are all entirely subjective value judgements which drive research governance at all levels and in all disciplines. The fact that social scientists and mathematicians have invented tools such as Cost Benefit Analysis and Fuzzy Logic does not mean that the subjective has been made objective. It does, however, point to the frequently ignored idea that subjectivity can be subjected to standards of rigour and evidence. Making the criteria for a subjective decision explicit and considering the question in as much detail and breadth as possible provide the framework for high-quality subjective research. The history of research in the arts and humanities has involved the subjective process of canon formation in which the aesthetic judgements of quality have been dressed up as an academic process (see Goehr, 1994). That process has come under increasing scrutiny but has also raised the scare mongering response that the logical outcome is that all music (or art) is of equal quality or value. That is, of course, only a logical outcome if you consider that quality and value are objective properties. If, like Moore's (2002) definition of authenticity, we consider them to be socially constructed, ascribed, subjective qualities then we return to the question of whose estimations of value are more important or numerous. And that is a question that goes beyond the scope of this book.

Aesthetics do not spring fully formed into the world. Their development in both individuals and communities is a process that is forever changing. By describing Practical Musicology as the study of how to 'do music better', I am not suggesting that musicology should be telling us what 'better' is – it has been doing that implicitly for a long time. Instead I want a musicology that explains how aesthetics emerge and practitioners embody those aesthetics in both their practice and their musical outputs. As this process is likely to emerge mostly from practice research where the practitioners reflect on the development of their aesthetics and judgements of quality, the research is likely to mostly be based on case studies. However, those case studies provide individual examples rather than sharable knowledge and there has to be a further process of extrapolating some more general but nuanced theory about how aesthetics emerge, quality judgements are made and how aesthetics tend to become embodied in practices and musical outputs. I would like to see a programme of experiments into the form that this new knowledge will take – hopefully leading to a multimedia journal with that as a focus.

This notion of extrapolating generalized and sharable knowledge from practice research and artistic research takes us back to Peter Osborne's keynote contribution to the Postresearch Condition where one of his conclusions is that 'Critically significant contemporary art practices are not likely to be generated within, and certainly not out of, the current higher-educational art institutional situation' (Slager, 2021, p. 13). This seems predicated on the idea that research through artistic practice should be aimed and creating examples of good art rather than knowledge about how to create good art. As I suggested during the 2021 RMA conference discussion about the Bulley and Sahin (2021) report, it would make sense for higher education to develop a two-pronged approach to quality judgements. Many students and academics would prefer to focus on the creation of 'critically significant contemporary art' and it might make sense, if we have to live in a world guided by such metrics, to develop a system that judges professional esteem rather than research quality. That, however, is not my focus in this book. When judging the results of Practical Musicology it is the research that needs to be good. The music doesn't need to be although life is obviously better when it is.

Bibliography

Adams, T.E., Holman Jones, S.L. and Ellis, C. (2015) *Autoethnography*. New York: Oxford University Press.

Ainsworth, C. (2015) 'Sex Redefined', *Nature News*, 518(7539), p. 288.

Akrich, M. and Latour, B. (1992) 'A Summary of a Convenient Vocabulary for the Semiotics of Human and Nonhuman Assemblies', in Bijker, W.E. and Law, J. (eds) *Shaping Technology, Building Society: Studies in Sociotechnical Change*. Cambridge, MA: MIT Press, pp. 259–64.

Allen, G.E. (2001) 'Is a New Eugenics Afoot?', *Science*, 294(5540), pp. 59–61.

Araújo, M.V. and Hein, C.F. (2019) 'A Survey to Investigate Advanced Musicians' Flow Disposition in Individual Music Practice', *International Journal of Music Education*, 37(1), pp. 107–17.

Aska, A. (2017) *Introduction to the Study of Video Game Music*. Lulu.com.

Auslander, P. (1999) *Liveness: Performance in a Mediatized Culture*. Abingdon, Oxon: Taylor & Francis.

Auslander, P. (2016) 'Musical Persona: The Physical Performance of Popular Music', in Derek B. Scott (ed.) *The Ashgate Research Companion to Popular Musicology*. Indianapolis, IN: Routledge, pp. 321–34.

Baily, P.J. (2015) *War, Exile and the Music of Afghanistan: The Ethnographer's Tale*. Farnham, Surrey: Ashgate (SOAS Musicology Series).

Bakhtin, M.M. (1982) *Dialogic Imagination: Four Essays*. New edition. Austin, TX: University of Texas Press.

Bakrania, F. (2013) *Bhangra and Asian Underground: South Asian Music and the Politics of Belonging in Britain*. Durham, NC: Duke University Press.

Bar, M. (2009) 'A Cognitive Neuroscience Hypothesis of Mood and Depression', *Trends in Cognitive Science*, 13(11), pp. 456–63.

Barclay, R. (2011) 'Stradivarius Pseudoscience: The Myth of the Miraculous Musical Instrument', *Skeptic (Altadena, CA)*, 16(2), pp. 45–51.

Bayley, A. (2011) 'Ethnographic Research into Contemporary String Quartet Rehearsal', *Ethnomusicology Forum*, 20(3), pp. 385–411.

Bayley, A. and Heyde, N. (2017) 'Communicating through Notation: Michael Finnissy's Second String Quartet from Composition to Performance', *Music Performance Research*, 8, pp. 80–97.

Bear, M.F., Connors, B.W. and Paradiso, M.A. (2007) *Neuroscience*. Philadelphia, PA: Lippincott Williams & Wilkins (Neuroscience: Exploring the Brain).

Behr, A. (2010) *Group Identity: Bands, Rock and Popular Music*. PhD. University of Stirling.

Behr, A. (2015) 'Join Together with the Band: Authenticating Collective Creativity in Bands and the Myth of Rock Authenticity Reappraised', *Rock Music Studies*, 2(1), pp. 1–21.

Benjamin, W. (1969) 'The Work of Art in the Age of Mechanical Reproduction', in Arendt, H. (ed.) Harry Zohn (trans.) *Illuminations*. New York: Schocken, pp. 217–52.

Bernays, M. and Traube, C. (2011) 'Verbal Expression of Piano Timbre: Multidimensional Semantic Space of Adjectival Descriptors', in *Proceedings of the International Symposium on Performance Science (ISPS2011)*, European Association of Conservatoires (AEC) Utrecht, Netherlands, pp. 299–304.

Berridge, K.C. and Kringelbach, M.L. (2013) 'Neuroscience of Affect: Brain Mechanisms of Pleasure and Displeasure', *Current Opinion in Neurobiology*, 23(3), pp. 294–303. doi:10.1016/j.conb.2013.01.017.

Berridge, K.C. and Kringelbach, M.L. (2015) 'Pleasure Systems in the Brain', *Neuron*, 86(3), pp. 646–64. doi:10.1016/j.neuron.2015.02.018.

Birt, L. *et al.* (2016) 'Member Checking: A Tool to Enhance Trustworthiness or Merely a Nod to Validation?', *Qualitative Health Research*, 26(13), pp. 1802–11.

Blacking, J. (1974) *How Musical Is Man?* Seattle, WA: University of Washington Press.

Blagden, I. (1869) *The Cown of a Life*. London: Hurst and Blackett.

Blier-Caruthers, A. (2010) *Live Performance – Studio Recording: An Ethnographic and Analytical Study of Sir Charles Mackerras*. PhD. Kings College London.

Blier-Caruthers, A. (2011) 'From Stage to Studio (… and Back Again)', in *Performance Studies Network International Conference*, University of Cambridge. Available at: http://www.cmpcp.ac.uk/online%20resource%20Thursday/PSN2011_Blier-Carruthers.pdf (Accessed: 28 May 2012).

Boden, M. (1994) *Dimensions of Creativity*. Cambridge, MA: MIT Press.

Boden, M.A. (2004) *The Creative Mind: Myths and Mechanisms*. Abingdon, Oxon: Routledge.

Borgdorff, H. (2012) *The Conflict of the Faculties: Perspectives on Artistic Research and Academia*. Amsterdam: Leiden University Press.

Born, G. (2005) 'On Music Mediation: Ontology, Technology and Mediation', *Twentieth Century Music*, 2(1), pp. 7–36.

Born, G. (2010) 'For a Relational Musicology: Music and Interdisciplinarity, beyond the Practice Turn', *Journal of the Royal Musical Association*, 135(2), pp. 205–43.

Bourbon, A. and Zagorski-Thomas, S. (2017) 'The Ecological Approach to Mixing Audio: Agency, Activity and Environment in the Process of Audio Staging', *Journal on the Art of Record Production*, 11. Available at: http://arpjournal.com/the-ecological-approach-to-mixing-audio-agency-activity-and-environment-in-the-process-of-audio-staging/ (Accessed: 10 February 2018).

Bourdieu, P. (1986) *The Forms Of Capital*. Hoboken, NJ: Wiley Online Library.

Bourdieu, P. (1993) *The Field of Cultural Production*. New York: Columbia University Press.

Bowden, R. (2004) 'A Critique of Alfred Gell on "Art and Agency" [Corrected title: A Critique of Alfred Gell on Art and Agency]', *Oceania*. Edited by A. Gell, 74(4), pp. 309–24.

Brooks, W. (2021) *Experience Music Experiment: Pragmatism and Artistic Research*. Leuven: Leuven University Press (Orpheus Institute Series). Available at: https://books.google.be/books?id=TnA-EAAAQBAJ.

Brosch, T. *et al.* (2011) 'Additive Effects of Emotional, Endogenous, and Exogenous Attention: Behavioral and Electrophysiological Evidence', *Neuropsychologia*, 49(7), pp. 1779–87.

Bruford, B. (2018) *Uncharted: Creativity and the Expert Drummer*. Ann Arbor, MI: University of Michigan Press (Tracking Pop).

Bruford, W. (2015) *Making It Work: Creative Music Performance and the Western Kit Drummer*. PhD. University of Surrey. Available at: http://epubs.surrey.ac.uk/810288/1/Bruford%20Thesis.%20Version%20of%20Record.pdf (Accessed: 30 January 2017).

Bulley, J. and Sahin, O. (2021) *Practice Research – Report 1: What Is Practice Research? and Report 2: How Can Practice Research Be Shared?* London: PRAG-UK. Available at: https://doi.org/10.23636/1347 (Accessed: 1 August 2021).

Burnard, P. (2012) *Musical Creativities in Practice*. New York, NY: Oxford University Press.

Burns, L. and Lacasse, S. (2018) *The Pop Palimpsest: Intertextuality in Recorded Popular Music*. Ann Arbor, MI: University of Michigan Press (Tracking Pop).

Buskin, R. (2004) 'Classic Tracks: The Sex Pistols "Anarchy In The UK"', *Sound On Sound*. Available at: https://www.soundonsound.com/techniques/classic-tracks-sex-pistols-anarchy-uk (Accessed: 18 August 2021).

Butler, J. (1988) 'Performative Acts and Gender Constitution: An Essay in Phenomenology and Feminist Theory', *Theatre Journal*, 40(4), pp. 519–31.

Butler, J. (1990) 'Lana's "Imitation": Melodramatic Repetition and the Gender Performative', *Genders*, (9), pp. 1–18.

Butler, J. (2006) 'Imitation and Gender Insubordination', *Cultural Theory and Popular Culture: A Reader*, 1, pp. 255–374.

Calì, C. (2013) 'Gestalt Models for Data Decomposition and Functional Architecture in Visual Neuroscience', *Gestalt Theory*, 35(3), pp. 227–64.

Callon, M. (1986) 'Some Elements of a Sociology of Translation: Domestication of the Scallops and the Fishermen of St Brieuc Bay', in Law, J. (ed.) *Power, Action and Belief: A New Sociology of Knowledge?* London: Routledge, pp. 196–223.

Candela, A.G. (2019) 'Exploring the Function of Member Checking', *The Qualitative Report*, 24(3), pp. 619–28.

Canestrari, C. et al. (2018) 'Pleasures of the Mind: What Makes Jokes and Insight Problems Enjoyable', *Frontiers in Psychology*, 8(2297).

Capulet, E. and Zagorski-Thomas, S. (2017) 'Creating a Rubato Layer Cake: Performing and Producing Overdubs with Expressive Timing on a Classical Recording for Solo Piano', *Journal on the Art of Record Production* [Preprint], (11).

Carroll, J. (1998) 'Steven Pinker's Cheesecake for the Mind', *Philosophy and Literature*, 22(2), pp. 478–85.

Case, A.U. (2007) *Sound FX: Unlocking the Creative Potential of Recording Studio Effects*. Burlington, MA: Focal Press.

Chaiklin, S. and Lave, J. (1996) *Understanding Practice: Perspectives on Activity and Context*. Cambridge: Cambridge University Press (Learning in Doing: Social, Cognitive and Computational Perspectives).

Chand, G.B. et al. (2017) 'Interactions of the Salience Network and Its Subsystems with the Default-Mode and the Central-Executive Networks in Normal Aging and Mild Cognitive Impairment', *Brain Connectivity*, 7(7), pp. 401–12. doi:10.1089/brain.2017.0509.

Chen, A.C. et al. (2013) 'Causal Interactions between Fronto-Parietal Central Executive and Default-Mode Networks in Humans', *Proceedings of the National Academy of Sciences of the United States of America*, 110(49), pp. 19944–9. doi:10.1073/pnas.1311772110.

Chica, A.B., Bartolomeo, P. and Lupiáñez, J. (2013) 'Two Cognitive and Neural Systems for Endogenous and Exogenous Spatial Attention', *Behavioural Brain Research*, 237, pp. 107–23.

Clark, H.H. (1996) *Using Language*. Cambridge: Cambridge University Press.

Clarke, E.F. (1999) 'Subject Position and the Specification of Invariants in Music by Frank Zappa and P. J. Harvey', *Music Analysis*, 18(3), pp. 347–74.

Clarke, E.F. (2005) *Ways of Listening: An Ecological Approach to the Perception of Musical Meaning*. New York, NY: Oxford University Press, USA.

Clarke, E.F. and Doffman, M. (eds) (2017) *Distributed Creativity: Collaboration and Improvisation in Contemporary Music*. New York, NY: Oxford University Press (Studies in musical performance as creative practice).

Clarke, M., Dufeu, F. and Manning, P. (2015) 'An Interactive Simulation of John Chowning's Creative Environment for the Composition of Stria (1977)'. *Computer Simulation of Musical Creativity Study Day*, University of Huddersfield, 27 June. Available at: http://eprints.hud.ac.uk/id/eprint/27151/ (Accessed: 28 April 2021).

Clayton, M. (2007) *Music, Time and Place: Essays in Comparative Musicology*. Delhi, India: B. R. Rhythms.

Clayton, M. (2012) 'Comparing Music, Comparing Musicology', in Clayton, Martin, Middleton, Richard, and Herbert, Trevor (eds) *The Cultural Study of Music*. Abindon, Oxon: Routledge, pp. 108–17.

Colbert, S.D., Jones, D.A. and Vogel, S. (2020) *Race and Performance after Repetition*. Durham, NC: Duke University Press.

Colley, I. et al. (2020) 'The Influence of a Conductor and Co-performer on Auditory-Motor Synchronisation, Temporal Prediction, and Ancillary Entrainment in a Musical Drumming Task', *Human Movement Science*, 72, p. 102653.

Collier, G. (1994) 'The Churchill Report on Jazz Education in America', *Jazz Changes Magazine*, 1(1), pp. 1–44.

Collins, K. (2013) *Playing with Sound: A Theory of Interacting with Sound and Music in Video Games*. Cambridge, MA: MIT Press.

Cook, N. (2000) *Music: A Very Short Introduction*. Oxford: Oxford Paperbacks.

Cook, N. (2002) 'Epistemologies of Music Theory', in Christensen, T. (ed.) *The Cambridge History of Western Music Theory*. Cambridge: Cambridge University Press, pp. 78–105.

Cook, N. (2018) *Music as Creative Practice*. Oxford: Oxford University Press (Studies in musical performance as creative practice).

Cook, P. et al. (2013) 'A California Sea Lion (Zalophus californianus) Can Keep the Beat: Motor Entrainment to Rhythmic Auditory Stimuli in a Non Vocal Mimic', *Journal of Comparative Psychology*, 127(4), p. 412.

Coppier, Y. (2021) 'Absurd Sounds', *Journal of Artistic Research*, 23. Available at: https://www.researchcatalogue.net/view/820939/821145.

Crawford, R. (2020) 'Beyond the Dots on the Page: Harnessing Transculturation and Music Education to Address Intercultural Competence and Social Inclusion', *International Journal of Music Education*, 38(4), pp. 537–62.

Csikszentmihalyi, M. (1988) 'Society, Culture and Person: A Systems View of Creativity', in Sternberg, R. (ed.) *The Nature of Creativity: Contemporary Psychological Perspectives*. New York: Cambridge University Press, pp. 325–39.

Csikszentmihalyi, M. (1997) *Creativity: Flow and the Psychology of Discovery and Invention*. New York: HarperCollins.

Cumming, J. et al. (2017) 'Developing Imagery Ability Effectively: A Guide to Layered Stimulus Response Training', *Journal of Sport Psychology in Action*, 8(1), pp. 23–33. doi:10.1080/21520704.2016.1205698.

Custodero, L.A. (2005) 'Observable Indicators of Flow Experience: A Developmental Perspective on Musical Engagement in Young Children from Infancy to School Age', *Music Education Research*, 7(2), pp. 185–209.

Damasio, A. (2000) *The Feeling of What Happens: Body, Emotion and the Making of Consciousness*. New edition. New York, NY: Vintage.

Damasio, A. (2011) 'Neural Basis of Emotions', *Scholarpedia*, 6(3), p. 1804.

Deco, G., Jirsa, V.K. and McIntosh, A.R. (2011) 'Emerging Concepts for the Dynamical Organization of Resting-State Activity in the Brain', *Nature Reviews. Neuroscience*, 12(1), pp. 43–56. doi:10.1038/nrn2961.

Deleuze, G. (2004) *Difference and Repetition*. Translated by P. Patton. New York, NY: Bloomsbury Academic (Continuum Impacts Series).

Deleuze, G. and Guattari, F. (2004) *A Thousand Plateaus*. Translated by B. Massumi. New York, NY: Bloomsbury Academic (Continuum Impacts).

Dewey, J. (1934) *Art as Experience*. New York, NY: Penguin Books.

Dibben, N. (2013) 'The Intimate Singing Voice: Auditory Spatial Perception and Emotion in Pop Recordings', in Zakharine, D. and Meise, N. (eds) *Electrified Voices: Medial, Socio-Historical and Cultural Aspects of Voice Transfer*. Göttingen: V&R University Press, pp. 107–22.

Dudley, S. (2003) 'Creativity and Control in Trinidad Carnival Competitions', *The World of Music*, 45(1), pp. 11–33.

Eastwood, J.D. et al. (2012) 'The Unengaged Mind: Defining Boredom in Terms of Attention', *Perspectives on Psychological Science*, 7(5), pp. 482–95.

Edgerton, D. (2006) *The Shock of The Old: Technology and Global History since 1900*. London: Profile Books.

Edmunds, B. (2001) *What's Going On? Marvin Gaye and the Last Days of the Motown Sound*. Edinburgh: Canongate Books.

Eisenberg, J. and Thompson, W.F. (2011) 'The Effects of Competition on Improvisers' Motivation, Stress, and Creative Performance', *Creativity Research Journal*, 23(2), pp. 129–36.

Ericsson, K.A., Krampe, R.T. and Tesch-Römer, C. (1993) 'The Role of Deliberate Practice in the Acquisition of Expert Performance', *Psychological Review*, 100(3), p. 363.

Ewell, P. (2019) 'Music Thbeory's White Racial Frame'. *Society for Music Theory 42nd Annual Meeting*, Hyatt Regency Hotel, Columbus, Ohio, 9 November. Available at: https://vimeo.com/372726003 (Accessed: 19 December 2020).

Fauconnier, G. and Turner, M. (2003) *The Way We Think: Conceptual Blending and the Mind's Hidden Complexities*. New York, NY: Basic Books.

Feldman, J.A. (2008) *From Molecule to Metaphor: A Neural Theory of Language*. 1st Cambridge, MA: MIT Press Paperback Ed. MIT Press.

Festinger, L. (1957) *A Theory of Cognitive Dissonance*. Stanford, CA: Stanford University Press.

Fodor, J. (2005) Reply to Steven Pinker 'So How *Does* The Mind Work?', *Mind and Language*, 20(1), pp. 25–32.

Fodor, J.A. (2000) *The Mind Doesn't Work That Way: The Scope and Limits of Computational Psychology*. Cambridge, MA: MIT Press.

Fransella, F., Bell, R. and Bannister, D. (2004) *A Manual for Repertory Grid Technique*. Hoboken, NJ: John Wiley & Sons.

Frith, S. (1998) *Performing Rites: Evaluating Popular Music*. New edn. Oxford: Oxford Paperbacks.

Gabrielsson, A. and Juslin, P.N. (1996) 'Emotional Expression in Music Performance: Between the Performer's Intention and the Listener's Experience', *Psychology of Music*, 24(1), pp. 68–91.

Galton, F. (1904) 'Eugenics: Its Definition, Scope, and Aims', *American Journal of Sociology*, 10(1), pp. 1–25.

Gama, J. et al. (2014) 'Network Analysis and Intra-Team Activity in Attacking Phases of Professional Football', *International Journal of Performance Analysis in Sport*, 14(3), pp. 692–708.

Gelding, R.W., Thompson, W.F. and Johnson, B.W. (2019) 'Musical Imagery Depends upon Coordination of Auditory and Sensorimotor Brain Activity', *Scientific Reports*, 9(1), p. 16823. doi:10.1038/s41598-019-53260-9.

Gell, A. (1998) *Art and Agency*. Oxford: Oxford University Press.

Gelman, S.A. and Roberts, S.O. (2017) 'How Language Shapes the Cultural Inheritance of Categories', *Proceedings of the National Academy of Sciences*, 114(30), pp. 7900–7907.

Gibson, J.J. (1979) *The Ecological Approach to Visual Perception*. Hove, East Sussex: Psychology Press.

Gilmore, B. and Johnston, B. (2002) 'Harry Partch (1901–1974)', in Sitsky, L. (ed.) *Music of the Twentieth-Century Avant-Garde: A Biocritical Sourcebook: A Biocritical Sourcebook*. Westport, CT: Greenwood Press, pp. 365–72.

Gilroy, P. (1993) *The Black Atlantic: Modernity and Double Consciousness*. London: Verso Books.

Gladwell, M. (2009) *Outliers: The Story of Success*. London: Penguin Books Limited (Penguin Psychology).

Glaser, B.G. (1992) *Emergence vs Forcing: Basics of Grounded Theory Analysis*. Mill Valley, CA: Sociology Press (Emergence vs. forcing).

Glăveanu, V. (2014) *Distributed Creativity: Thinking Outside the Box of the Creative Individual*. Heidelberg: Springer Science & Business Media.

Goehr, L. (1994) *The Imaginary Museum of Musical Works: An Essay in the Philosophy of Music*. New edition. Oxford: Clarendon Press.

Goffman, E. (1956) *The Presentation of Self in Everyday Life*. Edinburgh: University of Edinburgh, Social Sciences Research Centre.

Goffman, E. (1979) *Gender Advertisements*. London: Macmillan International Higher Education.

Goodman, N. (1968) *Language of Art*. Indianapolis: Bobbs-Merrill Company.

Gracyk, T. (1996) *Rhythm and Noise: Aesthetics of Rock*. London: I.B. Tauris.

Grimshaw, M. and Garner, T. (2014) 'Imagining Sound', in *Proceedings of the 9th Audio Mostly: A Conference on Interaction with Sound*. Available at: https://dl.acm.org/doi/10.1145/2636879.2636881 [accessed 7th Feb 2022] Article No.: 2, New York, NY: Association for Computing Machinery, pp. 1–8.

Habibi, A.A., Kemp, C. and Xu, Y. (2020) 'Chaining and the Growth of Linguistic Categories', *Cognition* 202, p. 104323.

Hacking, I. (1996) 'The Looping Effects of Human Kinds', in Sperber, D., Premack, D., and James Premack, A. (eds) *Causal Cognition*. Oxford: Oxford University Press, pp. 351–83. doi:10.1093/acprof:oso/9780198524021.003.0012.

Háden, G.P. *et al.* (2015) 'Detecting the Temporal Structure of Sound Sequences in Newborn Infants', *International Journal of Psychophysiology*, 96(1), pp. 23–8.

Haker, H. and Beyleveld, D. (2018) *The Ethics of Genetics in Human Procreation*. Abingdon, Oxon: Routledge.

Hanin, Y.L. (1980) 'A Cognitive Model of Anxiety in Sports', in Straub, W.F. (ed.) *Sport Psychology: An Analysis of Athletic Behavior*. Ithaca, NY: Movement Publications, pp. 236–49.

Harrison, B. (1997) *Haydn's Keyboard Music: Studies in Performance Practice*. Oxford: Clarendon Press (Oxford monographs on music).

Hawkins, S. (2016) *Queerness in Pop Music*. New York: Routledge.

Henry, L.G. (1988) *The Signifying Monkey: A Theory of African-American Literary Criticism*. USA: Oxford University Press (Oxford University Press paperback).

Heyde, N. *et al.* (2017) 'What Is It Like to Be an Improviser?', in Doffman, M. and Clarke, E.F. (eds) *Distributed Creativity: Collaboration and Improvisation in Contemporary Music*. New York, NY: Oxford University Press (Studies in musical performance as creative practice), pp. 314–16.

Hofstadter, D.R. (1979) *Gödel, escher, bach*. Hassocks: Harvester Press.

Hooks, T.Y. (2015) *Duct Tape and the US Social Imagination*. PhD Thesis, New Haven, CT: Yale University.

Huang, W. (2021) 'The Pragmatic Musical-Gestural Performer', in Brooks, W. (ed.) *Experience Music Experiment: Pragmatism and Artistic Research*. Leuven: Leuven University Press (Orpheus Institute Series), pp. 35–60.

Huron, D. (2008) *Sweet Anticipation: Music and the Psychology of Expectation*. Cambridge, MA: MIT Press.

Hyder, R. (2017) *Brimful of Asia: Negotiating Ethnicity on the UK Music Scene*. Abingdon, Oxon: Taylor & Francis.

Iacoboni, M. *et al.* (2005) 'Grasping the Intentions of Others with One's Own Mirror Neuron System', *PLOS Biology*, 3(3), doi:10.1371/journal.pbio.0030079.

Impett, J. (2019) *Artistic Research for Music – An Introduction* [Massive Open Online Course]. Available at: http://www.orpheusinstituut.be/mooc (Accessed: 17 September 2021).

Ingold, T. (2011) *Being Alive: Essays on Movement, Knowledge and Description*. Abingdon, Oxon: Taylor & Francis.

Ingold, T. (2013) *Making: Anthropology, Archaeology, Art and Architecture*. London and New York: Routledge.

Ingold, T. (2016) *Lines: A Brief History*. Abingdon, Oxon: Taylor & Francis (Routledge Classics).

Izhaki, R. (2008) *Mixing Audio: Concepts, Practices and Tools*. London: Focal Press.

Jackson, S.A. (1996) 'Toward a Conceptual Understanding of the Flow Experience in Elite Athletes', *Research Quarterly for Exercise and Sport*, 67(1), pp. 76–90. doi:10.1080/02701367.1996.10607928.

Jepma, M. *et al.* (2012) 'Neural Mechanisms Underlying the Induction and Relief of Perceptual Curiosity', *Frontiers in Behavioral Neuroscience*, 6, p. 5.

Jones, A.F. (2001) *Yellow Music: Media Culture and Colonial Modernity in the Chinese Jazz Age*. Durham, NC: Duke University Press.

Juslin, P.N. and Sloboda, J.A. (2001) *Music and Emotion: Theory and Research*. Oxford: Oxford University Press.

Kaastra, L.T. (2008) *Systematic Approaches to the Study of Cognition in Western Art Music Performance*. PhD. Vancouver: University of British Columbia. Available at: https://circle.ubc.ca/bitstream/handle/2429/678/ubc_2008_spring_kaastra_linda.pdf?sequence=1 (Accessed: 24 May 2013).

Kaastra, L.T. (2020) *Grounding the Analysis of Cognitive Processes in Music Performance: Distributed Cognition in Musical Activity*. Abingdon, Oxon: Routledge.

Karageorghis, C.I. *et al.* (2017) 'Music in the Exercise and Sport Domain: Conceptual Approaches and Underlying Mechanisms', in Lesaffre, M., Maes, P. and Leman, M. (eds) *The Routledge Companion to Embodied Music Interaction*. Abingdon, Oxon: Routledge, pp. 284–93.

Katz, M. (2004) *Capturing Sound: How Technology Has Changed Music*. Berkeley, CA: University of California Press.

Kaufman, J. and Beghetto, R. (2009) 'Beyond Big and Little: The Four C Model of Creativity', *Review of General Psychology – REV GEN PSYCHOL*, 13. doi:10.1037/a0013688.

Keep, A. (2005) 'Does Creative Abuse Drive Developments in Record Production', in *Art of Record Production Conference*, London: University of Westminster. Available at: http://www.artofrecordproduction.com/index.php/arp-conferences/arp-2005/17-arp-conference-archive/arp-2005/72-keep-2005 (Accessed: 26 July 2013).

Keil, C. and Feld, S. (2005) *Music Grooves*. 2nd edn. Tucson, AZ: Fenestra Books.

Kim, B. *et al.* (2021) 'Neural Networks Trained on Natural Scenes Exhibit Gestalt Closure', *Computational Brain & Behavior*, 4(3), pp. 251–63, 1–13.

Kitchin, R. and McArdle, G. (2016) 'What Makes Big Data, Big Data? Exploring the Ontological Characteristics of 26 Datasets', *Big Data & Society*, 3(1), p. 2053951716631130. doi:10.1177/2053951716631130.

Klotz, K. (2017) 'The Art of the Mistake: Why Flubs and Clinkers Are Part of the Myth of Authentic Jazz', *The Common Reader: A Journal of the Essay* [Preprint]. Available at: https://commonreader.wustl.edu/c/the-art-of-the-mistake/ (Accessed: 13 September 2021).

Knickmeyer, R. *et al.* (2006) 'Fetal Testosterone and Empathy', *Hormones and Behavior*, 49(3), pp. 282–92.

Krum, R. (2013) *Cool Infographics: Effective Communication with Data Visualization and Design*. Hoboken, NJ: John Wiley & Sons.

Kubiak, A. (2019) 'Creativity in New Music for Strings: Under Which Circumstances Does Creative Change Occur in Different Types of Performer-Composer Collaborations'. PhD Thesis. London: University of West London.

Kubovy, M. (1999) 'On the Pleasures of the Mind', in Kahneman, D., Diener, E., and Schwarz, D.N. (eds) *Well-Being: The Foundation of Hedonic Psychology*. New York: Russell Sage Foundation, pp. 134–54.

Laban, R. von and McCaw, D. (2011) *The Laban Sourcebook*. London: Routledge (Book Whole).

Lakoff, G. (1990) *Women, Fire, and Dangerous Things: What Categories Reveal about the Mind*. Chicago: University of Chicago Press.

Lakoff, G. and Johnson, M. (1999) *Philosophy in the Flesh: The Embodied Mind and Its Challenge to Western Thought*. New York, NY: Basic Books.

Lakoff, G. and Johnson, M. (2003) *Metaphors We Live By*. 2nd edn. Chicago, IL: University of Chicago Press.

Latour, B. (2005) *Reassembling the Social: And Introduction to Actor Network Theory*. New York: Oxford University Press.

Lehmann, A.C., Gruber, H. and Kopiez, R. (2018) 'Expertise in Music', in Ericsson, K.A. and Williams, A.M. (eds) *The Cambridge Handbook of Expertise and Expert Performance*. Cambridge: Cambridge University Press, pp. 535–49.

Lerdahl, F. and Jackendoff, R.S. (1996) *A Generative Theory of Tonal Music, Reissue, with a New Preface*. Cambridge, MA: MIT Press.

Linson, A. and Clarke, E.F. (2017) 'Distributed Cognition, Ecological Theory and Group Improvisation', in Clarke, E.F. and Doffman, M. (eds) *Distributed Creativity: Collaboration and Improvisation in Contemporary Music*. New York, NY: Oxford University Press, pp. 52–69.

Lock, C. (2004) *Different Stylistic Voices in Haydn's Piano Music*. Honours Dissertation. Oxford University. Available at: https://www.scribd.com/document/381181152/Dissertation-Cecily-Lock-pdf (Accessed: 19 April 2020).

Long Lingo, E. and O'Mahony, S. (2010) 'Nexus Work: Brokerage on Creative Projects', *Administrative Science Quarterly*, 55, pp. 47–81.

Lorenz, E. (2000) 'The Butterfly Effect', in Abraham, R. and Ueda, Y. (eds) *The Chaos Avant-garde: Memories of the Early Days of Chaos Theory*. Singapore: World Scientific (Nonlinear Science Series A), pp. 91–4.

Mani, C. (2021) *Reimagine to Revitalise: New Approaches to Performance Practices across Cultures*. Cambridge: Cambridge University Press (Elements in Twenty-First Century Music Practice). doi:10.1017/9781108903905.

Massey, H. (2000) *Behind the Glass – Top Record Producers Tell How They Craft the Hits*. London: Backbeat Books.

McCandless, D. (2012) *Information Is Beautiful*. London: Collins.

McClary, S. (2002) *Feminine Endings: Music, Gender and Sexuality*. Minneapolis, MN: Reprint. University of Minnesota Press.

McGrath, A. (2017) 'Dealing with Dissonance: A Review of Cognitive Dissonance Reduction', *Social and Personality Psychology Compass*, 11(12), p. e12362.

McGurk, H. and MacDonald, J. (1976) 'Hearing Lips and Seeing Voices', *Nature*, 264(5588), pp. 746–8. doi:10.1038/264746a0.

McIntyre, P. (2011) *Creativity and Cultural Production: Issues for Media Practice*. London: Palgrave Macmillan.

McIntyre, P. (2012) 'Rethinking Creativity: Record Production and the Systems Model', in Frith, S. and Zagorski-Thomas, S. (eds) *The Art of Record Production: An Introductory Reader to a New Academic Field*. Farnham, Surrey: Ashgate, pp. 149–62.

McNeill, W.H. (1995) *Keeping Together in Time: Dance and Drill in Human History*. Cambridge, MA: Harvard University Press.

McPherson, G., Miksza, P. and Evans, P. (2018) 'Self-regulated Learning in Music Practice and Performance', in D. H. Schunk and J. A. Greene (eds) *Handbook of Self-regulation of Learning and Performance*. Abingdon, Oxon: Routledge, pp. 181–93.

Menon, V. (2011) 'Large-scale Brain Networks and Psychopathology: A Unifying Triple Network Model', *Trends in Cognitive Sciences*, 15(10), pp. 483–506.

Mermikides, M. (2010) *Changes Over Time: The Theoretical Modeling, Analysis and Redeployment of Jazz Improvisational, and Time-feel, Mechanisms*. PhD. University of Surrey.

Merrotsy, P. (2013) 'A Note on Big-C Creativity and Little-c Creativity', *Creativity Research Journal*, 25(4), pp. 474–6.

Meynell, A. (2017) *How Recording Studios Used Technology to Invoke the Psychedelic Experience: The Difference in Staging Techniques in British and American Recordings in the Late 1960s*. PhD. University of West London.

Middleton, R. (1993) 'Music Analysis and Musicology: Bridging the Gap', *Popular Music*, 12(2), pp. 177–90.

Mills, C. and Christoff, K. (2018) 'Finding Consistency in Boredom by Appreciating Its Instability', *Trends in Cognitive Sciences*, 22(9), pp. 744–7.

Monson, I. (1997) *Saying Something: Jazz Improvisation and Interaction*. Chicago, IL: University of Chicago Press.

Moore, A.F. (2002) 'Authenticity as Authentication', *Popular Music*, 21(2), pp. 209–23.

Moore, A.F. (2012) *Song Means: Analysing and Interpreting Recorded Popular Song*. Farnham: Ashgate Pub Ltd.

Moylan, W. (1992) *The Art of Recording: Understanding and Crafting the Mix*. Waltham, MA: Focal Press.

Mynett, M. (2013) *Contemporary Metal Music Production*. PhD. University of Huddersfield.

Nattiez, J.J. (1990) *Music and Discourse: Toward a Semiology of Music*. Translated by C. Abbate. Princeton, NJ: Princeton University Press (Princeton Paperbacks).

Negus, K. (1992) *Producing Pop: Culture and Conflict in the Popular Music Industry*. London: Edward Arnold. Available at: https://research.gold.ac.uk/id/eprint/5453/1/Producing_Pop.pdf (Accessed: 26 August 2021).

Nettl, B., Russell, M. and University of Chicago (1998) *In the Course of Performance: Studies in the World of Musical Improvisation*. Chicago, IL: University of Chicago Press (Chicago Studies in Ethnomusicology).

Nimkulrat, N. (2016) 'Experience, Materiality and Articulation in Art/Design and Research Practices', *Studies in Material Thinking*, 14. Paper 07. Leeds: White Rose Publishing.

Noble, A. (2021) 'How Lin-Manuel Miranda's "In The Heights" Went From College Project to Major Motion Picture', *The Wrap*, 10 June. Available at: https://www.thewrap.com/in-the-heights-lin-manuel-miranda-road-to-movie/ (Accessed: 6 October 2021).

Noë, A. (2004) *Action in Perception*. Cambridge, MA: MIT Press (A Bradford Book).

Nooshin, L. (2017) '(Re-)imagining Improvisation: Discursive Positions in Iranian Music from Classical to Jazz', in Clarke, E.F. and Doffman, M. (eds) *Distributed Creativity: Collaboration and Improvisation in Contemporary Music*. New York, NY: Oxford University Press (Studies in musical performance as creative practice), pp. 214–35.

Nosofsky, R.M. (1986) 'Attention, Similarity, and the Identification–categorization Relationship', *Journal of Experimental Psychology: General*, 115(1), p. 39.

Oliveira, A. *et al.* (2021) 'Disentangling Motivation within Instrumental Music Learning: A Systematic Review', *Music Education Research*, 23 (1), pp. 105–22.

O'Regan, J.K. and Noë, A. (2001) 'A Sensorimotor Account of Vision and Visual Consciousness', *Behavioural and Brain Sciences*, 24, pp. 939–1031.

Oudshoorn, N. and Pinch, T. (eds) (2003) *How Users Matter: The Co-construction of Users and Technology*. Cambridge, MA: MIT Press.

Owsinski, B. (1999) *The Mixing Engineer's Handbook*. Milwaukee, WI: Hal Leonard Corporation.

Pender, A. (2016) 'Learning to Act: Tony Sheldon's Emotional Training in Australian Theatre', *Humanities*, 5(3), p. 72.

Piekut, B. (2014) 'Actor-Networks in Music History: Clarifications and Critiques', *Twentieth Century Music*, 11(02), pp. 191–215.

Pierce, J.R. (1983) *The Science of Musical Sound*. New York: Scientific American Library.

Pinch, T. and Bijker, W.E. (1987) 'The Social Construction of Facts and Artifacts: Or How the Sociology of Science and the Sociology of Technology Might Benefit Each Other', in Pinch, T., Bijker, W.E., and Hughes, T.P. (eds) *The Social Contruction of Technological Systems: New Directions in the Sociology and History of Technology*. Cambridge, MA: MIT Press, pp. 11–44.

Pinch, T. and Trocco, F. (2004) *Analog Days: The Invention and Impact of the Moog Synthesizer*. Cambridge, MA: Harvard University Press.

Pinker, S. (1997) *How the Mind Works*. New York: W. W. Norton & Co.

Pinker, S. (2005) 'So How Does the Mind Work?', *Mind & Language*, 20(1), pp. 1–24.

Porcello, T. (2004) 'Speaking of Sound: Language and the Professionalization of Sound-Recording Engineers', *Social Studies of Science*, 34(5), pp. 733–58.

Posner, M. and Rothbart, M. (1998) 'Attention, Self-regulation and Consciousness', *Philosophical Transactions of the Royal Society of London. Series B: Biological Sciences*, 353(1377), pp. 1915–27.

Power, J.D. et al. (2011) 'Functional Network Organization of the Human Brain', *Neuron*, 72(4), pp. 665–78. doi:10.1016/j.neuron.2011.09.006.

Preston, S.D. and De Waal, F.B. (2002) 'Empathy: Its Ultimate and Proximate Bases', *Behavioral and Brain Sciences*, 25(1), pp. 1–20.

Reyes, F.L. (2017) 'A Community Music Approach to Popular Music Teaching in Formal Music Education', *The Canadian Music Educator*, 59(1), pp. 23–9.

Robazza, C. (2006) 'Emotion in Sport: An IZOF Perspective', in Hanton, S. and Mellalieu, S. (eds) *Literature Reviews in Sport Psychology*. Hauppauge, NY: Nova Science Publishing, pp. 127–58.

Rogers, C.R. (2003) *Client-centered Therapy: Its Current Practice, Implications and Theory*. London: Constable (Psychology/Self-Help Series).

Rogers, D. (2005) *Warman's Vintage Guitars Field Guide: Values and Identification*. London: Penguin.

Roosevelt, T. (1913) *An Autobiography*. New York, NY: C. Scribner's Sons.

Rose, T. (1994) *Black Noise: Rap Music and Black Culture in Contemporary America*. Middletown, CT: Wesleyan University Press (Music Culture).

Rowley, J. (2002) 'Using Case Studies in Research', *Management Research News* [Preprint].

Savage, P.E. and Brown, S. (2013) 'Toward a New Comparative Musicology', *Analytical Approaches to World Music*, 2(2), pp. 148–97.

Sawyer, R.K. (2006) 'Group Creativity: Musical Performance and Collaboration', *Psychology of Music*, 34(2), pp. 148–65.

Schmidhuber, J. (2015) 'Deep Learning in Neural Networks: An Overview', *Neural Networks*, 61, pp. 85–117. doi:https://doi.org/10.1016/j.neunet.2014.09.003.

Seeley, W.W. (2019) 'The Salience Network: A Neural System for Perceiving and Responding to Homeostatic Demands', *The Journal of Neuroscience*, 39(50), p. 9878. doi:10.1523/JNEUROSCI.1138-17.2019.

Shah, D. and Scheufele, D. (2006) 'Explicating Opinion Leadership: Nonpolitical Dispositions, Information Consumption, and Civic Participation', *Political Communication*, 23(1), pp. 1–22.

Shercliff, E. and Twigger-Holroyd, A. (2016) 'Making with Others: Working with Textile Craft Groups as a Means of Research', *Studies in Material Thinking*, 14. Paper 07. Leeds: White Rose Publishing.

Sider, K. et al. (2017) 'Artistic Research: An Articulation', *Canadian Theatre Review*, 172, pp. 87–97.

Skov, M. and Nadal, M. (2020) 'A Farewell to Art: Aesthetics as a Topic in Psychology and Neuroscience', *Perspectives on Psychological Science*, 15(3), pp. 630–42.

Slager, H. (ed.) (2021) *The Postresearch Condition*. Utrecht: Metropolis M Books.

Sloman, A. (1990) 'Motives Mechanisms Emotions', in Boden, M. (ed.) *The Philosophy of Artificial Intelligence*. Oxford: Oxford University Press (Oxford Readings in Philosophy), pp. 231–47.

Small, C. (1998) *Musicking: The Meanings of Performing and Listening*. 1st edn. Middletown, CT: Wesleyan University Press.

Smalley, D. (1986) 'Spectromorphology and Structuring Processes', in Emmerson, S. (ed.) *The Language of Electroacoustic Music*. London: Macmillan, pp. 61–93.

Smalley, D. (1997) 'Spectromorphology: Explaining Sound-shapes', *Organised Sound*, 2(2), pp. 107–26.

Smalley, D. (2007) 'Space-form and the Acousmatic Image', *Organised Sound*, 12(1), pp. 35–58.

Smith, N. (1980) 'The Horn Mute: An Acoustical and Historical Study'. DMA Thesis, Rochester, NY: University of Rochester.

Spitzer, M. (2021) *The Musical Human: A History of Life on Earth*. New York, NY: Bloomsbury Publishing.

Srivastava, S. (2004) 'Voice, Gender and Space in Time of Five-Year Plans: The Idea of Lata Mangeshkar', *Economic and Political Weekly*, 39(20), pp. 2019–28.

Stein, M.I. (1953) 'Creativity and Culture', *The Journal of Psychology*, 36(2), pp. 311–22.

Stein, M.I. (1987) 'Creativity Research at the Crossroads: A 1985 Perspective', in Isaksen, S.G. (ed.) *Frontiers of Creativity Research: Beyond the Basics*. Buffalo, NY: Bearly Limited, pp. 417–27.

Stepánek, J. (2006) 'Musical Sound Timbre: Verbal Description and Dimensions', in. *Proceedings of the 9th International Conference on Digital Audio Effects (DAFx-06)*, Montreal: Citeseer, pp. 121–6.

Stévance, S. and Lacasse, S. (2018) *Research-Creation in Music and the Arts: Towards a Collaborative Interdiscipline*. London: Routledge.

Stock, J. (1995) 'Reconsidering the Past: Zhou Xuan and the Rehabilitation of Early Twentieth-Century Popular Music', *Asian Music*, 26(2), pp. 119–35. doi:10.2307/834436.

Stokes, M. (1994) *Ethnicity, Identity, and Music: The Musical Construction of Place*. Oxford: Berg (Berg Ethnic Identities Series).

Stratton, J. (2015) 'Popular Music, Race and Identity', in Bennett, A. and Waksman, S. (eds) *The SAGE Handbook of Popular Music*. Thousand Oaks, CA: Sage Publications, pp. 381–400.

Strauss, A.L. (1987) *Qualitative Analysis for Social Scientists*. Cambridge: Cambridge University Press.

Tabatabaie, A.F. et al. (2014) 'Neural Correlates of Boredom in Music Perception', *Basic and Clinical Neuroscience*, 5(4), p. 259.

Tagg, P. (2000) 'Analysing Popular Music: Theory, Method, and Practice', in Middleton, R. (ed.) *Reading Pop: Approaches to Textual Analysis in Popular Music*. New York, NY: Oxford University Press, p. 71.

Tang, A.C. (2016) *Repetition and Race: Asian American Literature after Multiculturalism*. New York, NY: Oxford University Press.

Taylor, J. (2010) 'Queer Temporalities and the Significance of "Music Scene" Participation in the Social Identities of Middle-aged Queers', *Sociology*, 44(5), pp. 893–907.

Taylor, T.D. (2001) *Strange Sounds: Music, Technology, and Culture*. 1st edn. Abingdon, Oxon: Routledge.

Thaut, M.H., McIntosh, G.C. and Hoemberg, V. (2015) 'Neurobiological Foundations of Neurologic Music Therapy: Rhythmic Entrainment and the Motor System', *Frontiers in Psychology*, 5, p. 1185.

Théberge, P. (1997) *Any Sound You Can Imagine: Making Music/Consuming Technology*. 1st edn. Middletown, CT: Wesleyan University Press.

Thompson, M. and Biddle, I. (eds) (2013) *Sound, Music, Affect: Theorizing Sonic Experience*. New York: Bloomsbury.

Thompson, P. and Lashua, B. (2016) 'Producing Music, Producing Myth? Creativity in Recording Studios', *IASPM Journal*, 6(2). Available at: https://iaspmjournal.net/index.php/IASPM_Journal/article/view/775/pdf (Accessed: 10 February 2021).

Till, R. (2019) 'Sound Archaeology: A Study of the Acoustics of Three World Heritage Sites, Spanish Prehistoric Painted Caves, Stonehenge, and Paphos Theatre', *Acoustics*, 1(3), pp. 661–92.

Tingen, P. (2001) 'Miles Davis and the Making of Bitches Brew: Sorcerer's Brew', *Jazz Times*, May 2001. Available at: http://www.jazztimes.com/articles/20243-miles-davis-and-the-making-of-bitches-brew-sorcerer-s-brew (Accessed: 6 November 2013).

Toynbee, J. (2017) 'The Labour That Dare Not Speak Its Name: Musical Creativity, Labour Process and the Materials of Music', in Clarke, E.F. and Doffman, M. (eds) *Distributed Creativity: Collaboration and Improvisation in Contemporary Music*. New York, NY: Oxford University Press, pp. 37–51.

Tufte, E.R. and Graves-Morris, P.R. (1983) *The Visual Display of Quantitative Information*. Cheshire, CT: Graphics Press.

Van Oort, B. (2000) 'Haydn and the English Classical Piano Style', *Early Music*, 28(1), pp. 73–89. doi:10.1093/em/28.1.73.

de Villiers, N. (2012) *Opacity and the Closet: Queer Tactics in Foucault, Barthes, and Warhol*. Minneapolis: University of Minnesota Press.

de Villiers, N. (2015) 'Afterthoughts on Queer Opacity', *InVisible Culture* [Preprint], (22).

Vygotsky, L.S. (1980) *Mind in Society: The Development of Higher Psychological Processes*. Cambridge, MA: Harvard University Press.

Waksman, S. (2001) *Instruments of Desire: The Electric Guitar and the Shaping of Musical Experience*. Cambridge, MA: Harvard University Press.

Wallin, N.L., Merker, B. and Brown, S. (2001) *The Origins of Music*. Cambridge, MA: MIT Press.

Wallis, C. (2011) 'Performing Gender: A Content Analysis of Gender Display in Music Videos', *Sex Roles*, 64(3–4), pp. 160–72.

Weinstein, D. (2004) 'Creativity and Band Dynamics', in Weisbard, E. (ed.) *This Is Pop: In Search of the Elusive at Experience Music Project*. Cambridge, MA: Harvard University Press, pp. 187–99.

Welch, G.F. (2006) 'The Musical Development and Education of Young Children', in B. Spodek and Saracho, O. N. (eds) *Handbook of Research on the Education of Young Children*. Mahwah, NJ: Lawrence Erlbaum Associates Publishers, pp. 251–67.

Wenger, E. (2010) 'Communities of Practice and Social Learning Systems: The Career of a Concept', in Blackmore, C. (ed) *Social Learning Systems and Communities of Practice*. London: Springer, pp. 179–98.

Windsor, W.L. and De Bézenac, C. (2012) 'Music and Affordances', *Musicae Scientiae*, 16(1), pp. 102–20.

Witek, M.A. *et al.* (2020) 'A Critical Cross-cultural Study of Sensorimotor and Groove Responses to Syncopation among Ghanaian and American University Students and Staff', *Music Perception*, 37(4), pp. 278–97.

Yin, R.K.(2009) *Case Study Research: Design and Methods*. Thousand Oaks, CA: SAGE Publications (Applied Social Research Methods).

Zagorski-Thomas, S. (2010a) 'Real and Unreal Performances', in Danielsen, A. (ed.) *Rhythm in the Age of Digital Reproduction*. Farnham, Surrey: Ashgate, pp. 195–212.

Zagorski-Thomas, S. (2010b) *Studio-Based Composition: How Can Performance and Production Methods Taken from Popular Music forms Create Expressive Meaning and Structure in My Composition?* PhD. Goldsmiths College, University of London.

Zagorski-Thomas, S. (2014a) 'An Analysis of Space, Gesture and Interaction in Kings of Leon's "Sex On Fire" (2008)', in Von Appen, R. et al. (eds) *Twenty-First-Century Pop Music Analyses: Methods, Models, Debates*. Farnham: Ashgate Publishing Limited, pp. 115–32.

Zagorski-Thomas, S. (2014b) *The Musicology of Record Production*. Cambridge: Cambridge University Press.

Zagorski-Thomas, S. (2016) 'The Influence of Recording Technology and Practice on Popular Music Performance in the Recording Studio in Poland between 1960 and 1989', *Polish Sociological Review* 4, (196), pp. 531–48.

Zagorski-Thomas, S. (2018a) 'Directions in Music by Miles Davis: Using the Ecological Approach to Perception and Embodied Cognition to Analyze the Creative Use of Recording Technology in Bitches Brew', *Technology and Culture*, 59(4), pp. 850–74.

Zagorski-Thomas, S. (2018b) 'The Spectromorphology of Recorded Popular Music: The Shaping of Sonic Cartoons through Record Production', in Fink, R., O'Brien, M.L., and Wallmark, Z. (eds) *The Relentless Pursuit of Tone: Timbre in Popular Music*. New York: Oxford University Press, USA, pp. 345–66.

Zagorski-Thomas, S. (2019a) 'Analysing the Product of Recorded Musical Activity', in Scotto, C., Smith, K., and Brackett, J. (eds) *The Routledge Companion to Popular Music Analysis: Expanding Approaches*. New York: Routledge, pp. 117–32.

Zagorski-Thomas, S. (2019b) 'Haydn in Modern Dress: Applying Experimental Contemporary Production Techniques to Classical Repertoire', in Zagorski-Thomas, S. et al. (eds) *The Art of Record Production: Creative Practice in the Studio*. London and New York: Routledge (Ashgate Popular and Folk Music Series), pp. 185–201.

Zatorre, R.J. and Halpern, A.R. (2005) 'Mental Concerts: Musical Imagery and Auditory Cortex', *Neuron*, 47(1), pp. 9–12. doi:https://doi.org/10.1016/j.neuron.2005.06.013.

Zollo, P. (2011) 'Leiber and Stoller: The Bluerailroad Interview', *Bluerailroad*. Available at: https://bluerailroad.wordpress.com/leiber-stoller-the-bluerailroad-interview/ (Accessed: 18 August 2021).

Index

Actor Network Theory 92, 181, 196
Adorno, Theodor 9
Akrich, Madeleine 68, 139
Alsop, Marin 207
Applebey, Stephen 190
Assassin's Creed Odyssey (music by The Flight) 71, 73
Auslander, Philip 6, 168
autoethnography 1, 5, 33–4, 37–8, 214
autographic and allographic 32

Bakhtin, Michail 60
    heteroglossia 6, 59, 145, 154, 168, 175, 190, 208
Bayley, Amanda 20, 156
The Beach Boys 182
The Beatles 102, 182, 189–90
Beghin, Tom 31
Bijker, Wiebe 51, 68
Björk 50, 98–9 107, 111
Blacking, John 165
Blier-Carruthers, Amy 8, 20, 73
Blige, Mary J., 101
Boden, Margaret 107, 191
Born, Georgina 7, 45, 138, 165
Bourbon, Andrew 8, 20–1, 25, 161
Bourdieu, Pierre 27, 75–6, 167, 178–9, 187, 193–4
    habitus 21, 26–7, 118–19, 161, 165, 179, 182–3, 203
Brown, Clifford 128
Brown, James 156
Bruford, Bill 130, 163, 187, 219
Burnard, Pam 6, 130, 163, 187–8,
Burns, Lori 47, 145, 190
Butler, Judith 6, 57

Cage, John 107
Callon, Michel 196
Camargo, Alex 213
Capulet, Emilie 8, 20–1, 161–2

Chijioke, Benedict (Ty) 110
Chowning, John 66, 139
Clapton, Eric 48
Clark, Herbert 92
Clarke, Eric 6, 54, 59, 162–3, 175, 185
Classical Music Hyper-Production AHRC Project 8–9, 20, 23, 26, 67–8, 82, 117, 161, 163, 166, 167, 169, 177
Clayton, Martin 45, 165
Clifford, Winston 36, 128, 186
Coleman, Ornette 107, 212
Coltrane, John 101
convergence and divergence 17, 26–8, 50–2, 59, 77, 88–90, 109, 130, 136, 152, 158–9, 172–6, 186–8, 190–2, 202, 205–6, 213
Cook, Nicholas 5, 138, 139, 200, 214
Cournarie, Louise 117, 119–20, 136
Cox, Courtney (guitarist with Iron Maidens) 74
Csikszentmihalyi, Mihalyi 92, 105, 107–8, 132, 181, 187
Cuban Music Room 43, 46, 63–5, 73

Damasio, Antonio 41, 91, 113, 131
Danielsen, Anne 20, 171
Davis, Miles 107
    Bitches Brew 131, 181–3, 195–6
de Assis, Paolo 2
Debussy, Claude 21, 48, 103, 107, 136, 161–2, 166–7, 169
Del Prete, Val 209
Deleuze, Gilles 54–5
Depper, Claude 186, 192
deterritorialization and reterritorialization (Deleuze and Guattari) 54
Dibben, Nicola 6
Doffman, Mark 162, 175
Dogantan-Dack, Mine 20
Doolin', 49, 50–1

El Alamacen Collective 44–5
embodied cognition 17, 78–9, 112, 125, 181, 196, 211
European Artistic Research Network (EARN) 2, 3
Ewell, Philip 6, 12, 30, 45, 200, 208, 214

Failing Upwards album (Zagorski-Thomas 2022) 30, 34–6, 182–3, 186, 188, 192, 195, 197
Fauconnier, Gilles and Turner, Mark 19, 120, 122, 148, 203
Feldman, Jerome 19, 79
Final Fantasy IX (music by Nobuo Uematsu) 71–3
Fournel, Josselin 49–50
Frith, Simon 6

Gaye, Marvin 140, 182
Gell, Alfred 137
Gibson, James 46–7, 59, 83, 133
  ecological approach to perception 41, 63, 65, 84, 89–90, 97, 100, 117, 162, 169, 181, 185, 196, 204, 206
Glass, Philip 76
Goehr, Lydia 215
Goffman, Erving 92, 175
  dramaturgy 6, 59, 168
Gordon, Wells 186
Gracyk, Theodore 32

Hawkins, Stan 57
Haydn, Josef 63, 67–8
Hendrix, Jimi 50, 54, 56, 58, 182
Heyde, Neil 156, 176–7
Hirst, Clare 186, 192
Hofstadter, Douglas 204
Howlett, Mike 20, 84, 86, 93

Impett, Jonathan 2, 31, 208
induction and deduction 8, 18–24, 27–9, 33, 47–59, 66–70, 73, 77, 79, 117, 119–20, 130, 133–5, 138–40, 148–9, 151–3, 155, 164–5, 175, 179, 187–8, 196, 203–4, 206
Ingold, Tim 59, 83–4, 108, 151, 191
intertextuality 2, 7, 47, 76, 82, 109, 130, 140, 145, 148, 154, 176, 190, 205, 208

Iron Maiden 74
Ives, Charles 174

Johnson, Mark 19, 31, 59, 79, 91, 148
Jones, Netia 76
Juslin, Patrik 72, 105, 124, 211

Kaastra, Linda 6, 92, 156
Kasongo, Kiamfu 36, 81–2, 103, 109–10, 186
Katz, Mark 63
Kayser, Jasmine 36, 186
Keep, Andy 68
Kina, Shoukichi 76–7
Kubiak-Kenworthy, Agata 156, 161, 186

Laban, Rudolph 128
Lacasse, Serge 20, 47, 145, 190
Lakoff, George 19, 31, 59, 79, 97, 148
Large-scale neural networks
  central-executive network 79, 96, 104, 119
  Default Mode Network 79, 112, 207
  Salience Network 79, 95–6, 112–15, 118–19, 132, 152, 202
Latour, Bruno 68, 92, 108, 139
Lave, Jean 108
Leiber and Stoller 140
Li Minghui 54

Macero, Teo 182
Mani, Charulatha 29, 30, 153
Martinez, Jimmy 186
Maruyama, Takeaki (Goth Trad) 200
Mason, Jeanette 186
McClary, Susan 109
McGuinness, Sara 43–4, 63–4, 81, 89
McGurk, Harry and McDonald, John 72, 85, 97, 141
McIntyre, Phillip 92, 181
Menzel, Idina 144
Mermikides, Milton 164
Meynell, Anthony 28
Michelsen, Morten 20
Middleton, Richard 103–4, 106, 109, 214
Miranda, Lin-Manuel 145–6, 148–9, 152–5
  Hamilton 145, 148, 152, 154–5
  In The Heights 148, 152, 154–5

mirror neurons and mirror systems 79, 88, 125, 150
Mitchell, Joni 67, 69, 107, 212
Monae, Janelle 130
Monk, Thelonius 212
Monson, Ingrid 6, 168
Moore, Allan 6, 89, 189, 196
    authenticity 9, 22, 49, 51, 55, 59, 74, 101, 138, 144, 191, 215
Morales, Yaniela 43–4
Morgan, Lee 128
Muñequitos de Matanzas 43–6, 73, 89
Mynett, Mark 159

Nattiez, Jean-Jacques 147
Negus, Keith 176
Noë, Alba 59, 78, 83, 87, 120, 151
Nooshin, Laudan 176

Ono, Yoko 107
Orpheus Institute 2, 4, 31, 192
Osborne, Peter 3, 216
Oudshoorn, Nellie 68

Parker, Charlie 101
Partch, Harry 66
Pérez Cassola, Sonia 43–4
Performance in the Studio AHRC Project 20, 84, 171
Piekut, Jonathan 92, 181
Pinch, Trevor 51, 65, 68
Pink Floyd 173
Pinker, Stephen 70–2
Porcello, Thomas 20, 156
Practice Research Advisory Group-UK (PRAG-UK) 1, 2, 219
    Bulley and Sahin Report 1, 3, 214, 216
Practice Research Assembly 1, 33
Public Enemy 212

Recorded Music Album / Sound To Picture Album (Zagorski-Thomas 2012 and 2019) 138, 140–1
representational systems 124
    'as if', 14–15, 18–19, 39, 41, 46, 88, 90, 147, 151, 162–3, 176, 181, 185, 187, 197, 204, 210, 214

schematic representation 14, 17, 35–6, 51, 136, 142, 202, 204–5, 210, 211, 213
restriction and affordance 5, 17, 28, 40–2, 46–7, 52–4, 57–60, 64–9, 76–9, 84, 89–90, 95–9, 103, 109, 112, 118, 120–38, 147, 153, 157, 162, 174–86, 192–6, 202–13
Richards, Keith 48
Rihanna 101
Rose, Tricia 6
Ruddick, Osbourne (King Tubby) 125–6

Schoenberg, Arnold 212
Sex Pistols 139
Sheldon, Tony 58–9, 211
Shostakovich, Dmitri 8, 161–7, 174–5
Simon, Paul 183
Size, Roni 183
Sloboda, John 72, 124, 211
Sloman, Aaron 41, 113, 131
Small, Christopher 4
    musicking 5, 64, 79, 82–3, 133, 147, 156, 199
Smalley, Denis 102
    spectromorphology 6, 79, 123, 169
Society for Artistic Research (SAR) 2
Spitzer, Michael 165
Stévance, Sophie 20

tacit knowledge 25, 32, 36–7, 48, 51, 77, 85, 93, 105, 147, 163, 188, 199
Tagg, Phil 37, 214
Taylor, Timothy
    technostalgia 67
Théberge, Paul 63, 65, 171
Thompson, Marie 6, 79
Thompson, Paul 92
three types of thought
    automatic 17, 40, 48, 81, 85, 96, 104, 108–13, 121, 130, 143–6, 173, 197, 202, 208, 214
    conscious 17, 19, 21, 28, 40, 48, 51, 58–9, 73, 81–2, 85, 91, 96, 104–19, 128–31, 143, 146–8, 165, 173, 187–8, 197, 202, 207–10, 214
    subconscious 17–18, 21, 23, 28, 40, 48, 51, 56–9, 81–5, 88, 90, 96, 104–12,

119–21, 129–31, 143–6, 164–5, 173, 187–8, 197, 202, 207–8, 214
Toynbee, Jason 162, 163
A Tribe Called Quest 140
Twenty-First-Century Music Practice (C21MP) research network 68

Vygotsky, Lev 23, 65, 118, 131, 167

Wenger, Etienne 108
Williams, Alan 20

Young, Jo Beth 84, 86, 93, 136

Zagorska-Thomas, Natalia 95, 100, 169
Zorn, John 171

www.ingramcontent.com/pod-product-compliance
Lightning Source LLC
Chambersburg PA
CBHW062143300426
44115CB00012BA/2020